WIDOWS Volume II

WIDOWS

VOLUME II

North America

Helena Znaniecka Lopata, editor

Duke University Press Durham 1987

Printed in the United States of America on
acid-free paper ∞
Library of Congress Cataloging-in-Publication Data
appear on the last page of this book.

dedicated to all the women
in all the countries
who helped us learn of the
many paths of widowhood

Contents

List of Tables

Preface

As those of you who read the preface to volume I, *Widows: The Middle East, Asia, and the Pacific,* know, these two volumes have a very pleasant history. When I first thought of editing a book on the situation of widows in other countries as well as many places in North America, the prospects did not look good. Except in the United States, very little research was being done on widowhood, or so I thought. I attended international gerontological congresses and talked with social scientists familiar with several other countries. After placing an announcement of my plans in the *Gerontological News,* I found so many good, original chapters that the book, originally called *Widows: Other Countries, Other Places,* became much too long. The solution? Make two volumes out of it. Volume I has chapters on widowhood in India, China, Korea, Turkey, Iran, Israel, the Philippines, and Australia. The remaining chapters on Canadian widows, American widows in Columbus, Ohio, a retirement community in Florida, among urban blacks, and among the ethnic poor in California were supplemented with additional chapters for volume II. I had met the authors of the already existing chapters several places. Shirley O'Bryant contacted me . some time ago, and we have met in several pleasant places, including San Antonio and New York. I have known Anne Martin Matthews for many years and was very pleased that she could contribute a chapter on Canada. Jessyna McDonald, Anne Neale, and the team of Anabel Pelham and William Clark responded to the *Gerontological News* announcement and I was able to meet with them at the Gerontological Society of America meetings in San Antonio.

In order to round out volume II, I called friends whom I knew to be studying widows in North America or who might know of research on this topic. I had met Phyllis Silverman years ago when I visited the Widow-to-Widow program at the Harvard Medical School, and I have been on several platforms with her since then. I have also read many of her books and articles. I have long been familiar with Carol Harvey's work. We just missed each other at the International Congress of Sociology in India and, upon my return, I called her in Manitoba just in time to get her and her colleagues to organize data from the Canadian Health Survey into a chapter.

Trudy Anderson has been a postdoctoral fellow at the Midwest Council for Social Research on Aging. Linda Rosenman had written to me earlier, stating that their American data was very rich and could be used for another chapter, this in addition to the one she and her husband had written on Australia for volume I. I had asked Gordon Streib, while eating Indian food in New Delhi, if he knew anyone studying widows, and he called upon his return with the name of Rubye Beck, who had just completed a dissertation at the University of Florida. Thus, with ease, volume II emerged.

I have already thanked several people for their help, but I would like to stress my appreciation to those who were especially helpful with the Chicago support-systems study. Here I must add the name of Rod Coe, who turned to me once at a Midwest Council for Social Research on Aging dinner and asked when I would repay the postdoc fellowship by studying something relevant. (The Council had helped me to get my data analyzed for *Occupation: Housewife.*) Without hesitation, and completely unexpectedly to myself, I responded that I would study widows. Many years have now been devoted to that subject, and it is a pleasure to have so many people now realize that widowhood is a significant subject to social gerontology. Ethel Shanas, Bernice Neugarten, and Robert Winch advised me in the first study. Hank Brehm was the project officer for *Women as Widows: Support Systems* research and proved to be a very active contributor, as everyone can see in our coauthored *Widows and Dependent Wives: From Social Problem to Federal Policy*. The members of the Center for the Comparative Study of Social Roles, especially Frank Steinhart and Sister Gertrud Kim, helped in the many stages of the support-systems research.

Finally, thanks go again to my colleagues at the Department of Sociology, Loyola University of Chicago.

Part I
Relatively Homogeneous Populations

1 Widows: North American Perspectives

HELENA ZNANIECKA LOPATA

In volume 1 of *Widows: The Middle East, Asia, and the Pacific,* we examined the support systems and life-styles of widows in many "less developed" countries, most of which fall into the Third World category. The various authors analyzed not only the traditional situation of widows in these countries or in specific cities but also the consequences of change in the support systems into which the older women, and even many younger ones, had been socialized. The Westernization of economic and social development has brought with it greater industrialization, shifts of population, urbanization, and mass communication and education. However, many of these trends have affected women, especially older widows, mainly indirectly by changing the lives of their support networks rather than directly by changing the women themselves. Thus, many are left with very limited support systems.

As previously defined, a support is "any object or action which the giver and/or the receiver define as necessary or helpful in maintaining a style of life. A support system is a set of similar supports and a support network consists of those persons and groups who provide these supports." Resources from which supports are drawn depend on the society, the community, and the personal characteristics of the widow. Societies differ considerably in both formal and informal resources that they create and make available to different categories of members. Formal resources range from laws and the provision of different forms of economic security to communal work and life-styles as well as to complex organizations. Informal resources exist primarily on the community level in the form of neighbors, places where people congregate, norms concerning behavior, and status criteria. Personal resources include health, material possessions, self-confidence, the ability to understand and take advantage of societal and community resources, and the network of children, relatives, friends, co-workers, comembers of voluntary associations, neighbors, and any other persons, groups, or objects that facilitate initial social engagement and reengagement following life-disorganizing events.

In this volume we will examine the life-styles and support systems of widows who reside in two allegedly very developed, "modernized" societies: the United States of America and Canada. Both countries are "new" compared to most of the rest of the world in that they have built themselves up without the baggage of social structure and tradition, which makes social change difficult in more established societies. Lipset (1979) wrote of *The First New Nation*, referring to the United States. Other new nations have been created since, such as Canada, Australia, and New Zealand, all three of which are former territories of larger units who have won their independence. Their circumstances have really been different, however, than those of the United States. Both Canada and America (I shall refer to the United States as America since no other concept refers to the society and its people rather than just to the political state; see Znaniecki, 1952) have gone through dramatic social and economic changes within a relatively short period of time. These changes have included not only all the major upheavals of what is called social development but also the absorption of masses of immigrants, many of whom are involuntary immigrants. Canada has experienced some of the same changes, though on a smaller scale and with a different ideology regarding its population.

The transformation of America and Canada from rural and mainly subsistence economies into industrialized, urbanized, and capitalistic countries was accompanied by mass education as a means of preparing children for adult roles. Most work has been organized into income-paying jobs, which are entered by preparatory achievement (with some ascribed paths still in evidence) and performed in standardized ways within limited time frames. Housing is now available for rental or purchase rather than through inheritance or self-construction. Family life has changed dramatically. Education and paid employment have freed young adults from dependence upon their families of orientation, into which they were born and socialized. American family ideology allows mate selection by mutual choice, neolocal residence, and the formation of a nuclear unit that provides most of its own supports, creating its own support networks. For over a hundred years and until recently, American society has insisted on the husband/father as the main breadwinner, the wife ideally devoted to full-time homemaking and care of the family. However, the ideal nuclear family "of Western nostalgia"—as Goode (1963) has labeled the stereotype of one bread-winning husband, one full-time homemaking wife, and two children in a suburban home—was never fully representative of Americans and represents fewer and fewer families now. Some remain single, by choice rather than by alleged inability to attract a spouse. The decision to become a parent has become complicated by refusal, willingness to have children without a cooperating coparent, or to give them up, as well as by the less-than-universal use of contraceptives. Divorce, as well as remarriage, is common. However, decreased control by the patrilineal family upon children, which was traditional in most of the societies from which North Americans migrated and in the early years of their history, also means a decrease of traditional kin support networks.

Changes in the definition of the roles of women and their behavior vis-à-vis the world of work outside of the home have occurred with dramatic intensity since the 1950s. The 10th anniversary issue of *Working Woman* (November 1986) was devoted to "How Working Women have Changed America." The repercussions have not yet been fully realized.

American and Canadian cities have become increasingly volunteeristic; that is, social engagement or integration is dependent upon individual initiative to decide what is wanted, search out the resources, and undertake the steps necessary to achieve the goal. There are fewer connecting links to automatically engage and reengage people after former links are broken. Fewer links are available now than in the past, in the countries studied in volume 1, or in small, stable communities. Disengagement by the elderly (Cumming and Henry, 1961) was due partly to the fact that so many of them had been socialized to expect support networks that would remain throughout the life course. These elderly did not possess the social skills and personal resources necessary to utilize the existing formal and informal societal and community resources for reengagement.

One of the characteristics of some of the more traditional areas of the newly developing countries noted in the previous volume is the responsibility of the male line for support systems for widows, usually that of the late husband rather than that of the father and brothers. This obligation is often written into law, supported by religion, and backed by strongly enforced folkways. In such cases, it is usually the mother–son relationship that is most important to the woman. Dependence upon a son in future widowhood and the norm requiring the daughter to become part of her husband's kinship group—thus moving away from the mother's territory and unable to assist her in old age—meant that the mother–daughter tie was traditionally weak. When the widow lived in the home of her son and daughter-in-law, or they in her house, interaction was apt to be continuous and competitive, often to the point of conflict (Blumberg, 1985).

The transformation of societies and families in relatively recent years has begun to weaken feelings of responsibility on the part of the son for parents, widowed mothers, and younger siblings. The independence of the younger nuclear unit from the male line, which is typical of the more developed societies and was observed long ago by Goode (1963) and later by Hareven (1976), has decreased the strength of this obligation. Simultaneously, the daughter is no longer cut off from relations with her family of orientation, especially her mother, by the demands of the husband's family. She now has more freedom throughout the life course than in many societies. This, as we shall see, is particularly true of daughters in urban America. Similarity of gender identification and experiences results in the daughters, rather than the sons, becoming the main suppliers of most supports (Fisher, 1986). This does not mean a complete absence of the son, only the removal of the full burden of responsibility from him. It is he who usually still makes the final decision, or is at least the main adviser, over major changes in the lives of elderly parents, such as residential moves. As we shall see in the case of Columbus, Ohio, he often helps with male-ascribed services, such as repairs and heavy work for a homeowning mother (O'Bryant, this volume).

Both male and female offspring are now released from the obligation to economically support the widow both in America and Canada. The governments of these societies, and of some of those discussed in the previous volume, have taken over that obligation through the provision of social security, welfare, and medical care. This economic support, when it exists, frees the elderly from a dependence on their offspring that requires reciprocity of services, the parent continuing to provide labor. A major difference between the lives of widows in these societies and those in much of the Third World has been this relative economic independence. As mentioned before, adult children have reached independence from their parents and are able to create their own households. A son does not have to remain in the parental home to care for it and his parents in their old age (Hareven, 1976). On the other hand, the widow does not have to give up her own household and move into the son's home, becoming a peripheral member of the family of her son and daughter-in-law, or of a daughter and her family. There is a great amount of independent residence on the part of, especially, middle-class American widows.

Having sketched in some of the characteristics of modern urban America and Canada, we can now examine in greater detail the support systems of different widows in metropolitan Chicago. It is this research (Lopata, 1979) that provided the theoretical basis for several of the studies represented in both volumes of *Widows*.

Metropolitan Chicago Widows

The support systems and life-styles of Chicago area widows are strongly influenced by social class and, especially, by the educational achievement of the women (Lopata, 1973a).

Resources

Many of the widows researched in the 1970s in two large projects —one focused on the modification of social roles of older women brought about by the death of the husband (Lopata, 1973b), and the other on the support systems of widows of all ages (Lopata, 1979)—were first- or second-generation urbanites.[1] Four-in-ten of the parents in the second study were born in rural areas, and over half of all the fathers and mothers were immigrants. Very few of the fathers, and only 10 percent of the mothers, were born in Chicago (Lopata, 1979:61). The older the widow, the more likely it was that her parents were born outside of the United States. Many of the homes did not use English as the primary language. The parents of the black widows were almost inevitably born in the American south. Almost half of the respondents did not even know the educational level attained by their father. Both parents about whom schooling was known usually reached no higher than eight grades of schooling, and often not that many (see also Hyman, 1983). Such a parental background was not apt to provide the daughters with sufficient knowledge of urban America to prepare them for multidimensional use of its resources. As far as the woman and her late husband are concerned, the younger they were, the more education they had obtained. Even so, only 13 percent of the sample had entered college, and 58 percent never graduated from high school.

The widows in the Chicago support systems study, as well as those in the Chicago *Needs Assessment Survey* (Chicago Mayor's Office for Senior Citizens, 1973), and those in other parts of the country definitely underutilized community resources (Lopata, 1978a). Pelham and Clark (this volume) report a very limited use of resources such as recreational, health, legal, and financial facilities, which are all services provided by governmental agencies, helping professionals, self-help groups, job training, and related programs. Many of our respondents did not even experience satisfactory supports from religious personnel and church membership. They explained this neglect as due to a focus on families, which made them invisible after the funeral and official mourning was over. In most cases the underuse of societal resources can be accounted for by a lack of knowledge about the city and what is available. In addition, these women were often hesitant to focus bureaucratic or even personal attention on themselves and lacked self-confidence for seeking out and demanding services. The women most apt to turn to formal networks were those with higher education and a history of resource utilization.

Most of the women in the Chicago sample had not obtained occupational training, either before or after becoming widowed. They lack occupational skills and knowledge. Forty percent never held a paying job while married, and only 8 percent were employed throughout marriage. Others have an "on-and-off" work history. On the other hand, almost half had been forced, or anyway decided, to work for pay since widowhood, with 28 percent employed at the time of the interview. Unfortunately, they had not sought jobs in the most rational methods available in modern societies, such as employment agencies and advertisements. Instead, they utilized friends or went to a place in the neighborhood where a job might be found. As a result, they are concentrated in the traditional women's low-paying jobs in clerical, operative, service, and household worker occupations. Many needed the job because they fell in the "blackout" period of the life course—that is, with no Social Security benefits. They had no young children covered by the program, they themselves were ineligible for old age benefits, or neither spouse had worked in included occupations.

The widows were generally in their late 50s at the time of the death of the husband, who was likely to be under the age of 65 and working in his usual occupation. At the time of the interview, few had living parents, although those who did and whose parents were healthy and available, found them very supportive. One of the surprising findings of the support systems study was the infrequency with which the extended family appears in the support networks of these women. Although all but a fifth of the respondents had living siblings, such relatives are absent from most supports, except those immediately surrounding the death of the husband and in other crisis situations (Lopata, 1978a). They are not active in the economic or service supports, and relatively few women report frequent social interaction with a brother or sister. If a sibling does appear, he or she (most often she) tends to be strongly involved. Even when given the chance to list up to three providers of 65 different supports, most widows did not list members of the extended family, not even as major confidants or comforters. This finding challenges some of the traditional literature on American elderly (Litwak, 1965; Shanas, 1979; Sussman and Burchinal, 1966) but supports Blau's (1961) findings that such supports are most common among same-age peers who are not part of the kinship network.

Friendship and membership in voluntary associations are more typical of middle- than of working-class Chicago-area widows, although the blacks of both classes report strong involvement in church groups. Some of the respondents are still embedded in neighborhood networks, often with people of the same ethnic background and around whom they have lived for years. However, many of the previously compact communities have dispersed; half of the widows have moved since their husband's death, often to smaller quarters (Lopata, 1971). Two-thirds still live in private homes, which is typical of this metropolitan area. Over half own their place of residence, while a third rents, and the remaining live with others. Eight out of ten widows are heads of their households; only 12 percent list an offspring as head. They are very pleased to be able to live independently and do not wish to give up the rights to space, choice of food, and time. Having visited their sons and daughters often enough, they know that they would experience trouble in the relationships if they lived together. As one respondent explained, her daughter invited her to come live in their large house, but only on the condition that she "keep my mouth shut—now you tell me, what is the fun of living if you have to keep your mouth shut?"

American society has no rigid norms about the remarriage of widows, an unusual situation compared to several of the societies discussed in volume 1. The levirate system—by which a male agnate (relative on the same patrilineal side) of the deceased "enters her hut" to "raise up his seed," referred to even in the Bible, which guarantees birth of children of whom the late husband is social father—is not practiced among most Americans or Canadians (Bohannan, 1963); neither is widow inheritance, or the automatic transfer of the role of husband from the deceased to one of his male "agnates," i.e., close relatives. In addition, the tendency of men to marry younger women, especially in second and later marriages, and the greater longevity of women, results in a scarcity of potential husbands, especially as the woman ages. Remarriage is not a strong statistical possibility. Most women know this and, anyway, claim not to want to enter marriage again. They do not wish to invest again in an emotionally charged relationship in anticipation of reexperiencing grief, to care for another ill man, or to give up their new independence. Some fear negative reactions from children. In addition, these women tend, with some definite exceptions, to idealize the late husband. This tendency was so strong in the pretest interviews that I constructed a "sanctification scale," the bottom line of which states, "my husband had no irritating habits" (Lopata, 1981). The process by which sanctification is accomplished performs some important functions: it makes the widow feel more worthy, since such a saintly person married her, and it "cleans up" the spirit of mortal jealousies and other sentiments that can complicate the restructuring of her life without the husband. However, it has a major drawback in that it antagonizes friends who knew the husband as a mortal with irritating habits, and, it can interfere with the development of relations with other men, who cannot compete against this idealized image. Of course, some women are unable, or unwilling, to sanctify their late husband. We found that black widows were less likely to do so, and the extreme levels were not reached by either the least or the most educated women.

The studies of widows in metropolitan Chicago found many lifestyles and support systems, reflective of a variety of factors. The amount of disorganization in prior systems and styles—as well as in the changed self-concepts of the women brought about by the death of the husband and the direction and form of reorganization—varied by such differences as the degree of interdependence between the woman and her husband, the size and form of the larger unit of which both were a part, and the composition of the household. The source of control over the household before the man's death and the strength of the kinship network and of its control over the widow and her children both influence the widow's life. Also important are the sources of economic supports, legal status, rights to inheritance, the availability of social roles outside of the family, and personal resources such as education, health, and income. These factors, and others particular to special situations, are important in any society and are discussed throughout these volumes.

The Chicago-area research led to the conclusion that middle-class American urban women suffer a greater degree of disorganization in their lives after the death of the husband than do working- or lower-class women (Lopata, 1972; 1973b; 1979). The more education a woman has, and the more middle-class a life-style she and her husband developed while he was living, the more disorganization she experiences in her support systems, life-style, and self-concept following his death. There are many reasons for this. Briefly, middle-class couples become strongly involved in each other's lives, and women tend to reconstruct the reality of their world, including themselves, upon marriage (Berger and Kellner, 1970; Lopata, 1984). They coparent with the husband, participate in couple companionate relations, are comembers in voluntary associations, and engage in many activities together. Several other studies have concluded that such couples communicate with each other more fully than do working-class couples (see, for example, Komarovsky, 1967). If the wife is not actively involved in her own roles outside of the home, and her husband is in a two-person single career, much of her life is dependent upon his (Fowlkes, 1980; Kanter, 1977; Ostrander, 1985; Papanek, 1973; Seidenberg, 1973). A two-person career involves one of the partners in a career outside of the home, which is made possible through the contributions of a backup person. It is usually the husband who is the external jobholder, with the wife working both in the home and in the community, often with the husband's co-workers or clients to build, maintain, and enhance the family social position (Papanek, 1979).

In such situations, the whole base of the life-style collapses when the husband dies (or divorces). The extent of its being dependent upon the husband is evident in the forms and components of loneliness reported by the Chicago-area widows (Lopata, 1969). A widow can be lonely for: the late husband as a specific person, having him as a love object, being a love object, having someone treat her as an important human being (even to fight with), a companion, a sexual partner, an escort to public places, part of a team in social events, the father of the children, a person around whom time and work are organized, or simply as another presence in the home. She also misses the whole life-style made possible by his being alive: activities focused around his job and earnings, and being part of a couple companionate circle that tends then to drop her. Finally, she can be lonely for everything connected with being married and being married to that particular husband. Even some of the obligations previously found irksome because of career demands are now missed.

Lindemann (1944) found the need for "grief work," by which ties with the deceased are cut and the widow learns to live in a world without him. I have added to this process the need to reconstruct the self-concept (Lopata, 1984). To the extent that the woman had constructed herself into a wife, and the wife of that husband (and certainly not all women do so), she has to develop another central identity. This does not happen early in the grieving period; rather it happens when she starts looking to the future (Lopata, 1986). There is no status role of widows in America similar to the one that appears in some other societies. The large and volunteeristic urban centers enable a woman to become Mary Smith instead of Mrs. John Smith. However, some of the Chicago-area respondents reached a point of limbo with the question, "What am I going to do with the rest of my life?" (See Rubin [1979] for a discussion of the same problem in *Women of a Certain Age*.) The reconstruction of the self-concept can often be painful, although some women are not aware of changes taking place.

On the other hand, the more educated and middle-class a woman, the more personal resources she has to develop a new support network and life-style when the period of heavy grief is over. Such women have a wide range of options unavailable to women in many other societies or to their less well-positioned counterparts suffering from minimal education and understanding of the community, or who have health or financial problems. Although most of the widows suffered a drop in financial resources, some were able to maintain themselves relatively comfortably by utilizing their own earnings, social security, some insurance, and any combination of resources. The more resources, the better off the widows (Lopata and Brehm, 1986). They can build their social life space around a job, the family, friendships, voluntary associations, neighborhood networks, and so forth. As individuals, they can date and remarry, live with another man, or join forces with other housemates. Often they still have children at home when the father dies.

The less-educated and lower-class women are often less disorganized in their life-styles and self-concept than are the middle-class widows because they are less deeply interdependent. Their world tends to be more sex-segregated; the level of involvement of husband and wife with each other is less intense. On the other hand, these widows may become more isolated than before with the break of this connecting link to the world. This is especially likely if the children have already left home, the neighborhood has changed, or if they themselves are forced to move. They usually lack the social skills required of volunteeristic engagement in organizations, even the religious ones, and they do not know that one can actually make friends in the later part of life.

Although the concept of disorganization implies negative and unpleasant events, this is not necessarily so. An event such as the death of a husband can disrupt what went on before, but the process or results of reorganization can be very pleasant, often creating a freer life and greater happiness than the woman experienced in marriage. This is certainly true if the husband had been an abuser, an alcoholic, a person unable to earn an income equal to the one the widow now receives, or was someone not wishing his wife to have personal social contacts and activities and who did not engage in couple friendships. Being released from the marriage and all the work it entails, the widow is also often freed from in-law relations, can do what she wants, and can build new support networks. Younger women sometimes return to their natal families, and widows of all ages can enter new relationships and social roles, changing whatever of their past they wish to discard, modify, or forget. Women in the Chicago area often reported feeling more competent and independent after widowhood than before, thus filling out their self-concept into a whole rather than a part of a couple. However, unless they take over the husband's business or political office, which few do, they are not apt to experience an increase in power or influence, as do some women in the many localities who gain status as the matriarch once the patriarch dies.

Whatever direction and form of reorganization of the support systems, life-styles, and self-concepts a widow chooses, alternatives are indeed present in the urban centers of modern societies. One of the alternatives, as stated above, can be social isolation, or a high dependence upon a very limited number of persons. Alleged legal equality of women still does not protect many from being cheated by unscrupulous entrepreneurs, ignored or made confused by bureaucracies, subject to bad advice from significant others, or lowered in status in the eyes of even close relatives and married friends. There can easily be a mismatch between a society's or community's life-style and the abilities of many of its members to lead satisfactory lives.

Let us now examine specifically the support systems of the metropolitan Chicago widows.

Support Systems

The supports about which we asked the respondents in the last Chicago study, of whom there were 82,078, when weighted, fit into four support systems: economic, service, social, and emotional. In all, there are 65 supports, and each respondent was given the chance to list up to three persons. Thus, each widow could list up to 195 different people. She could list herself, no one, or a present husband only 65 times (see Table 2 in Lopata, 1979:74). The women themselves were selected randomly by the statisticians of the Social Security Administration from lists of current beneficiaries with eligible children, current recipients of old age benefits, women who received only "lump sum" benefits to help defray funeral costs because they were not otherwise eligible, former beneficiaries who remarried, and former beneficiaries whose children had grown beyond the age of eligibility (Lopata, 1979).

Most of the widows do not exchange economic supports in the form of inflow or outflow of gifts, "payment or help in the payment" of rent or mortgage, food, clothing, or other bills such as medical or vacation expenses, or any other financial help (see table 1.1). In fact, they are more likely to see themselves as givers of gifts rather than recipients, the main recipients besides the children being the grandchildren. In this they are unlike many elderly in other studies, who are receivers more often than givers (Decker, 1980; Hess and Markson, 1980). Certainly the flow both in and out is mainly focused on the children. In addition, as I shall document later, it is mainly the daughter who is involved in most of the support systems. The main fact that is evident from table 1.1 is that 9 percent or less of the widows report receiving financial aid, indicating one of several things: that the widows simply do not report receiving financial aid or do not consider some forms of supports to be such aid, that they are so well off that they do not need it, or that such exchanges are not part of the norm of reciprocity among urban Americans. The second explanation is not likely to be true since, "on the whole, more than two-fifths (43 percent) of the Chicago-area widows were poor, as measured by the SSA low-income index" (Lopata and Brehm, 1986:126).

Many more widows are involved in the exchange of services, but there is no consistency in the figures, mainly due to the unique features of life of particular widows (see table 1.2). The one pattern that is visible is the traditional gender division of labor. None of the widows offered car care, and only a few offered house repairs, yard work, or legal aid. More give child care than receive it, mainly because of the ages of the people, including offspring, involved in the network. About the only support the widows offer is care during illness. However, even this is a very infrequent support, both in the inflow and, especially, in the outflow from her. In fact, it is surprising that only 55 percent of the widows living in a city with imperfect public transportation receive such a service.

Here again, it is mainly the child who is the provider and receiver of most supports, although other relatives and secondary or formal people or groups enter as providers. Few parents are able to do more than child care and, if alive, they are important receivers of service supports. Friends are seen as recipients of services, mainly transportation and shopping, which are probably connected activities. It is interesting to note that, although the few women who have remarried or have a boyfriend report these men as providers, the women do not report them as recipients of supports. We discovered when going through some of the interviews that the widow does not list people living with her as recipients of, for example, housekeeping or shopping services. Such are listed only if specially arranged for, or if they are not part of the normal flow of life in a household, or require leaving it.

The third support system, that of mutual engagement in social activities, brings in the friends, a category less active as giver of economic or service supports. Social supports drew in many more people than the previously discussed support systems had, so table 1.3 contains both the first person listed and the total number of people

Table 1.1 Significant Others Contributing to the Inflow and Outflow of Economic Support Systems of Chicago-area Widows (in percentages).*

Economic support	Number of first listings**	No one: do not receive or give	Parents Total	Children Total
Inflow				
Gifts, money	7,210	91	2	83
Rent	7,201	91	2	70
Food	9,193	98	1	77
Clothing	4,685	94	0	92
Bills	6,168	92	2	58
Outflow				
Gifts	10,844	87	2	43
Rent	4,380	84	5	81
Food	4,523	75	5	67
Clothing	2,811	97	1	60
Bills	3,554	96	3	68

*Percentages are computed from the universe of widows represented by our sample.

**First listings indicate the number of widows who receive or give this support out of 82,078.

specifically mentioned by each widow. There are some very interesting totals and distributions here. The most frequently engaged in activity with other people, and the largest number of people so listed, is celebration of holidays. (The reader should remember that we could list only three persons per support, and the interviewers sometimes accepted "the family," although they were trained not to do so.) One suspects that even more people are involved with the widow in celebrating holidays and in visiting than is indicated in table 1.3. On the other hand, 51 percent of the women claim to never go to public places such as movie theaters or restaurants, and 58 percent do not play games such as cards or sports with anyone. The difference in the number of people whom widows "visit" and those they entertain" must be due to these concepts. I suspect, unfortunately too late, that the term entertaining is a middle-class one, indicating a formality that visiting does not imply.

It is here that we are again struck by the relative absence of siblings. Other relatives include grandchildren with whom holidays are spent and who are entertained by the grandmother, as well as who are visited, usually in the home of adult children. Those women who do

Siblings	Other relatives	Friends	Other people or groups	Present husband or boyfriend***
Total	Total	Total	Total	Total
5	4	2	0	3
5	—	13	6	4
7	2	0	8	4
5	1	0	1	1
4	0	0	30	6
4	29	1	20	2
10	3	1	—	—
14	5	1	4	4
9	17	2	11	—
8	10	8	4	0

***Most widows do not have a husband or boyfriend.

play games tend to do so primarily with friends, who are also luncheon companions and hosts or guests. Other people with whom lunch is shared are primarily organization comembers. The woman may go to church alone, but she meets people there. Going to church with children usually means that they live together or very close nearby.

Finally, there is the emotional support system, which is divided, with the help of symbolic interaction theory, into sentiments of interaction and feeling states about oneself (see table 1.4). The women were asked, for example, whom they feel closest to, or who most often makes them feel important. Here we have the largest number of people involved with the widow, or at least the largest for any single support, since the same person is often mentioned for many of the supports. In addition, many of the women mentioned more than one person for any single support. Parents are dead so do not appear often, although some women still feel closest to them, particularly to a mother even if she is no longer alive. Children are again frequent contributors to both types of emotional supports, though not as often to feelings of independence or self-sufficiency. The self appears here as a provider of those sentiments, as well as that of security. The response "no one" is cer-

Table 1.2 Significant Others Contributing to the Inflow and Outflow of Service Support Systems of Chicago-area Widows (in percentages).*

Services	Number of first listings**	No one: do not receive or give	Parents total	Children total
Inflow				
Transportation	44,771	45	0	57
House repairs	34,863	57	1	55
Housekeeping	18,702	77	3	69
Shopping	32,060	61	1	67
Yard work	25,836	69	2	55
Child care	2,806	96	21	28
Car care	10,787	87	2	50
Sick care	45,723	44	4	65
Decisions	33,663	59	2	70
Legal aid	15,670	81	0	19
Outflow				
Transportation	14,763	82	8	19
House repairs	1,320	98	25	34
Housekeeping	9,842	88	8	56
Shopping	10,727	87	20	13
Yard work	2,948	96	17	23
Child care	16,689	80	0	52
Car care	108	100	68	0
Sick care	29,302	64	10	44
Decisions	14,694	85	6	44
Legal aid	508	99	22	35

*Percentages are computed from the universe of widows represented by our sample.
**First listings indicate the number of widows who receive or give this support out of 82,078.

tainly prominent in this system. It is different from "I do not do that" in the social system in that it distances the respondent from people rather than from activities. It certainly is surprising to social psychologists to find out that 63 percent of the widows do not find anyone who most often makes them angry. One cannot help but feel sorry for the women who do not have anyone as confidant or comforter. Siblings are again absent in that, given the chance to list three people who provide emotional supports, only one tenth of the total are siblings, and that is as the closest (mainly to women, by the way, who do not have children), or to whom the widow would turn in times of crisis.

Siblings total	Other relatives total	Friends total	Other people or groups total	Present husband or boyfriend*** total
8	6	18	7	5
9	11	4	10	11
2	7	5	11	4
5	4	12	6	5
4	13	2	14	11
4	9	12	10	17
4	6	5	17	17
9	4	8	6	4
10	5	2	2	9
8	10	5	55	2
7	10	39	16	0
3	9	20	3	4
10	8	12	6	0
9	8	34	16	0
20	6	13	17	2
3	30	8	6	0
6	18	8	0	0
10	10	14	16	2
11	7	24	4	4
2	9	24	8	0

*Most widows do not have a husband or boyfriend.

Friends certainly do not appear in the emotional support systems as often as in the social support systems—an indication that the relation must be quite superficial, though probably pleasant, for many of the respondents.

Seeing much more frequent references to daughters than to sons in most of the supports, I decided to actually count their numbers in the emotional system. All in all, there are 303,949 references to daughters and 236,156 to sons, with a surplus on the side of the women of 67,793 (Lopata, 1979:198). Sons appear less often in *each* support, coming the closest in making the mother feel secure, with a surplus of only 157.

Table 1.3 Significant Others Contributing to the Social Support Systems of Chicago-area Widows (in percentages).*

Social	Number of first listings**	Total number of listings***	Does not engage in activity	Parents total	Children total
Public places	40,243	59,944	51	1	28
Visiting	64,869	110,063	21	2	29
Entertaining	48,964	88,970	40	1	23
Lunch	51,399	79,607	37	1	18
Church	62,078	79,318	24	1	35
Sports, cards, and games	34,337	56,709	58	0	12
Travel out of town	48,460	68,046	40	1	35
Celebrate holidays	73,853	142,108	8	2	52
Other activity	3,291	4,064	96	1	17

*Percentages are computed from the universe of widows represented by our sample.
**First listings indicate the number of widows who engage in this support out of 82,078.

They are the least likely to have her feel closest to them, or to be the comforter when she feels depressed. Thus, the argument I was making earlier here, and also in volume 1, that daughters are the main suppliers of supports to the mother applies not only to service and social supports but also to emotional ones. Of course, other social scientists have found the same regarding American urban elderly and their daughters, explained mainly by the claim that women are socialized to be more nurturant and emotionally demonstrative than are men (Farrell, 1975; Decker, 1980; Hess and Markson, 1980; Shanas, 1979; Townsend, 1968). This is certainly a different situation than that reported in societies such as India. It is possible that we should reexamine the statement that the mother–son tie is most important in many societies.

One of the main findings of the two metropolitan Chicago studies of widows is their tremendous heterogeneity. Part of this diversity is in the social life space, or the roles and dimensions along which they extend themselves into the society. Some are relatively socially isolated, living vicariously through television soap operas and occasionally seeing other people, usually an offspring. At the other extreme are the cosmopolitan women, who relate to a variety of people in a multidimensional life space—that is, in roles in several institutions. They are active in the family, religious, recreational, and even political groups and are not geographically restricted. In between are women in traditional

Siblings total	Other relatives total	Friends total	Other people or groups total	Self total	Present husband or boyfriend**** total
6	6	38	6	3	12
11	10	40	5	2	2
6	19	43	5	0	2
7	5	51	12	2	4
6	5	15	3	33	3
5	10	58	8	2	4
11	9	15	2	21	6
10	25	7	2	0	2
0	0	24	6	47	3

*Total listings refer to all the people (up to three) the widows listed.

**Most widows do not have a husband or boyfriend.

neighborhoods, committed totally to their church, working in jobs with which they identify, active in friendship networks, or in any combination of these. The advantage they have as urban Americans is the range of choice of resources available to them. The problem they face is the need to volunteeristically engage in these resources and to continuously build and rebuild social networks as their situation and that of their associates change. Socialized in the traditional style—of women focused on the private sphere of home and related spaces—as the elderly of these widows were, our sample contains fewer of the cosmopolitan types and more of the minimally or single-dimensionally engaged women. Chicago, a large modern urban center in an allegedly *very* developed society, contains many "traditional" women and many who have no traditional supports but who are unable to develop "modern" ones.

Let us now briefly meet the widows in other parts of the United States and in Canada. The chapters in this volume point to the fact that even such highly developed countries as Canada and America contain a variety of support systems and life-styles in widowhood within the same location or in contrast to widowhood in another community. Although each chapter develops its own theme, commonalities emerge. Social class remains a very important factor, even above income, as measured by the widow's own education, as well as by the life-style

Table 1.4 Significant Others Contributing to the Emotional Support Systems of Chicago-area Widows (in percentages).*

Emotional supports	Number of first listings**	Total number of listings***	Parents total	Children total	Siblings total
Sentiments					
Closest	80,044	144,277	3	60	10
Enjoy	80,706	145,463	2	52	8
Problems	81,664	112,996	2	42	9
Comfort	81,304	117,671	2	45	9
Angry	80,320	89,275	0	22	3
Crisis	80,170	114,490	3	54	10
Feeling states					
Important	79,630	128,246	2	57	4
Respected	81,035	114,162	2	52	4
Useful	80,459	126,334	2	50	4
Independent	79,819	96,552	0	20	4
Accepted	77,698	128,472	1	40	4
Self-sufficient	78,953	100,140	1	21	4
Secure	79,883	111,801	1	36	4

*Percentages are computed from the universe of widows represented by our sample.

**First listings indicate the number of widows who receive or give this support out of 82,078.

she and her husband built when he was alive. Ethnicity is also important in many places. Stability of the community and mobility of the woman influence the resources from which she pulls together a support network. Several chapters point to the importance of social engagement and of religion as a system of beliefs and a source of social involvement. I have tried to organize the chapters by the amount of homogeneity of the population of widows being studied, although there is overlap. Many of the authors have sufficient data to be able to contrast the support systems of widows to those of widowers or to married women. The range of methodologies and types of samples is also quite broad.

Relatives total	Friends total	Others total	Self total	No one total	Present husband or boyfriend**** total
9	10	2	1	2	3
13	16	3	0	5	4
4	12	5	6	21	4
4	11	5	4	21	5
4	2	9	1	63	2
5	7	4	3	12	5
7	9	4	4	12	5
7	12	13	4	4	4
2	7	9	11	13	4
2	3	7	50	7	2
7	19	14	7	10	4
3	6	5	49	10	3
7	4	9	30	10	5

Total listings refer to all the people (up to three) the widows listed.
*Most widows do not have a husband or boyfriend.

Relatively Homogeneous Populations

Momence, Illinois

This is a small, stable, and relatively homogeneous working-class town in which people build a continuity of social networks. Christine Fry and Lauree Garvin found in their research, which forms part of a large, multicommunity and even cross-cultural project, that widowhood does not dramatically disorganize life for the woman, mainly because of the continuity of social relationships. It is not a "significant marker of the life course," being taken for granted and weakened in its effect by the strong gender segregation of interactions. This supports the Chicago finding that it is the middle-class widow whose life is more disorganized by the death of the husband than is that of the working-class widow.

Columbus, Ohio

A somewhat similar picture emerges when we turn to the homeowning widows in Columbus, Ohio, studied by Shirley O'Bryant. In some ways these women, all but a few of whom were born in the United States, provide a glimpse of future cohorts of American widows, unlike those in the central cities such as Chicago. These widows have benefited from the society's middle-class urban life-style in that they are property owners in their own right and have been able to maintain their homes after the husband's death—even though their present economic circumstances are still judged by many to be "unfair" when compared to those of men. They are better educated than most women; in fact, better educated than almost all the women discussed in these two volumes. This education provides them with more effective coping strategies for reorganizing their support systems after the heavy grief is over. They thus have many advantages typical of only the better educated Chicago-area widows, and they enjoy the freedom provided by this more developed society to individualistically utilize its resources. On the other hand, they also have the advantages of the Momence widows in the stability of their social network.

These Columbus women are living alone in a "typical" American community and are highly attached to their homes, having no intention or need to move. Although children predominate in their support networks, there is greater heterogeneity of people contributing to the systems. The major need of these older women, who are generally healthy and able to do many things for themselves, is help with male-stereotypical chores that require physical strength and masculine skills, such as household repairs and yard work. Some have enough money to pay for help, others enlist assistance from sons, sons-in-law, brothers, male neighbors, and friends. Sons are more often mentioned as support givers than is true of the Chicago-area widows (Lopata, 1973; 1979). The same is true of siblings. The ability to retain their home and the proximity of many children who are active support suppliers results in a sense of well-being on the part of these women. They have also developed a high degree of self-sufficiency. On the one hand, they have relative independence of action, and on the other hand, they are more isolated than is true of women in less modernized societies.

A Retirement Community in Florida

A very different form of social integration is found among widows living in the retirement community in Florida that was studied by Anne Victoria Neale. Both formal and informal support networks abound, as they do in the previous two communities, and are similar to those of communities in Chicago. However, the community is age-segregated and voluntarily created by the residents away from prior homes. The argument of whether or not the elderly are more socially engaged in age-segregated, rather than in age-integrated, communities has a long history among gerontologists, although Rosow's (1967) and Hochschild's (1973) research results favor locations with age homogeneity. This community is also ethnically homogeneous, the people having migrated mainly from the same city, Detroit, usually as couples, in order to avoid the disadvantages of climate, unsafe urban neighborhoods, and household maintenance. The atmosphere of leisure-time enjoyment and the availability of contact through community activities make friendship formation easier than in most urban areas. Children are not frequent contributors to the support systems of those widows who do not return to their prior neighborhoods after the death of the husband. This means that their ties are closer, or life-style more satisfactory than "back home." They have moved by choice rather than because they could not maintain themselves in the previous location, a situation not as typical of the Chicago widows. Living in a retirement community with people similar to oneself is one of the options available in modern societies.

Urban Nebraska

Omaha, Nebraska, is a medium-sized, relatively homogeneous city with multiple resources for social engagement. The wives and widows studied by Trudy Anderson live in a section of the city that forms a little community by itself, with a concentration of elderly people. Anderson compares and contrasts the support networks of wives to those of widows, showing that the absence of a husband as a supplier of supports leads to the use of other relatives and long-standing friendships. It is interesting that hardly any of her respondents could not name at least one very close interpersonal tie. Widows, more than wives, report engaging in social activities with children, but a surprisingly large proportion of all these women do not feel close to their offspring. The

Omaha findings support the "principle of family substitution," in that widows rely first on their children, then, if these are not available, on their family of orientation and other relatives for emotional, social, and instrumental supports. Wives depend first upon their husbands. As in the case of Chicago women, friends appear to form a different type of support network, one not compensating for unavailable kin.

Comparisons and Contrasts

American Blacks

Jessyna McDonald decided to concentrate her study of wives and widows on American blacks living in several metropolitan areas. One aspect of their supports that is immediately apparent is the failure of the social security system to cover so many. These women are, therefore, much more likely to be living in poverty than is true of American widows as a whole, most of whom are not very well off. In other words, their economic situation lies at the bottom of the averaged bottom. Many of the older black women worked in occupations that are not covered by social security, such as domestic service. They have either not been married long enough to be covered by the husband's work record, or the husband was also not eligible. Racism and all forms of discrimination, dating back to slavery days but still prevalent now, make it unlikely that lower-class black men, predominant among the elderly, were able to support their families or gain sufficient education or other ladders out of that class to break the vicious cycle of poverty, un- or underemployment, and family conflict.

One source of supports utilized by black widows, in contrast to those, for example, in Australia, is religion and the church as a social group. Both McDonald and I found these resources to be very important to urban black widows. In addition, the whole socialization process of black women stressed their need to be psychologically strong, and the widows express such feelings about themselves. In this chapter we find a strong negative attitude toward remarriage, which was also often voiced by the Chicago and the St. Louis widows of all races. Loss of economic benefits for those eligible for them was one reason, but unpleasant experiences with a past marriage are also a definite deterrent. McDonald found the same importance of the extended kin in providing all kinds of supports as did Stack (1975). Although four in

10 of the women McDonald studied, and two-thirds of those who fell into my early sample (Lopata, 1973), did not have an offspring living with them at the time of data collection, there had been considerable inflow and outflow of people through the home and an exchange of service and social supports, even economic ones in the form of payment for food and clothing. However, the point still remains that many widows in the black community are very poor and are therefore restricted in what they can do for others. Most of their associates share the same fate.

The Remarried and the Unremarried Widows of St. Louis

Margaret Gentry, Linda Rosenman, and Arthur Shulman focused their study on a different aspect of widowhood, the comparison between women who remarried, those who considered remarriage but did not do so, and those who did not even consider such a step. A new husband can provide security and companionship, as well as emotional supports, in addition to many more instrumental supports. Of course, there is a great imbalance in the number of widows and widowers available for remarriage, and the number is not in favor of the women. In addition, men tend to marry younger women, even more so on the second or later time around. Although younger women saw more advantages to remarriage than did older ones, they also recognized more problems. As in Chicago, a very high proportion of widows did not wish to remarry, especially not wanting to give up their independence. We now have more evidence as to the heterogeneity of widows to add to our findings in volume I. In Omaha, Chicago, and St. Louis a husband, in this case a new husband, was or becomes the main provider of supports, while widows use secondary or tertiary resources. Unlike Momence, the gender segregation within marriage is insufficient to provide separate support networks, the wife's networks surviving the death of the husband.

Widows and Widowers

Phyllis Silverman studied widows and widowers who have in common membership in mutual aid organizations for the widowed. The heterogeneity she contributes to this volume is not only in the differences between the genders but also in the response to widowhood. Since these people joined and continue to be involved in mutual aid associations, they obviously feel a need to share their grief among people going through the same experience. They tend to be well educated and articulate—the men, however, less able to express themselves than the women. Their construction of reality around widowhood is varied. Some hark back to what they define as a happy marriage and cannot accept their current situation. One wonders whether they have been going through the husband sanctification process. Several of the widows seemed particularly distraught over decision making since they had depended previously either upon the husband alone or upon a joint experience. Although the differences between the men and the women are strong—their involvement in marriage was from different viewpoints and behavior and they vary in their ability to express their feelings—there were commonalities. Silverman found the women moving toward autonomy while the men increased their ability to "take the role of the other" and to take greater responsibility for maintaining ties with others.

Low-Income Racial and Ethnic Californians

The picture of low-income widows of Hispanic, Asian, black, and white backgrounds living in California and receiving the Supplemental Security Income/State Supplemental Payment (SSI/SSP), as well as benefits from the Medicaid health-care program is similar in several ways to the urban blacks studied by McDonald. They are poor, but many are fortunate in having an extended family and neighborhood networks to fall back upon. In addition, these Californians are living in a state with many benefits for the poor, and they have taken advantage of some of these opportunities, otherwise they would not be in the study. The overall profiles Anabel Pelham and William Clark present are very different from those in other chapters in that they focus on the formal support resources. The authors found the Asian and Hispanic widows to be functionally illiterate but to have many informal supports. They live in large families from which they receive extensive supports. The whites have smaller families and households, and the blacks have fewer children. All four groups, however, receive informal assistance when needed and maintain frequent contact with their children. The differences among the groups are definite but more marginal than substantive in terms of supports rather than structures.

The authors, in fact, do not consider ethnicity itself to be the decisive factor in predicting the level of informal supports; it is the combination of family size and shared residence that is more significant. The needs are serious, but the informal support networks provide sufficient care so that the formal support network is not used as much as it could be. As it is, the In-home Supportive Services and medical care expenditures of the state are enormous and would be overwhelming were the informal systems not in place. There is an interesting variation among the ethnic/racial groups: the Asians do not use the formal system, either because their needs are already satisfactorily met or because of a cultural reluctance to admit need.

What is unique about California is its highly developed program for older people, among the best in any state. This chapter presents a detailed description of the kind of services a government can undertake to help the elderly poor, including widows, and the frightening possibility of expenditures such an organization would have to meet without the informal networks, especially as the number of elderly increases in coming years.

The Big Picture

Widows in Canada

Two chapters deal with widows in Canada as a whole society, but each uses different sets of data and focuses on different characteristics of the women and of widowhood. Anne Martin Matthews found the support systems and life-styles of Canadian widows similar to those of the Chicago area. They face a drop of income and many live near the poverty line. Although Canada and the United States have created a vast network of resources to help people in times of crisis and to assist in reorganization of lives following such events, the widows, particularly the most needful and older ones, underutilize these resources. One difference between the Canadian widows and those of Chicago, which Matthews and I have discussed on several occasions, is the presence of siblings in the support systems. As stated before, we asked respondents to name the main contributors to 65 different economic, service, social, and emotional supports. Brothers and sisters, and other members of the extended family, appeared very rarely in the Chicago sample (Lopata, 1978b). This is not true among the Canadians. Matthews hypothesizes that the difference may be due to the fact that so many widows in Canada are still living in the area in which they grew up, while those in Chicago have been experiencing much social and geographical mobility, even on the part of the widows themselves and their older family members. More siblings are available to the Canadians.

Friendship appears also to have greater salience for the Canadians. Part of the research reported by Matthews was her own replication of my study, so the differences are bound to be in the culture and structure of Canada vis-à-vis Chicago rather than a product of differences in what is being studied.

More Canadian Widows

The final chapter in this volume also focuses on Canadians and, rather than using many studies, as did Matthews, depends upon a single piece of research, a large Canadian Health Survey. Selecting measures hypothesized to influence morale among the elderly on the basis of known research, the authors conclude that, in the combination of gender and marital status, widowed women have the lowest morale, followed by widowed men, married women, and married men. They find eight "predictors of positive morale" among women, including better income, marriage, better education (reminding us of other studies), good health, smaller families, participation in more solitary activities as well as in social activities, and religiosity. Religion thus appears as an important part of life in several samples of widows. The authors also found fewer differences between widowed people in Canada and the United States. The results of the study favor an activity theory of aging, but it is interesting that solitary action was also important.

Summary

This volume, thus, contains chapters describing the support systems and life-styles of widows in two allegedly highly developed or modernized societies, America and Canada. Yet, it will be apparent as we go through these analyses that there is great heterogeneity of resources and supports offered, or pulled together by a great variety of women. This is not surprising since people tend to continue levels of social engagement throughout their adult lives. The societies, and the communities in which the widows are located, provide different types of resources, and the women have been socialized to engage at different levels and types of social roles and relations. A major factor influencing the life frameworks of widows, as of other people, in modern societies is their personal set of resources enabling volunteeristic engagement. This does not mean an absence of automatically engaging informal networks, as we will see in all the communities or categories of widows, from Momence to the ethnic poor in California or to all the Canadians thus far studied.

2 American After Lives: Widowhood in Community Context

CHRISTINE L. FRY and LAUREE GARVIN

Widowhood is a life stage experienced by a majority of women. It is an ascriptive stage in the sense that widows exert little choice in the deaths of their husbands. In spite of the loss of a partner, life goes on. How these "after lives" unfold and develop is shaped by the social arena in which the woman is located. With few exceptions (e.g., Lopata, 1972; Levine, 1986), we know comparatively little about the influence of this social context upon the way in which widowhood is experienced. Communities provide meaning, offer norms and role models, and place restrictions on or provide opportunities for widows. The relation between community context and widowhood is an important factor in determining what can happen as the woman's life after marriage continues. It also points to diversity in the way widows experience and shape their lives.

This chapter examines widowhood in one community, Momence, Illinois.[1] Momence is a small town that was the focus of a cross-cultural project on age in community contexts, Project AGE. The social arena in Momence is what we call a "life-term arena" (Moore, 1978). It is marked by residential stability and continuity. Although people do move in and out of the community, the majority are long-term residents living among kin and friends. In the life-term arena one's life develops in a social field where one is known in his or her entirety as a person and one's social history is known to all. Also, lifelong patterns develop with continuity as cohorts grow old together.

What are the consequences of this life-term arena for the life after the death of a husband, widowhood? Increasingly, as we have focused on the lives of older people, widows become the subject of scientific research. The pioneering work of Lopata (1973; 1979) has mapped the phenomenon of widowhood and the support systems of widows in Chicago. Our current knowledge, however, is anchored in this and other urban populations or in a framework of intervention (Silverman, 1986) to ameliorate the deficits of the urban environment. Of necessity, most of this research is based on a survey design and obtains selected information about the women who are widowed. Although located in an urbanized county (greater than 50,000), culturally Momence is not urban, nor is it rural. Momence is a community, a small town. The data from this study is both qualitative and quantitative. In this chapter we first describe the social arena and context. We then look at the significance of widowhood as a marker of a stage of life. Finally, we examine the experiences of widowhood in this life-term arena.

Momence: The Old Border Town

Momence is a "cosmopolitan small town." Key informants were consistent on this point. It is located 50 miles directly south of the Chicago Loop along the Dixie Highway (Illinois 1) on the Kankakee River. The proximity of Chicago makes access to some of the nicer qualities of urban life easier. As recently as 12 years ago one could take a train into the Loop for shopping and a show and be home before midnight. Now this can be accomplished by an hour's drive. Momence is far enough from Chicago that it has not experienced suburbanization. The cultural boundary to the south for the Chicago SMA coincides with the 312/815 area code and the Will County/Kankakee County line. This is about 12 miles north of Momence between Beecher and Grant Park. North of this line the distribution of the *Kankakee Daily Journal* falls off and the frequency of tract housing and commuting increases. Although Chicago is a positive in availability of cultural resources and jobs, it has its negative side. Most informants express fear of the expressways (e.g., the Dan Ryan), getting lost, and the neighborhoods on the South Side.

Momence views itself as a unique and vital community. An "Old Border Town" is the phrase used by local residents to describe the community. This comes from the early days in the 1830s and on through the 1860s and 70s when life in Momence was pretty rough-and-tumble. Momence was the border between civilization and the outlaws in the Kankakee Marshes. Momence has maintained another kind of border to the west. Momence looks east toward the state line separating Indiana and Illinois. In 1853, when Kankakee County was established, an election was held to decide in which community the county seat would be located. Momence at that time was the largest community and the "rightful" choice. However, the railroads stuffed the ballot boxes by letting their road gangs vote several times, and Kankakee, 13 miles to the west, became the county seat. It isn't the fact that Momence lost the election that is significant, rather the fact that people still remember. Although many residents work in Kankakee and shopping expeditions are fairly frequent, boundary maintenance is quite high. The "they" in Kankakee is somewhat negative (e.g., the *Journal* is not interested in what goes on in Momence; they act like "big city hot shots"; or the Chamber of Commerce was self-congratulatory when it crossed the boundary and donated $200 to the Kankakee Chamber for a postal campaign to encourage the President to reinstate the Joliet Arsenal—"Who would believe it"). To the east is farmland and a 19-mile course of the Kankakee River as it winds its way from the state line seven miles away. To the south the border is even sharper. Pembroke and Hopkins Park are black communities settled in the 1870s. A caste line corresponds with the township line. Finally, to the north is Chicago, the "up north."

Thus, Momence is a bounded unit with a nucleated town and a sustaining area of about 70 square miles. The population is not evenly distributed. Population density is greatest along the river, in the three subdivisions in town, and in the less well-to-do sections of town. It is lower in the farmlands that exist two per square mile in one section to the east. In population numbers, the City of Momence has 3,297 people with an estimated 4,000 in the 70 square miles around the town. Of this number, 22 percent are over 60; when looking at the adult population (over 18 years of age), 32 percent are over 60. The population we identified on our sample blocks (from which we drew our sample) within the city closely resembles the U.S. Census figures. In our sample of 210 men and women, we have 11 widowers and 25 widows. All are over the age of 60 years. This age group was intentionally oversampled because of our interest in old age. Of the women, 13 are among the younger old (less than 75 years) and 12 are among the older old (75+ years).

Change and Stability

Population size has been stable over the past three decades, expanding at a rate of about 200 per decade. The U.S. Census indicates that the percentage of population change is 16 percent. Somewhat consistent figures from the Haines Criss-Cross Directory indicate a 13 percent change in phone listings per year. This latter figure is a little problematic since many of those changes are simply corrections of incorrect listings.

Economy

The economy of Momence is diversified. Its business community is differentiated, with business oriented to the service sector, agribusiness, retail, and industrial. We counted over 300 firms within the study area (not including farms). The biggest issue facing Momence is the economic situation, which has stagnated. Local small business has expanded, but the business district has too many vacant buildings. Major stores—a men's clothing store, the Western Auto store, a bar, a shoe store, the shoe repair, and a fabric shop—have all closed. Merchants complain about small profit margins and even report subsidizing their businesses from their own capital.

The biggest change in Momence has been this decline in the economy. At the time we were interviewing informants, the unemployment rate in Kankakee County was 17 percent, among the highest in the state of Illinois. With an unemployment rate that high, the community was fearful of losing community members, who would go elsewhere for work. It is the young who are seen as being most affected by this change; they are starting out but are without jobs. The old are insulated from these changes in that they have pensions and social security as well as their accumulated savings.

Project AGE

The research reported here is a part of Project AGE[2], a cross-cultural project designed to examine the effects of community characteristics on the well-being of older people. Work has been conducted in Momence, Illinois, Swarthmore, Pennsylvania, and in four neighborhoods in Hong Kong. Work is also being conducted in two communities in Ireland and two in Botswana in southern Africa. By selecting communities of markedly different characteristics, the intent is to provide data from these communities that makes possible an evaluation of hypotheses about the consequences of macrosocial features for the well-being of older people. The system-level factors include such features as societal scale, economies, type of changes, demographic stability, and cultural values. Intervening mechanisms such as the meaning and clarity of age norms, resource control, peer ties, intergenerational relations, and health and functionality constitute pathways through which system-level factors exert their influence on well-being in old age.

The methods of comparative community study must be multiple. Five strategies are essential to obtain relevant and comparable data. First, participant observation is used to anchor the dynamics of age to the arena of community life. Second, a structured interview is employed to obtain data on residential history, kin location, educational and work histories, community participation, self-assessment of health and functionality, and self-assessment of well-being. Third, the "Age Game" was developed. This is a sorting task to obtain data on perceptions of the life span—including normative definition and evaluation of life stages and transitions—and on social contacts with individuals in stages defined as "old." Fourth, life histories examine lives over time, subjective views of the life span, and community change. Finally, community inventories of formal organizations and commercial establishments are undertaken to establish age relations within the public domain of community life.

The life course, not widowhood, was the target of this comparative project. However, because widowhood is characteristic of the later life stages, we will consider its importance as a marker in the life course. Also, because the methods involve observations of public life and collections of life histories, qualitative data is available on the experience of widowhood.

Significance of Widowhood as a Marker of the Life Course

Since we wanted to examine the life course and the meaning of age, an instrument we call the Age Game was developed. This was designed to intellectually involve respondents in an ethnosemantic[3] interview and to investigate the meanings of the life course in each community. The development of this instrument involved intensive and repeat interviewing of a number of key informants. The initial question asked was, "What do I need to know to make a judgment about a person's age?" Besides asking directly about the stages of life in each community, we reversed roles with each informant by playing a game of "twenty questions" (Spradley, 1979). Informants asked investigators questions about people in the community to guess correctly their age. From the questions asked we were able to ascertain the significant markers that signaled greater or lesser age. For Momence these markers are work status, marital status, children's status, education, organizational involvement, and housing tenure, especially if the mortgage is paid or not.

From these initial interviews we returned to our key informants to work out age norms by asking them to define real people using the age markers. Key informants took the markers (we also could call them attributes of age) and created first themselves and then others of different ages. On the basis of 140 real people in Momence we created age-norm tables. Finally, using these age norms, hypothetical people or "social personae" were described using the markers of age. Our key informants approved them for their cultural appropriateness or grammaticality. From this point, we introduced our personae to a sample of 210 people in Momence who played the Age Game.

These respondents were asked to examine the social personae (presented as descriptions on 3 × 5 cards) and to evaluate their age and then to place them into an age group. Respondents were not instructed on the number of divisions of adulthood; they were told there was no "correct" way, that we were interested in their view. The median number of divisions of adulthood in Momence was five, with the majority of variation ranging between three and six stages of adult life. The divisions people saw constituted the meaningful point of reference for a battery of questions. These included a judgment on the markers of age; the transitions across the stages of adult life as well as chronological end points; and qualitative dimensions of good things, hard things, and concerns of the respective age groups.

Respondents and informants were not asked about widowhood. Instead they were asked to focus on the life course. Interestingly, when looking at the life course in its entirety, widowhood is not seen as either a major marker or as a defining transition into a stage of adulthood. This is a surprising and somewhat unsettling result of the research in Momence, both when considering data anchored in self and questions of generalized life stages. These results, as we will argue, are linked to a community context that eases the transition from married to widowed and reflect the age-saliency of statuses as age markers at different points of the life course.

Defining Features of the Life Course

Once respondents had sorted personae into age groups, they were asked to give a name to the respective groupings and to indicate why they had placed the particular persona in each group. Widowhood was never used to name an age group, either young or old. However, in describing what the personae have in common as they were grouped into life stages, widowhood seems to be more significant. For the older life stages, the range is 10.6–22.9 percent of respondents mentioning it. The 22.9 percent is for an age grade with a threshold of 75 years.

Transitions into Generalized Life Stages

Following the sorting of personae into age groups, respondents were asked, "How does one become a member of this group? What marks the turning point at which a person enters this group?" A low percent of respondents saw widowhood as a threshold to the older life stages. The range is between 5.6–8 percent.[4] Widowhood, not unexpectedly, is never referenced for the younger groups. We find that retirement, poor health, and chronological age are of greater significance than widowhood as a point of entry into the older age categories.

Own Transition

Following the playing of the Age Game, respondents were asked to identify their age group, when they became a member (year), and what event signaled membership. Again references to widowhood are low. Only two out of 25 widows saw widowhood as the event that moved them into an older age group.

Widowhood as a Theme in Life Histories

Three of the women invited to record their life histories are widows, and a fourth was widowed while the multiple-session life histories were being obtained. Widowhood in the lives of these women is very important and an experience about which they talk freely. The metaphor used to elicit the life history is that of book chapters, not age. Our framing question was, "If I were to write a book about your life, what would be the chapters?" Each person then looked at their life as a sequence of meaningful divisions. Interestingly, only one widow (a young widow at the time of the event—age 49 years with children still to launch) saw a chapter beginning with the death of her husband and continuing with its aftermath. "Widowhood" was the title given to this chapter. Since that event occurred early in her life, there were other chapters to follow. For the older widows, the chapters are titled "Semi-Retirement" or a continuation of "Life in Momence" and "A Learning Experience." The latter referred to widowhood but also to multiple deaths in her family and other transitions for family members.

Clearly, when integrating their lives and their experiences into a meaningful framework, widowhood has shaped their lives. Widowhood, however, seldom stands alone as a separate chapter, except when major reorganization is required and the event is "off time." In looking at the meaningful divisions in their lives, these women focus on the substance of the event and its aftermath, not the event itself. They see their lives ordered by many things, with widowhood being only one among many. When widowhood is disruptive of the other things, then it becomes *the* major thing.

Interpretation

The empirical data indicates that widowhood is not a significant marker of the life course, either as a threshold for generalized transitions or for one's own transition. It is a little more important as a defining feature of life stages, especially for life stages that begin at 75 years (the oldest, old). On the other hand, when organizing one's own life, the experience of being widowed is a part of other stages, seldom being the central feature in looking at a meaningful division as that life has unfolded. Two explanations can be offered concerning widowhood and age. The first examines what information on age and life course the status of widowhood reveals. The second looks at the context of Momence.

1. *Widowhood and life stages*. Death is beyond the control of humans and hence is a natural event. Although widowhood is a status that increases after age 60, it is not inevitable, with some husbands surviving into their 90s. As a transition and as a marker of a life stage, it is

somewhat random. Culture is not random as humans superimpose order onto nature. Very rarely are random features used as a cultural marker.

Marital status, on the other hand, is an important marker of age and life stage. In the younger age ranges marital status is more important. In older age groups it follows in importance retirement, grandchildren, great grandchildren, and loss of abilities to retain the independence associated with adulthood as a defining feature of the life stage. The reason for this is that marriage is normatively linked to children. Our key informants found marital status to be critical in making judgments about age. Information about marital status was second in their sequence of questions, with work being first. Not surprisingly, the third question was about children's status. The question about marital status politely cleared the way for questions about children. (If single was our reply, very few people ventured to ask about children.)

A reason why widowhood is not seen as a marker of age is that if marital status is linked with children, then widowhood provides very little information about age. If a widow has children they are likely to be adult children and grandchildren. Because adult children are usually not co-resident with the widow, and the presence of grandchildren is dependent on their children's reproductive decisions, the saliency in indicating age of the widow declines. One can be a grandparent as early as 30 or may have to wait until the 50s or 60s.

The implication is that certain statuses correspond fairly well with chronological age and hence serve well as social markers of age. However, these may be salient only at specific life stages. Age norms, legal norms, or biological maturation and capabilities calibrate the age markers. As one gets older, what worked well as a marker earlier in the life course may not work as well in indicating age later in life. For instance, one graduates from high school around age 18, but one still can be a high school graduate at age 85. The same may be said for marital status, children's status, grandchildren and great-grandchildren, and work status, although the age norms are different.

2. *Socioeconomic status and gender differentiation*. Momence is a working-class community. The range of variation on the Trieman (1977) occupational prestige score is 18–75, with means around 41 and standard deviations of 12. Seventy-seven percent of those people interviewed in our sample were below the score of 50. Using the Warner scale (Warner et al., 1949), we find the full range of prestige scores (1–7) and means of 3.9, with standard deviations of 1.4. Consistent with this

is the educational level of those interviewed. Almost 70 percent had only a high school education or less, while only 9 percent had a college or advanced degree. The mean income reported for the zip code in which Momence is located in 1980 was a little over $10,000. This figure is somewhat depressed by the fact that a portion of Pembroke, a black community, is partially located in the same zip code as Momence.

Gender differences in activities and social networks are markedly differentiated. Male and female social networks follow the patterns suggested by Bott (1957) for working-class families in London. Female networks are usually kin based and, in the more public arena, display considerable female bonding after the age of 40. Males, on the other hand, are less kin based but are bonded in the political, commercial, and formal arena on an ability (and visibility) and not age basis. Although married couples are seen as a couple, their networks are differentiated. Consequently, when a woman loses her husband, she doesn't also lose her social network. In other communities where marital roles are less differentiated, and where coupling is the pattern, widowhood may be a more significant marker of the life course. Here, when a woman loses her husband, her network becomes disrupted with the stage of life initiated by widowhood becoming, indeed, a new stage of life.

In the life-term arena, we find that gender differentiation extends beyond the marital role. In Momence the public arena (in contrast to the domestic sphere—Ortner, 1974) are differentiated by age and gender. Participation for women generally begins after children are launched. There is a visible female social sphere within churches, female organizations (Women's Club, female auxiliaries to male organizations), and informal cliques. The male sphere is much more diffuse, being linked to business and politics. It is the availability and continuity of involvement in this female sphere that has the potential of minimizing the disruption of social relations inaugurated by widowhood. Although the event of becoming a widow is traumatic, the aftermath sees the widow reincorporated back into a world of peers.

The Experience of Widowhood

Although the size and interdependency of Momence with other communities precludes a total face-to-face community, the majority of the cast of characters is known. For those who remain in Momence or return to Momence, it is a life-term arena. One's personal history is built up over time, it is known, and one's present actions and circumstances are interpreted in light of the past. The life-term arena has its costs and benefits. The costs are familiar to urbanites who enjoy the "freedom" and choices in cities. Freedom from community and past identities, however, can have their costs in anomie and social isolation if major linkages are disrupted. In spite of the potential negatives in remembering past identities, continuity in social relations brings benefits to widows. They lose one significant relationship but do not lose their entire social network with the death of their husband.

Becoming a Widow

As a rite of passage, widowhood transforms a woman from married to formerly married. Rites of passage involve a state of separation (Van Gennep, 1960) or a liminal state (Turner, 1969). Such a liminal state places the widow in an in-between status of neither fully married, but not yet widowed. For the duration of her husband's terminal illness, dependent on the severity and limitations of that illness, the widow-to-be is in limbo, isolated from normal social relations.

The consequences of the liminal state can be quite profound. One widow had nursed her husband for five years, becoming housebound along with him. Following his death, she was filled with anger and found the process of reestablishing social ties overwhelming. On the other hand, terminal illnesses that are short in duration or not isolating do not result in a long in-between period. Consequently, reintegration on the widow's side proceeds more rapidly.

Reintegration into Community

In a life-term arena, a "culture of widows" exists. It is not community-wide but exists in the form of informal networks often formed through membership in formal organizations such as clubs or church groups. Women who are already widowed or still married carefully monitor the progress of the new widow as she adjusts to life without her husband. Discussions of her progress and readiness ultimately results in invitations to join the more public and service functions of the community. Volunteer jobs such as working a food concession stand for a fund-raising activity, serving as a hostess at the flower show or the museum, or helping out at public events brings the widow back to the community and visibility in women's groups. Literally, the widow is "grabbed" by her peers and her liminal state terminated. Nearly 75 percent of the older women visible in the public life of the community are widows.

Peers and the Culture of Widows

The culture of widows is by and large a peer culture bonded by homophyly in gender, widowhood, and common experiences built around long-term participation in community life. The informal basis of this peer culture can be seen in cardplaying, eating in the local restaurants, and, for those who can afford it, travel to exotic places.

Cardplaying is ubiquitous and is not an exclusive activity of the widowed or the old. Formalized cliques play bridge, and the results are reported in the local paper under the heading "Bridge-o-Rama." Informally, couples or groups of women, both married and widowed, play bridge or pinochle usually in the evening. At fund-raising events a salad lunch is provided and tables are set for an afternoon of cards. People, mostly older female and widowed, arrive in foursomes, claim their tables, eat lunch, and then play cards, with the winner taking home the centerpiece (usually a potted plant). Continuity is found in cardplaying. Widows report that 20 years ago as a couple they would visit other couples and play cards. Now, as widows, they continue, but without the men. These informal cliques sometimes are named—e.g., "The Widows Club." Also, widowhood does not separate the widow from the married women who join their friends, who may be widowed, as a part of the prearranged networks that arrive at fund-raising luncheons for an afternoon of cards.

Community life is also seen in the local restaurants. Here widows are not excluded but constitute a major set in the cast of characters. What we call "commensality cliques" of widows are most visible in this context. Friendship cliques often begin the day with breakfast or meet for coffee and lunch. In the evenings widows join each other for supper at the evening restaurants on a regular and predictable basis. Widows also report frequenting restaurants in Kankakee or elsewhere in the area as a part of shopping expeditions.

A few widows are visible within the community because of annual expeditions to foreign countries. For a change of scenery and a new experience, they team up, make plans for a different part of the world, and go. They return with new experiences, treasures to give to their families, and stories to recount to others and each other.

Because the culture of peers is informal, its public visibility represents only the "tip of the iceberg." Peers are extremely important in linking a widow to a part of the community. In a life-term arena, peer culture extends back to high school for those who are lifelong residents. Continuity in networks and activities throughout adulthood means continuity in spite of changes brought about by the change in marital status.

Formal Organizations and Widows

The formal organizations that structure the female public domain are both age graded and age heterogeneous. The women involved are mostly over the age of 40. These groups are the female church groups and the Women's Club, which crosscuts the entire community. The church groups are the most age graded but incorporate both the married and the widowed. The Women's Club recruits women of all ages, but members do acquire seniority as they mature and move through the ranks of office. These formal groups link widows with the married and single women of the community. It is here where knowledge of each other is acquired and, once widowhood occurs, the process or reincorporation into the informal peer culture of widows can begin.

Family and Widows

Residential stability in Momence is high. The 16 percent change in population per decade and the 13 percent change in telephone listings must be interpreted in the face of family continuity. Over one-third of our sample had lived in Momence for 30 percent of their lives. Thirty-three percent of our sample was born in Momence and 46 percent within Kankakee County. The mean number of years lived in Momence was 33, with a standard deviation of 20. Of those in our sample, nearly 50 percent have or had parents in Momence.

These statistics are consistent with what impressed us in early observations as obsession with genealogies. Several informants explained to us that children, regardless of their gender, are often referred to by their mother's name. Kinship is at the core. To be on the map you need kin, otherwise you are an outsider because you cannot be placed and have no roots in the community. Some people leave, especially the young. Here the success stories are counted: the basketball star who is presently a star in the NBA, the high school football star who plays in the NFL, the university professor, and the architect who designs hotels all over the world.

In this context of residential and familial continuity, widows are not significantly different than the rest of the over-60 population. We estimate that people over 60 years of age have an average of nearly 12 kinship members within an hour's drive of Momence. Widowers have significantly less kin available. The support from kin is nearly invisible since it is in the domestic domain. Yet it is there and is very strong. On a nearly daily basis some widows receive a short visit from a daughter or daughter-in-law. Family events and holidays bring kin together, with some widows forced to choose between local kin or a trip to children who have moved elsewhere. Widows talk about their descendants and siblings, while children and grandchildren talk about their mother (grandmother) and usually about how "active" and how well they are doing.

Formal and Informal Supports

Support systems in Momence are by and large informal. Formal supports exist but are rarely seen as a viable alternative, only as the last resort. Informal supports are not highly visible.[5] Instead, they are the support given by beauticians who give a client a ride to the grocery store or take them to the doctor over in Kankakee (often for a nominal sum or lunch and gas money). Cleaning ladies not only keep houses clean and do house maintenance, they are known to provide further support by preparing one hot meal during the day. Thus, a support network exists that works on a cash basis but that is not state supported. Elderly widows are able to purchase rides to the store or maintenance of their household (inclusive of cooking) at reasonable rates. Formal (state supported) support is comparatively rare. For instance there are only four people receiving "meals on wheels" in Momence.

Effects of Community on Widowhood

A life-term arena has its benefits, and the benefits for widows are considerable. With continuity in social networks with kin and with peers (females), the effects of limnality are reduced. Widows are welcomed back to public life and to the formal organizations when they are ready. Informal cliques of widows congeal and continue recreational and social activities that are continuous with those of the younger years when husbands were alive.

Although we have seen the continuity in Momence as positive for the experience of widowhood, life-term arenas are not without their costs. Continuity means that one's personhood has a history that is known in considerable detail. Reputations are built and difficult to modify. In terms of support systems, one builds and discharges social capital across their lifetime. Even in a lifetime arena, where informal supports are available, when acute need arises, it may be difficult to draw on one's social capital. People remember the past and who one was. To call on supports alters that image most likely for the worse.

Widowhood in this arena is not seen as marking the threshold into a life stage or as being a life stage in and of itself. However, it is seen as a significant characteristic of the oldest age categories among other characteristics. Widowhood provides very little information about age. Women who talk about their life experiences see their own widowhood, liminal states, and the aftermath as major events in their lives. Yet, unless these events created major reorganization (as in early or "off time" widowhood), widowhood is not seen as a distinct division in their lives.

The parts of the life-term arena that are visible are the public contexts of formal organizations or the activities of informal groups that take place in a public context or are talked about. The widows participating in this part of the arena are the "active/outgoing" women. They are the "successful" widows and older women. They are not isolated and have not become the polar opposite of "active," disinterested and deteriorating. However, there is a continuum from those who are active and those who are not active. In a context of continuity, this too is a lifelong pattern. If one is not involved as a young or middle-aged adult, then one will not be active as an older adult. This does not mean they are isolated but that they are not visible. Their linkages to others are through kinship and neighboring.

Since social contexts are noted for their diversity, the case study of Momence raises many questions that can only be resolved by examining widowhood in other social contexts. The two issues raised here center on widowhood as a marker of age and as a stage in the life course, and reincorporation of the widow following her limnality after the death of her husband.

In Momence we found that widowhood is not a strong marker of age and that it is not an event widows use to retrospectively organize their lives. Is this a product of the continuity we find in Momence where widowhood is not disruptive of the woman's social network unless it is "off time?" Is it a product of marital status not being an age-salient marker late in the life course, or death of a spouse being a natural rather than a cultural event? The significance of widowhood as a life-course event and organizing principle of later life remains an empirically unexplored topic.

Widows in Momence have available a female public domain that can reintegrate them into community life if their own understandings of themselves and lifelong patterns permit them to be drawn into the culture of widows. Because of the size and established traditions in the community, this is visible to an observer and to the actors themselves. Do we find this in more urbanized communities, only in much more fragmentary and much less visible form? To discover this requires more qualitative discovery procedures. On the other hand, in more rural communities, is this public domain not as developed and not as available to women who are widowed?

Life after the death of a husband, in many ways an "after life," is an issue that is central to research on aging. Partners cannot expect to die together. For the survivor life must go on. The arena in which that life continues to unfold and develop conditions what eventually happens. Communities in their diversity are natural laboratories in which to explore the causes and consequences of social context on the meaning and experience of widowhood in the life course of widows.

3 Attachment to Home and Support Systems of Older Widows in Columbus, Ohio

SHIRLEY L. O'BRYANT

American culture, especially in the case of today's older cohorts, has attached great importance to homeownership. Many older couples have lived in the same house for an extended period of time. Usually husbands die first, often leaving their widows as sole homeowners. The extent of the vulnerability of these older widows, who remain living alone in their own homes, is related to a number of factors. Of particular interest is what impact the availability and viability of an older widow's family, friends, and neighbor support networks have on her sense of well-being and ability to remain in her home.

The Place

The circumstances, support systems, and well-being of older widows living alone in their homes have been studied extensively among older women in Columbus, Ohio. Columbus, as referred to throughout this chapter, includes 10 small urban and suburban incorporated cities within and bordering the city limits of Columbus, proper. All of these urban areas are within Franklin County, Ohio, and the large city of Columbus dominates the life-styles and economies of the county. The greatest advantage that Columbus offered to this research was that it is so typical of the *average* American life-style; thus, it provided an excellent socioeconomic environment for the study of widowhood. The

This research was supported by a grant from AARP Andrus Foundation. Their support is gratefully acknowledged.

validity of describing Columbus as an average American city is based on demographic, historic, economic, and social data.

The 1980 Census showed 1,167,460 people aged 65 or older living in Ohio. They represent 10.6 percent of the state's entire population, or about one in every nine persons—quite comparable with the national percentage of 11 percent. In Ohio, women account for three-fifths (60.5 percent) of the 65+ population. With regard to marital status, there are more than five times as many widows as widowers, with nearly half (45 percent) of all women aged 65 or older being widowed (Ohio Department on Aging, 1984). With respect to living arrangements, older Ohioans are close to national figures, with 71 percent of older persons being homeowners. Smith and Hiltner (1977) studied the characteristics of elderly residents in the United States and concluded that Ohio was one of the eight states where the housing situation of elderly persons was "typical" of that which exists nationwide.

Demographically, whereas many midwestern cities were declining in population during recent years due to economic problems and people moving to the Sun Belt, Columbus has remained relatively stable. The 1983 population of the city was 564,871, that of Franklin County was 876,893, and that of the Columbus Standard Metropolitan Area, consisting of seven counties, was 1,401,403 (Columbus Regional Information Service, 1984). Although a highly populated area, Columbus also covers a large geographical area; thus, it retains much of the charm of a small community (Bowman, Giuliani, and Mingé, 1981). In the 1920s the people of Columbus liked to refer to their town as the biggest small city in the nation and the phraseology has lasted. Peirce and Hagstrom (1984) recently described the city as a "well-scrubbed, provincial, complacent, spacious plains city . . . which is quite content to be characterized as the largest small town in America" (pp. 312–13).

In their book, *Columbus: America's Crossroads*, Garrett and Lentz (1980) quote Columbus-born humorist James Thurber, who wrote, "Columbus is a town in which almost anything is likely to happen and in which almost everything has" (p. 10). Garrett and Lentz go on to relate that the city did not inherit its history and reputation but built them from scratch. Approximately 200 years ago the fertile area of what is now central Ohio, where rivers converge and flow south to the Ohio River, was populated by various Indian tribes. Early settlers subsequently formed the small community of Franklinton at the confluence of the Olentangy and Scioto rivers. The settlement became a strategic location on these waterways and was a stopover point on the Indian trail to Lake Erie from the Ohio River. Later the location was important to the canal system and, in more recent times, to railroads, expressways, and air routes. Today, two large nationwide retail stores have placed giant distribution centers in Columbus. Thus, the city has always held a key location for commerce in mid-America.

Following the American Revolution, major land grants took place in the Midwest. The small settlement of Franklinton offered the advantage of being located between two major conflicting cultural areas —the Western Reserve area in the northern part of the state, which was settled by Yankees from New England, and an area in the southern part of the state that was settled by persons of Appalachian heritage from south of the Ohio River (Garrett and Lentz, 1980). Although a few remnants of these cultures are still visible today when contrasting the northern and southern sections of the urban area, Columbus does not have any identifiable ethnic neighborhoods other than a somewhat diversified area of blacks, who constitute approximately 16 percent of the city's population.

Between 1803, when Ohio became a state, and 1812, the state's fledgling legislators operated out of temporary capitals. In 1812 an area across the river from Franklinton was selected to become the new capital of the state. Surveys were made, plots of land were set aside, and very wide streets were laid out in a grid. This new and permanent state capital was named after Christopher Columbus. The early population was primarily English, German, and Scots-Irish. Most of the settlers were not farmers or state lawmakers but were professionals, businessmen, and craftsmen (Garrett and Lentz, 1980). The early trend of professionals and businessmen gravitating to the city has continued to the present day, with some of America's top companies being headquartered in Columbus.

Although Columbus grew rapidly during World War II, when numerous military aircraft were produced there, it does not have large, smoke-belching industries in the city. Instead, there is a finely balanced business economy consisting of light manufacturing and local entrepreneurs. The latter not only have personal stakes in the city but also sway its development (Peirce and Hagstrom, 1984). In addition, governmental interests play a strong role in Columbus. Almost 20,000 individuals employed by the State of Ohio, as well as numerous federal employees, are found in various governmental agencies based in different locations throughout the city; closely associated with these agencies are various interest groups and lobbyist organizations. Furthermore, separate governmental structures are operated by Franklin County and the City of Columbus, both of which provide numerous services for the general population of the area through the employment of thousands more civil servants. In addition, this large urban area contains not only stable businesses and functional government but also an intellectual component. There are 12 colleges and universities in the metropolitan area, the largest of which is The Ohio State University with an enrollment in excess of 50,000, thereby constituting a city within itself. Also, Columbus is the headquarters of the world-renowned Battelle Memorial Institute, the largest nonprofit research facility of its kind. Overall, with respect to the city's balanced milieu, 24 percent of the labor force is employed in retail business, 22.4 percent in services and education, 20.3 percent in government, 17.4 percent in manufacturing, and the balance in finance, insurance, transportation, utilities, and construction (Ohio Bureau of Employment Services, 1984).

Given the foregoing description, it is no surprise that Columbus is utilized by the business world as one of America's leading test markets for new products (Columbus Area Chamber of Commerce, 1984). The consistently stable economy, lower rates of unemployment than in other Midwestern cities, and demographic diversity all lead to a socioeconomic balance that is considered ideal for market testing. In addition, the various attributes of Columbus provide a very fertile environment for research in the social sciences. The qualities of the population have created a city that is not only symbolic of average America but also one that has proven itself to be exactly that throughout its history and development. Consequently, it is believed that widows in Columbus are representative of a much larger population of urban widows, though generalizations beyond the present group should be made bearing in mind the place in which they live.

Living Arrangements

The most common type of living arrangement in the United States, accounting for 44 percent of all older households, is one in which an older husband and wife reside in their own home, with no other family members present. The second most frequent type is the single homeowner who lives alone, representing 37 percent of the 65 + population (Pastalan, 1983). The majority of these single homeowners are widows who have outlived their husbands and have continued to reside in the same single-family dwellings. Rix (1984) reports that nearly two-thirds of all elderly female householders own their dwellings and most of them—80 percent—live alone.

Generally, older persons' homes represent their major financial asset; however, homeownership is seldom a sign of economic security, especially for elderly women. In the United States, as of 1981, the median value of the houses owned by older women living alone was $39,600, as compared to a median value of $55,300 for all owner-occupied houses (Rix, 1984). Although poverty is less prevalent among owners than among renters, nearly one-quarter of elderly female nonfamily homeowners have incomes below the poverty level (Rix, 1984). These women had to maintain their homes on an income much lower in proportion to the value of their homes than is the case of other elderly homeowners. An important point here is that many women shift from high- to low-income status when they are widowed, yet their housing expenses —mortgage payments (if any), utility costs, maintenance, insurance, and repairs—remain virtually the same. Not surprisingly, economic considerations have been shown to be a leading predictor of older widows' intentions to move from their homes (O'Bryant, 1983b).

Attachment to Home

Rather than move, the majority of older widows choose to remain in their homes for a variety of reasons. Among these may be that the elderly widow's home is usually fully paid for and may represent the most economical place for her to live because she does not pay rent and can postpone many maintenance costs (Scholen and Chen, 1980). Also, the widow may feel that her health is good enough to manage staying in her home, but not good enough to move. Most importantly, as Lopata (1979) points out, a widow's home is an important resource and serves as a symbol of ownership and independence.

Many housing experts typically view the phenomenon of older persons' remaining in their homes negatively. To wit: "It is not uncommon for old people to cling to their own homes for sentimental reasons or from fear of change. Since they have spent so much of their lives there, they often do not realize when their homes become inadequate for their needs. This attachment may make them less likely to take advantage of available social assistance and often leads to isolation and loneliness" (Goldenberg, 1981, p. 4).

The present author was among the first to study empirically the subjective factors that enter into an older person's "attachment to home" (O'Bryant, 1983a). This research identified four factors: (1) competence derived from living in a familiar environment; (2) status provided through homeownership; (3) a cost versus comfort trade-off—e.g., uncomfortable homes are seen as more of a financial burden; and (4) a traditional family orientation that sees the home as a part of the family, both in terms of memories and as a domicile for future generations. For widows, in particular, being a homeowner serves as a symbol of status and competence (O'Bryant and Nocera, in press). In addition, the attachment-to-home factors have been shown to be related to the general housing satisfaction (O'Bryant 1982; O'Bryant and Wolf, 1983) of older persons and are also good predictors of widows' intentions to stay in their homes (O'Bryant, 1983b).

Other studies suggest that older people have important attachments to their neighborhoods (Cantor, 1975; Hartmann, 1977). It is quite likely that the widows have lived in their homes for a number of years and may be very socially integrated into the surrounding community. Arling (1976) found that "friendship-neighboring is clearly related to less loneliness and worry, and a feeling of 'usefulness' and individual respect within the community" (p. 757). On the other hand, if the neighborhood is deteriorating, increasing crimes against property and assault rates may cause the widow concern and fear (Patterson, 1978). Social integration in specific neighborhoods may be decreasing due to the loss of friendly neighbors through mobility or death. Furthermore, it is quite likely that neighborhoods may become unsuitable in other ways as widows grow older. Many older women either do not drive or no longer feel comfortable driving automobiles; thus, the convenience of public transportation, facilities, and services takes on new significance upon the death of a husband.

Vulnerability

Doborf (1979) points out that systems of aid do exist for the urban elderly, yet the reality is also that older people who live alone—simply by virtue of their living alone—are a particularly vulnerable group. One could argue that many widows live alone in their residences by "default." Unlike either single women or some divorcées, widows have not chosen to live alone; when the time comes, they may have little preparation for a single life-style. Kahana and Kiyak (1980) contend that, for women whose major previous roles were those of wife and mother, living alone during later life may represent a crisis. Approximately 70 percent of all older widows inherit the role of homeowner —one they have played previously only as a member of a team. Their husbands were often the managers and "handymen," assuming responsibility for major and minor household repairs, yard work, and car care. Consequently, widows may have limited experience in handling these functions and dealing with legal or financial matters related to the home, such as taxes and insurance. In addition, widows would be especially prevalent among those elderly who are "overhoused"; they remain in family homes which originally served at least two and probably more individuals. These are likely to be older houses, which are generally more difficult and expensive to heat and cool and are often in need of more repair (Struyk and Soldo, 1980).

Furthermore, concern has been expressed for those older persons who are isolated and lonely because they live alone. Should the widow suffer sudden illness or an accident, will such an event be known and responded to? Isolation and loneliness are not by any means the same problem, but they are inextricably related. Lopata (1973; 1980) found that one-half of the widows in her study mentioned loneliness as their greatest problem. This was particularly true for more recent widows.

In summary, older widows who are homeowners and live alone may be vulnerable for a number of reasons. They may: (1) have a reduced income following their husbands' deaths; (2) have depended on their husbands for taking care of many maintenance and repair jobs; (3) have limited experience handling legal or financial matters related to homeownership; (4) have problems with transportation; (5) be more isolated and at risk in the event of accident or illness; (6) suffer from loneliness in homes previously shared with loved ones; and, (7) live in inappropriate or deteriorating neighborhoods.

In response to widows' vulnerability, it appears that there are at least three options. The first would be for them to sell or rent their homes and move to more appropriate residences; however, only some of the husband's household functions would disappear as a result of moving. The available data do not bear out the notion that widows choose to move in any great numbers following their husbands' deaths. Lopata (1979) observed that, after an average of 11 years of widowhood, over half of the women in her Chicago sample lived in the same housing units. Recently, O'Bryant (1983b) reported that 91 percent of older Columbus widows who lived alone and were homeowners planned to continue living in the same homes—73 percent for "as long as they could manage" and 18 percent for the "rest of their lives."

Provided that economic and environmental conditions are relatively satisfactory, a second option is for a widow to assume the functions and roles of the former husband. In many cases widows perform male-stereotypic homeowner tasks even before their husbands' deaths. For instance, in those cases where the husbands are seriously ill or bedridden for long periods of time, many wives develop whatever skills and abilities are required. In other cases, following the husband's death, widows are "fast learners," raising their own levels of competence and becoming proficient sole homeowners. There are many times, however, when being completely self-sufficient is neither practical nor possible. A third possible option, then, is for widows to have families, friends, and neighbors who will provide supports whenever and wherever they are needed. The remainder of this chapter is devoted to an examination of the availability and the viability of the support systems of Columbus widows who live alone in their own homes. It is hypothesized that good support networks contribute to older widows' more positive subjective well-being and enable them to remain in their homes longer and more comfortably.

Support Systems of Widows

In the last decade social scientists have seriously pursued the issues with respect to how widows' support systems differ from those of married women (Anderson, 1984; Kohen, 1983; Lopata, 1979). It has become increasingly clear that widowed persons are more dependent on their adult children than are married persons (Mutran and Reitzes, 1984; Powers, Keith, and Goudy, 1975). Support networks have special significance to Columbus widows who live alone in their own homes. The age-integrated communities in which these women live do not provide as many supports to the aged as do retirement villages or elderly housing projects. Thus, instrumental or "service" supports may be critical to the widow's ability to remain in her home. Nevertheless, usually the widow's goal is to manage on her own and not be a burden to others.

Scholen (1980) takes an interesting analytical approach to understanding the older person's desire to maintain an independent household. He observes: "Dignity is more important than the illusion of total independence for most older people. Indeed, the critical aspects of maximum independence for the old are not the total absence of support services or the complete lack of interpersonal assistance. More precisely, the key elements are individual autonomy, control, choice, and access. The singular ability to choose how much and to determine when support and assistance are needed and desired is more important. . . ." (p. 46).

The availability of direct assistance from kin and friends to older persons is limited by their numbers and the proximity of their residence to that of the older person (Hays, 1984). Two historical and social phenomena affect the support networks of the current cohort of older women in the United States. First, women who were born between 1900 and 1920 had the lowest fertility of any cohort of women in American history (National Institute of Health, 1979). Thus, there are more childless women among today's 70-year-olds and more who have only one or two offspring. Secondly, the mobility of families has a greater impact on low-fertility cohorts. Given that only children and firstborns are apt to be high achievers and college graduates (Brophy, 1977), the fewer offspring of today's older parents may be quite widely dispersed and no longer residing within easy range of their parents. This usually does not become a major problem for adult children until their mothers are widowed—then proximity becomes a key issue.

It has been shown that, because older widows are "attached" to their homes for a variety of valid reasons, they generally wish to continue living in them after their husbands' deaths (O'Bryant, 1983b). It is believed that they are not necessarily striving for greater independence but are, instead, trying to maintain their dignity and a reasonable degree of control and choice in their lives. Consequently, supportive services, when they are provided by others without undue hardship and in socially prescribed manners, are predicted to be related to older widows' greater sense of well-being.

Older Widows in Columbus and Franklin County, Ohio

Older persons comprised 9 percent of the population of Franklin County in 1983,[1] with a total of 70,733 persons over 65 living in households and 4,500—5 percent—in institutions or group quarters. Older men comprised 36.6 percent of all individuals over age 65, with approximately 13 percent of them being widowers. Older women comprised

63.4 percent of the older population, with almost two-thirds of them being widows. Thus, there are more than six older widows for every older widower. With respect to household types, an estimated 18,860 older widows in Franklin County live alone (Columbus Regional Information Service, 1984).

The widows whose support systems are discussed here were 226 white women between the ages of 60 and 89 ($M = 71.6$), who had annual incomes of $15,000 or less. All respondents had remained alone in their homes following their husbands' deaths, which had occurred within 7 to 21 months ($M = 13$) prior to the time of the interviews.[2] These respondents were derived from a population of widows who had been systematically identified through public records by using a three-step process. The first step was the use of newspaper obituary notices of men over the age of 65 who died between September 1, 1981, and October 31, 1982. Newspaper obituaries were a rich source of information; they usually provided the deceased's full name, his occupation, names of surviving wife and children, and other pertinent information. However, they often did not provide the home address of the deceased. Consequently, as a second step, it was necessary to access the county death records for this purpose. In addition, the death records also provided information with regard to the race of the deceased. Unfortunately, due to the small number of black widows in this age group who were homeowners and lived alone, black women were not included.[3] The third step of the identification process was to cross-check the names and addresses of potential respondents against the Homestead Exemption tax rolls of Franklin County in order to ascertain whether the surviving widow was a homeowner, her age, and income status. Eligibility for the Homestead Tax Exemption in the state of Ohio is based on being age 65 or older and a ceiling of $15,000 income. Finally, general property ownership tax rolls were also checked to assist with the verification of the widow's eligibility for the study.

Altogether, names and addresses for almost 400 widows were compiled. At the time of the initial personal contacts, widows who were under age 60 (8 percent), were seriously ill (2 percent), or who had others residing in their homes (23 percent) were only briefly questioned; they were then eliminated from inclusion in the study. In addition, it was found that 33 widows (8 percent) no longer resided in their homes: nine had moved voluntarily to other locations, 13 had been moved to nursing homes by their families, and 11 had died —following their husbands in death in less than a year's time. Of the remaining potential respondents ($N = 260$), 15 percent refused to be interviewed. Subsequently, an analysis of the information available on this group indicated that these refusers were not significantly different from the 226 respondents who agreed to participate.

Interviewers were four middle-aged women who were chosen on the basis of their previous experience in interviewing, knowledge and understanding of older persons, personality, and maturity. In addition, three of the four interviewers were also widows. Prior to contact by the interviewer, each potential respondent was mailed a letter of introduction, which very briefly described the study, its support from the AARP (American Association of Retired Persons) Andrus Foundation, and named the interviewer who would be contacting her. The following week the interviewer called on the widow and, if the widow agreed, an interview was conducted at that time. Otherwise, an appointment was arranged for a more convenient time. All interviews took place in the widows' homes and, on the average, lasted 1½ hours.

The interview schedule contained items covering demographic, health, family, housing, and neighborhood characteristics, and included scales measuring "attachment to home" (O'Bryant, 1983a), relations-restrictive attitudes (Lopata, 1973), and "subjective well-being" (Bradburn, 1969). The latter measures two distinct variables, *positive affect* and *negative affect*, which are orthogonal factors. Positive affect includes feeling: (1) particularly excited or interested in something; (2) proud because someone complimented you on something you had done; (3) pleased about having accomplished something; (4) on top of the world; and (5) that things are going your way. Negative affect includes feeling: (1) so restless you can't sit long in a chair; (2) very lonely or remote from other people; (3) bored; (4) depressed or very unhappy; and (5) upset because someone criticized you. In the present study, examination of the intercorrelation matrix revealed that these two sets of items were functioning somewhat differently. Negative-affect items were more closely related to other variables—e.g., loneliness, husband's death and deaths of other family members, possible psychosomatic problems, and poor social-emotional adjustment (as rated by the interviewers). On the other hand, positive-affect items had stronger and clearer relationships to the support-system variables. These findings agree with recent psychometric analyses of various measures of well-being by Lawton, Kleban, and diCarlo (1984). These researchers report that, of the two constructs, negative affect appeared to be more closely related to psychophysical symptoms and neuroticism, whereas positive affect was more closely related to external gratifications and various quality-of-life indicators. Consequently, at present, only results related to positive affect will be presented and discussed. First, however, it is necessary to describe Columbus widows and their support systems in more detail.

Description of Columbus Widows

Seventy-five percent of the Columbus widows reported that they had lived in Ohio most, if not all, of their lives, with 72 percent reporting they had been born in Ohio. Of the remaining 28 percent, half had been born in states that border Ohio. Only 4 percent of the sample were born in foreign countries, arriving in the United States at an average age of 12 years and living in the United States for an average of slightly over 50 years. This residential stability also characterized these older women's homeownership patterns. Only 5.3 percent had lived in their present homes for less than 10 years, whereas 50 percent had lived in their homes for 25 years or more. For the total sample, the mean number of years of residence in the present dwelling was 25.9 years, with many indicating they had lived in the same house most of their married lives.

With respect to health, 63.8 percent of the Columbus widows reported their health as "good" or "excellent," 30 percent indicated "fair" health, and the remainder, 6.2 percent, rated their health as "poor." Consistent with the often-acknowledged presence of chronic illnesses in older women, 49 percent reported having at least one long-standing physical condition that limited their activities in some way. Arthritis and other musculoskeletal impairments represented approximately one-half of the reported conditions—a figure comparable to that from national surveys of noninstitutionalized older women (Hing and Cypress, 1981).[4]

Rix (1984) reports that, as of 1983, U.S. households consisting of unrelated individuals headed by a person 65 or over, who was typically a woman, had a median annual income of $6,938. In the present Columbus sample of female homeowners who are 60 and over, the median income was approximately $7,500 annually. Slightly over 12 percent thought they were "well-off"; the majority described their economic status as "comfortable," whereas 17 percent felt they had to restrict their activities because of finances. Only 6 percent of the widows had incomes below the 1981 poverty level for one-person households. For the total sample, having a higher income was related to being younger ($r = -.15, p<.01$), being in better health ($r = .15, p<.01$), having a higher educational level ($r = .40, p<.01$), and having worked outside the home for more of their lives ($r = .24, p<.01$).

Educational levels for the present group of widows were as follows: 14.8 percent had eight years or less of schooling; 23.4 percent had some high school; 38.2 percent had completed high school; 17 percent had some college; and 6.8 percent had completed college. Approximately 3 percent of the group had some graduate-level education or special training. Higher educational levels were related not only to income but also to better health ($r = .12, p<.05$). Given that the median number of school years per women over age 65 was 9.4 years in 1975 (Block, Davidson, and Grambs, 1981), these Columbus widows are somewhat better educated. Comparisons of different educational levels with census data (U.S. Bureau of the Census, 1981) suggest that women with less than eight years of education are underrepresented in the present sample.

With respect to marital history, 82 percent of the Columbus widows had been married only once, with 22.8 years being the average age at marriage and 46.8 being the mean number of years married. There was a relationship between having a higher educational level and marrying only once ($r = .13, p<.03$). Those who had been married more than once (only two women had been married more than twice) had spent an average of 43.2 years of their lives married, suggesting that most of them had spent little time as single persons before they had remarried.

Few studies have investigated the work-history characteristics of older women. Lopata and Steinhart (1971) found, in their study of women over age 50, that the average respondent had a very uneven employment history and had dropped out of the labor market several times during her life, withdrawing to the home to perform the roles of wife, mother, and housewife.[5] With regard to the present cohort of older women, not only family events but also historical events affected their labor-force participation. Some had to overcome the effects of the Great Depression, which meant dropping out of school early to work at whatever jobs were available. The prosperity of the late 1930s allowed many to return to their homemaking and childrearing. Soon, however, World War II pulled women into the labor force to perform so-called "men's work." After the war, many working wives returned to their homes to once again perform the traditional female roles of wife and mother. In the present study Columbus widows were asked how much of the time during their married lives they had held jobs outside their homes: 11.6 percent reported "all of the time"; 27.2 percent reported "most of the time"; 44.2 percent reported "some of the time"; and 17 percent reported that they had "never" worked outside the home.[6] As already reported, those women with prior employment histories had significantly higher present incomes and, as might be expected, significantly fewer children ($r = .16, p<.01$).

As a group, Columbus widows had a mean of 2.0 children, with a range of from 0 to 10 living children. As is true of the general population of older persons, approximately 80 percent of these widows had living children.[7] These "children" ranged in age from 22 to 69 years, with a mean age of 43.[8] Of those who had children, 71 percent had at least one child who lived in Columbus, whereas 29 percent had children residing elsewhere. For the latter group, almost half of them had children somewhere in Ohio and, thus, within an automobile drive of from one to two hours. There were differences, however, in the frequency with which these two groups of widows saw their children. When children lived in the same city, they were seen on an average of once a week; when children lived in another Ohio city, they were seen slightly less than once a month. Columbus widows had more siblings than children, with a mean of 2.5 sisters or brothers still living. In terms of their residential proximity, however, only 50 percent of the widows with siblings had one or more who lived in Columbus.

Types of Support

The support systems of Columbus widows discussed here include 11 different types of support: transportation, household repairs, housekeeping, shopping, yard work, car care, sick care, emotional support, help with decision making, legal assistance, and financial support.[9] Each respondent was asked to indicate the one person who most often provided her with each type of support (inflow of assistance) since her husband's death, and, secondly, the person to whom she most often provided that support (outflow of assistance). Persons in the support networks were identified as to their sex and their relationship to the widow. This chapter focuses only on the *inflow* of support to the widow and the *relationship* of the person whom she names as most often providing each type of support. Relationships were coded into one of seven categories: adult child or child-in-law; grandchild; sibling or sibling-in-law; another relative; friend; neighbor; or other (including professionals and hired help).[10] In those instances where the widow listed no person as providing a particular type of support, there are two possible explanations. First, she may not have had this person in her support network. As already discussed, 20 percent of the sample had no children (and, therefore, no grandchildren) and 16.4 percent had no siblings. Second, the widow may have indicated there had been no provider because she either did the task herself or had not needed that type of support—at least not yet. Finally, in addition to indicating if she received a particular type of support and the person who provided it, each widow also indicated how frequently, on a nine-point scale from "never" to "daily," she received this type of support.

Table 3.1 presents the percentages of widows who received assistance with respect to each of the 11 types of support and, also, percentage breakdowns of the persons most often named as providing that support. Types of support are listed in the left-hand column in order of the number of widows who indicated they had received that type of support, from high to low. It is clear that more Columbus widows received assistance with male-stereotypic tasks, such as yard work, minor household repairs, and transportation. These are the most likely supports to have been provided by the husband before his death. It is also important to note that the rank order of the types of support received reflects the fact that these women were recently widowed—on an average of 13 months prior to the interview. Therefore, legal assistance had been necessary and had required the help of others, usually professionals. However, although more widows received legal aid than other types of support, it had been provided only once or twice during the previous year. The most frequent type of support received was help with yard work; when combined as a single group, children and grandchildren were the most likely providers. Also, and not surprisingly, neighbors assisted with yard care, being named by 22 percent of the respondents.

Transportation is often crucial for older persons who live in single-family dwellings. Many widows who are now over age 60 never learned to drive an automobile, and, in addition, many suburban areas do not have public transportation conveniently available. Fifty-seven percent of the Columbus widows did own and drive automobiles; some of these also exchanged rides with friends and neighbors. Another 5 percent owned automobiles but did not use them frequently. Thirty-eight percent did not drive at all; 8 percent of these also did not live near a bus stop. As can be seen on table 3.1, almost half of transportation support for those who needed it came from adult children, with most of the remainder being provided by friends and neighbors. Although 66.8 percent of the sample indicated that transportation was never a problem for them, over one-third of these widows had problems with transportation, with 24.8 percent reporting they "sometimes" did and 8.4 percent reporting that, since the husband's death, they "always" had transportation problems.

Chevan and Korson (1972) report that the greatest personal need among older women is for home-repair services. With respect to minor household repairs, table 3.1 indicates that 64 percent of the Columbus widows have received support with such repairs—the majority of which came from their adult children. When questioned in more detail regarding the maintenance of their homes, 34 percent of the widows reported that their homes had also needed *major* repairs since their husbands' deaths. Fifty-one percent of the widows had used hired help for such repairs, with 95 percent reporting that the repairs had been done satisfactorily and 92 percent reporting that they had had no problems with the persons who did the repairs. For the 49 percent of the widows who did not use hired workers, children, other family, friends, or neighbors had contributed to major household repairs. Of those widows who had children, 27 percent indicated they planned to bequeath their homes to their children; thus, the contributions children made to the maintenance of the home might presumably have some future benefits for them.

Overall, because of the age of these widows, the fact that they had all been married most of their lives, and the recency of their widowhood, it was expected that they would receive more types of support and more frequent support than they actually received. Consequently, the most interesting aspect of the data presented on table 3.1 may well be the extent to which the widows in this study were managing on their own. Twenty-four percent did their own yard work, 30 percent provided all of their own transportation, and 34 percent managed to do the necessary minor household repairs.

Persons in Support Networks

Since their husbands' deaths, 99 percent of the sample reported that they had received support on at least one occasion; however, only 78 percent of the respondents named persons who provided support

Table 3.1 Types of Support Received from Persons in Widows' Support Networks (in percentages; $N=226$).

Types of support[a]	Self-help or no help	Child	Grandchild
Legal assistance	22	19	1
Yard work	24	18	12
Transportation	30	29	1
Minor household repairs	34	35	4
Help when feeling blue	38	17	1
Decision making	39	39	1
Care of car	47	22	2
Assistance when ill	56	22	1
Shopping	72	16	2
Housekeeping	84	5	2
Financial support	96	3	0

[a] Types of support are listed in the order of the numbers of widows who indicated they receive

more than a few times. Columns 2 through 8 of table 3.1 present the percentages of times seven types of persons were named as members of widows' support networks. Many of the results are consistent with findings that have been reported previously by other researchers. It is clear that adult children comprise the group that most often provides support, and they do so for almost all of the 11 types of support. Children were named most often by widows as providers of home repairs and transportation. Interestingly, whereas children were most frequently mentioned as helping with decision making, the modal frequency of such help occurred only several times a year.

Hired help and other professionals provided legal assistance, yard work, and car care. However, these more "formal" support persons were seldom mentioned and rarely used for other services, such as emotional support. Despite the recency of these women's widowhood, counselors were rarely sought out. In the particular set of 11 support items reported on here, emotional help had been measured by a single question, "Who helps you by being available when you feel blue?" In line with other researchers' findings (Arling, 1976; Blau, 1973; Pihlblad and Adams, 1972), friends and neighbors were more often named than adult children, representing a combined 30 percent of the persons who gave this type of emotional support.

In addition, as with other studies of older persons (Scott, 1983) and widows (Lopata, 1979), siblings did not contribute substantially to

Sibling	Other relative	Friend	Neighbor	Hired/Other
2	2	2	1	52
1	2	6	22	15
5	4	18	12	0
4	5	5	10	3
10	4	18	12	1
8	5	6	1	3
2	3	4	6	14
5	3	4	6	1
2	2	3	3	0
0	0	1	1	6
1	0	1	0	0

at type of support.

Columbus widows' support systems. Only 22 percent of the sample named siblings as providing one or more types of support. This can be partially explained by the ages of siblings, and by the fact that siblings resided less often in Columbus, and even fewer resided in their widowed sister's neighborhood. The specific type of support most often provided by siblings was being available when the widows felt blue; however, even in this instance, only 10 percent of the widows named their siblings. Siblings were less often named than were children, friends, or neighbors. Not surprisingly, those who did name siblings were more often childless, and the siblings who served as emotional supports were often widowed.

Frequency of Support

In those cases where support was received, the frequency with which it was received varied according to the particular type of support. The modal frequency for the various supports, when they did occur, is as follows: provision of transportation most often occurred once or twice a week; assistance with housework, yard work, and shopping most often occurred once a week; and, assistance with household repairs, car care, sick care, and financial support most often occurred only several times a year. As previously indicated, legal help was seldom received. Unexpected was the finding that, for the 62 percent of the widows who received support when they felt blue, the modal frequency was only several times a year—despite the relative recency of their bereavement.

In general, the frequencies with which a particular support was provided were at approximately the same level regardless of which persons provided that support. There were some interesting exceptions, however. First, siblings not only provided emotional support in fewer cases than children and friends but also provided it less frequently. The same pattern was true also for sick care; whereas children provided such support several times a year, siblings provided it at a frequency of about once a year. In addition, the findings for neighbors are also interesting. Emotional support and sick care provided by neighbors is more frequent than that provided by children and siblings. These differences, though small, suggest that neighbors, because of their proximity to older widows, can play very important supportive roles (Cantor, 1975; Lopata, 1979; 1982).

Finally, a series of analyses of covariance[11] were used to assess the number of types of support provided and the frequency of each support for three subgroups: childless widows ($N = 46$), widows with one or more children in the city ($N = 127$), and widows whose child(ren) lived elsewhere ($N = 53$). There were several findings of interest. Not surprisingly, widows who had children in the same city received more types of support than widows who were childless or whose children lived elsewhere, $F\ (4, 221) = 3.50$, $p<.03$. Obviously, the number of persons readily available to widows with children in the same city is quantitatively higher; but, in addition, this greater number of persons also can offer a greater variety of skills and abilities. The latter could be viewed as a "qualitative" aspect of a larger support system—i.e., the likelihood increases that at least one of the persons in the network is able to perform the particular needed assistance. Second, and not surprisingly, the overall frequency of support received was significantly less for childless widows than for the other two groups, $F\ (4, 221) = 12.87$, $p<.001$. In terms of particular types of help, the greatest difference was noted for household repairs, for which childless widows received significantly less-frequent support than did the other two subgroups, $F\ (4, 221) = 10.33$, $p<.001$. It would appear, then, that social programs that offer assistance with home maintenance might be most effective if they "target" their services toward childless widows in particular.

Support Systems and Their Relationships to Positive Affect

Initially, partial correlations were derived, controlling for health and income, to investigate the relationships of positive affect with the frequency of receipt for each type of support. For the total sample, positive affect was significantly related to receiving a greater variety of types of support ($r = .23, p<.001$) and, also, more frequent support ($r = .21, p<.001$). In addition, positive affect was related to more-frequent help with household repairs ($r = .15, p<.01$), car care ($r = .15, p<.01$), yard work ($r = .17, p<.02$), legal assistance ($r = .13, p<.02$), and help with shopping ($r = .13, p<.03$).

Next, for the purpose of gaining further insights into how the availability and proximity of support persons are related to widows' well-being, further comparisons were made among the three subgroups of widows. Partial correlations were derived for the frequencies of support provided by each of the seven categories of persons. These are presented in table 3.2. Although significant, the sizes of the correlation coefficients are small. Nevertheless, based on the *direction* of various relationships, these figures suggest some interesting patterns that exist among the various persons in the support network. First, for widows with children in the same city, positive affect is related to receiving more frequent amounts of support; but, for widows with children residing elsewhere, there is a *negative* relationship between frequency of support and positive affect. This finding suggests that perhaps widows are less happy when their children must come from longer distances to help them.

A second interesting finding suggests that widows may not feel good about getting help from siblings when they also have children living in the same city; i.e., there is a negative relationship between sibling support and positive affect for this subgroup. On the other hand, for childless widows, there was a *positive* relationship between sibling support and higher levels of positive affect. It will be recalled that only 22 percent of all the widows received one or more of the 11 types of support from their siblings; however, childless widows more often mentioned siblings in their support networks than did widows with children, $F(4, 221) = 12.73, p<.001$. The present findings suggest that such support has a positive impact on the well-being of childless widows.

Finally, frequency of support from friends is related to higher positive affect for all three subgroups; however, such support appears to be

Table 3.2 Partial Correlations of Positive Affect with Frequency of Support from Various Persons.

Frequency of support from:	Total sample ($N=226$)	Widows with child in city ($N=127$)	Widows with child elsewhere ($N=53$)	Childless widows ($N=46$)
Children	.15***	.20***	−.18*	—
Grandchildren	.01	−.07	−.02	—
Siblings	.04	−.18**	.08	.29**
Other family	−.03	−.04	.00	.05
Friends	.14**	.15**	.26**	.12
Neighbors	−.04	.02	−.01	−.04
All persons	.22***	.18**	.11	.30**

Note: Widows' self-rated health and income levels have been partialed out.
*$p<.10$.
**$p<.05$.
***$p<.01$.

of most importance to widows with children living elsewhere. The relationship between interactions with friends and higher morale has been reported by a number of other researchers (Arling, 1976; Blau, 1973; Lee, 1979; Wood and Robertson, 1978).

Conclusions

Older widows who lived alone in their own homes in Columbus, Ohio, in nearly all instances were "attached" to their homes and did not intend to move. Due to the loss of their spouses, these older widows had become the sole owners and caretakers of their homes. Many of the "services" that their husbands had previously contributed to the households had to be assumed by either the widows themselves or by others within the widows' support networks. Most often others provided male-stereotypic tasks, such as yard work, household repairs, and transportation. Data on these widows have not yet been analyzed in terms of the sex of the persons providing support; however, a provocative hypothesis for future analysis is that widows with more male persons in their support networks are "better off" in terms of the amount of support they receive, and that this, in turn, is related to a greater sense of well-being.

As in Lopata's study of Chicago widows, adult children were the most predominant persons in Columbus widows' support networks. Furthermore, the proximity and availability of children affect the extent to which they provided support to their mothers. When children lived in the same city, receipt of more frequent support from them was positively related to their mothers' greater sense of well-being. When children lived elsewhere, frequent provision of support was negatively related to their mothers' well-being.

Among the other persons in Columbus widows' support networks, siblings played a very small role. Less than one-fourth of the respondents reported any type of support from siblings—even less than that reported by Lopata (1979). Comparisons of childless widows with other groups revealed that, in terms of amount of contact, the childless widows did not see siblings more often than did widows with children. On the other hand, there was a strong relationship between the frequency of receiving sibling support and the positive affect of childless widows. Apparently, the nature of these sibling relationships changed, at least for some, from *social* to *service* supports after their widowhood. Cicirelli (1981) points out that siblings often help to fill some of the roles of a deceased spouse. Also, the conclusions drawn here are in line with Lopata's (1979) observation that support roles must be "reorganized" after women become widows. When a support system is viable and flexible enough to reorganize in more supportive ways, the result may well be an increased sense of well-being on the part of the recipients. A future question of great interest is what are the characteristics of support systems that are able to reorganize and respond in appropriate ways to the older widow?

There are intriguing implications for the patterns of support found in this study of older widows. Family sociologists have long wondered why older persons' morale, or well-being, is not related to, or greatly enhanced by, the family support they receive. The usual explanation for the lack of relationship is that children's assistance is obligatory and, therefore, does not make parents feel any better. However, particular circumstances—such as living arrangements and location of children—may be more important factors than has been generally recognized. Widows who live alone may be more receptive to family supports, particularly if they can accept or reject them depending upon their needs. Also, widows may be more affected, either positively or negatively, by the presence or absence of particular types of supports, than are widowers or married persons. For example, childless older women, more than childless older men, may suffer more from the impact of being childless once they are widowed.

In summary, most of Columbus widows were "attached" to their homes and wanted to remain in them. After using their own abilities for achieving this goal, receipt of particular service supports from their adult children was their major resource; furthermore, when children were proximal, their support was related to widows' greater sense of well-being. In the absence of children, other family and friends sometimes substituted for missing children and, although not fully compensating, also provided supports that enhanced the well-being of these older widows. It is hoped that this study will serve as a reminder for the need to explore the complexities of support systems in greater detail; therein will lie the discovery of many clues toward understanding widowhood.

4 Widows in a Florida Retirement Community

ANNE VICTORIA NEALE

This research examined the relationship of marital status with social networks and psychological well-being among residents of a Florida retirement community. Widowed and married women were contrasted on social networks, psychological well-being, and attitudes related to living in a retirement community. The data reported here are from a larger study of voluntary relocation among the elderly that was conducted in 1979 by the Elderly Care Research Center at Wayne State University. Data were collected through a self-administered questionnaire distributed to residents of the Century Village retirement condominium community in Deerfield Beach, Florida.

Middle-Class Retirement in the United States

While in many cultures the elderly widow would almost always live with other relatives, this is not the case for a large number of widows in American society. After the death of the spouse, elderly widows frequently live alone. Remarriage after the death of the husband is still unusual for older widows (Cleveland and Gianturco, 1976; Treas and VanHilst, 1976). Yet elderly American widows have many life-style options that were not available to earlier generations and are still not common in some other societies. One of these options is the freedom to relocate

The author wishes to acknowledge Dr. Eva F. Kahana for her support during this research, which was funded by NIMH Grant No. MH-29687-04.

to another region of the country and live independently after the spouse's death. The United States is a highly mobile society, and many Americans who are financially independent relocate after retirement.

Since its inception in the 1950s, age-segregated housing for the elderly has become very popular, and retirement communities are found throughout the country. For the widow, living in a retirement community is an opportunity to find new activities to replace those previously shared with her husband. Thus, independent living in leisure-oriented communities far away from other relatives is sanctioned, if not encouraged for the retired widowed woman in some subcultures of the United States.

Retirement communities located in the South tend to attract elderly migrants from all regions of the United States, and research has indicated that such migration is commonly of two types: returning to the area of childhood origin, and retirement in the Sun Belt states (Serow, 1978; Golant, 1975). The women who participated in this research were all from the northeastern coastal area of the United States (primarily New York, New Jersey, and Connecticut) and moved into a retirement community in the southern state of Florida.

The financial independence of many retirement-age people in the United States makes it possible to migrate and settle into a new community. The foundation of financial security among retired workers is the government-sponsored Old Age, Survivors and Disability Insurance Program, popularly known as Social Security (SS). Monthly SS checks are based on the individual's earning history, and even women who did not work outside of the home receive an allowance in the amount of 50 percent of that of the husband's. The average SS benefit paid to women retiring in 1979 was $224.00 per month. In addition to SS, 40 percent of unmarried women have some income beyond the SS benefit (Sommers and Shields, 1979). Additional income most often comes from sources such as personal financial investments, a private pension, and/or the widows' benefits from the deceased husband's policies, such as his Social Security benefit, private pension, or life insurance, if any.

Constructed in 1975, Century Village at Deerfield Beach is one of the largest retirement communities in the United States, with 8,500 living units. Century Village was built for middle-income retirees (mortgage payments for year-round residents were in the range of $350 to $400 per month in 1979). Property taxes and the monthly maintenance fee are additional. Residents at Century Village must provide their own furniture, but the units include central air conditioning, wall-to-wall carpeting, smoke detectors, garbage disposals, dishwashers, and patios. Each apartment is also equipped with a medical emergency alert and intrusion alarm. Storage and laundry facilities are close to each unit. Exterior and landscape maintenance is covered by the monthly maintenance fee. Other services covered by this fee are free transportation to nearby shopping facilities, security patrols, and cable television. A wide variety of entertainment and recreational opportunities are also available. These include tennis, golf, swimming, billiards, fishing, table tennis, and shuffleboard. Self-improvement or hobby classes in areas such as painting, sewing, and exercise are available. In the evenings there is dancing and nightclub-type entertainment.

There is no single set of characteristics that will describe all retirement communities, although they usually consist of uniform one- or two-story condominium units. Every condominium development has a homeowners' association that is comprised of all the condominium owners in a given complex. Bylaws are generally established by the association's board of directors. Many condominium communities prohibit residents from changing the landscaping or from hanging laundry out-of-doors in an effort to maintain the complex's appearance in its intended state.

Some retirement communities offer a variety of services and recreational activities. Social clubs, game rooms, swimming pools, and homeowners' associations are common. Transportation services to local shopping areas are also typical features. In addition, some communities have a combination of independent living, optional meal programs, and skilled-nursing facilities, depending on the needs of the resident. (See Slivinske and Kosberg, 1984, for an example of a health-care program within a retirement community.) Some communities are no different than any other age-integrated housing complex, where there may be no particular organized activities or health services available.

A number of researchers have attempted to characterize retirement community residents. The people studied by Longino (1980) were from a relatively homogeneous middle-class background. Carp (1978) noted that activity, morale, and longevity were positively related among elderly people living in senior-citizen housing. Shely (1974) interviewed male residents of a retirement community in Florida and reported an overwhelming number of them not only satisfied with retirement in general but also relatively free of the feelings of disengagement often associated with retirement.

Mangum (1973) has summarized data on the reasons older persons migrate to retirement villages. Dissatisfaction with the old neighborhood was the major reason given for relocating, followed by climatic considerations and the few maintenance responsibilities of the condominium. Heintz (1976) found that the reasons older people moved into retirement communities revolved around economic considerations, such as lower taxes and property maintenance, and an antipathy toward city life, including a desire for more safety in the neighborhood. An additional inducement was the frequent availability of hobby classes and social and recreational facilities. In contrast, moving away from retirement communities more often depended on health or personal variables, such as death or financial problems.

A few research studies have examined social networks in retirement communities. The respondents in Christopherson's (1972) study felt the greatest advantages of living in a retirement community were the ease with which new friends are made and the variety of social activities. Lemon et al. (1972) found that participation (although not frequency) in an informal friendship group was an important correlate of life satisfaction. Sherman (1975) examined the networks of mutual assistance among 600 healthy elderly people who lived in retirement housing. She found that there were no more supports in such settings than among neighbors in age-integrated neighborhoods. In addition, retirement housing residents did not suffer from a lack of assistance from their children, as was hypothesized. Martin (1973) reported that residents of a southern-California retirement community who had a life-style that suggested structural disengagement (retirement, low family interaction, and age-integrated activities) were still socially active and high on life satisfaction. Hochschild (1973) was a participant-observer in a senior-citizen housing building and documented an "unexpected community" with an extensive network of mutual social and psychological support among the (largely widowed) residents.

Longino and Lipman (1981) have published the only study known to explore the relationship of support networks to marital status in retirement communities. They found that the married had more primary relations than did the nonmarried, with married women having the most and unmarried men the fewest. Their data indicated that the unmarried compensated for the deficit in social supports through the presence of more casual or secondary relationships.

The Deerfield Beach Women

This research investigated the social networks, emotional support, and attitudes toward life in the retirement community among a sample of widowed and married women. The three-part questionnaire was designed to obtain personal support or demographic information, level of social support, and emotional well-being. The personal support variables included marital status, length of marital status, age, religion, race, country of birth, health, and financial and occupational status. The social support measures were the amount of time spent in various informal activities, memberships in voluntary associations, and friendships. The emotional support variables were a three-item self-concept index and the Life Satisfaction Index A (Neugarten et al., 1961).

Four hundred fourteen individuals responded to the questionnaire, from which the data reported here is a subset. Forty-five percent (N = 187) of the respondents were married men; 41 percent (N = 171) were married women; 12 percent (N = 48) were widowed women; and 2 percent (N = 8) were widowed men. The responses from all 48 widows were compared to 48 randomly selected married women. Sex differences could not be examined due to the small number of widowed men. All respondents were white and had migrated to Florida from the northeast coastal region of the United States (primarily the states of New York and New Jersey). Nearly all the sample was Jewish, and eight in 10 were born in the United States. The others came mainly from Eastern Europe.

It is notable that the sample migrated from the area of the United States with the heaviest concentration of Jews into a community populated largely by Jewish retirees. It is likely that a relocation where one remains within one's ethnic community alleviates some of the stress associated with moving to a new area and leaving family and friends behind. Data was not available on how the decision to relocate was made or whether or not the respondents knew each other or any other community residents at the time they moved.

The average age of the widows who participated in this research was 70 years. Almost all lived alone. Slightly more women were widowed when they moved into Century Village than had become widowed while residing there. In terms of financial status, half of the widows said they had "just enough" income to live on, and four said they couldn't "make ends meet" (see table 4.1).

This sample of widowed women is more highly educated than the

Table 4.1 Background Characteristics of the Study Sample (in percentages).

Background characteristics	Widowed	Married
Number	48	48
Mean age	70 years	66 years
Length of marital status	9 years	35 years
Religion		
Jewish	89	88
Other	11	12
	100	100
Level of education completed		
Grade school	6	13
Some high school	21	21
High school graduate	40	40
Some college	13	23
College graduate	19	4
	100*	100*
Financial status		
Can't make ends meet	9	0
Just enough	50	45
Comfortable, more than enough	41	55
	100	100
Reported health status		
Excellent	6	14
Good	69	55
Fair	19	25
Poor	6	6
	100	100
Recent health changes		
Better	17	8
Same	73	79
Worse	10	13
	100	100

*Totals do not always add up to 100 percent due to rounding.

entire elderly population in the United States of the same age. Two in five completed high school, and a third went to college. United States Census data (1978) suggests that this widowed group has more formal education than the average for their generation: nationally, 22 percent of white women over 65 had graduated from high school, 8 percent had some college education, and only 6 percent had a college degree or beyond.

Three-fourths of the widows rated their health as either good or excellent. About the same proportion also stated that their health had remained stable over the past year, while eight women reported their health had improved. The literature on health and marital status indicates the widowed are at excess risk of morbidity and mortality (Koskenvuo et al., 1980; Kraus and Lilienfeld, 1959; Morgan, 1980), but the widows who participated in this study may be more healthy than the general widowed population. Most of them had been widowed long enough (the average was nine years) to be past the high-risk period after the husband's death when mortality rates among the widowed rise (Kraus and Lilienfeld, 1959; Parkes et al., 1969; Rees and Lutkins, 1967; Talbot et al., 1981).

Age-segregated housing is a predominant characteristic of retirement communities. A number of authors have suggested that age segregation should be related to both morale and social activity among the elderly (Messer, 1967; Teaff et al., 1978; Lowenthal and Robinson, 1976). One of the earliest works was Rosow's classic study (1967), which found more friendships among those elderly who lived in neighborhoods with high concentrations of older people than those in age-integrated areas. In addition, this relationship was particularly strong among the widowed. However, not all studies have found that residential segregation is consistently related to morale or friendships (Carp, 1975; Deimling et al., 1979; Gubrium, 1970; Poulin, 1984).

The questions on age segregation frequently elicited conflicting responses. Even though Century Village is an elderly-exclusive neighborhood, most widows stated they did not prefer age-segregated living. Over half said they would prefer living with all ages, while three stated a preference for living among young people. Only one-third said they preferred the age-segregated environment. However, living with people in one's age group was mentioned as an advantage of Florida life by over four in 10 widows. In order to get more specific attitudes about age segregation, the women were also asked whether they preferred to do things alone, with any age group, or with their own age group. The widowed were divided in their attitudes: half said they had no preference for age-segregated activities, while almost as many said they preferred interacting with their own age group; and 5 percent said they preferred solitary activities. One interpretation of the seeming lack of consistency in the attitudes toward age segregation is that life in the age-segregated retirement village has the advantages of easy access to peers, plus relief from any annoyances that neighborhood children can create. While many women may have missed the dynamics of an intergenerational neighborhood, they may also have enjoyed their current arrangement.

Respondents were asked about the advantages and disadvantages of living in Florida. The "advantage" that was overwhelmingly endorsed by these displaced northerners was the climate. This was not surprising in light of the predictably warm Florida weather. The available activities were seen as an advantage for three-fourths of the widows. Six in 10 reported that transportation was a disadvantage, which probably reflected the superior public transportation of the greater New York City area to which many respondents were accustomed. Medical care was also seen as a disadvantage for one-third of the widows.

The Widows' Social Support System

The social support literature has confirmed the importance of frequent social contact for maintaining psycho-emotional well-being (e.g., Adams, 1971; Knapp, 1976; Larson, 1978; Lemon et al., 1972; Tobin and Neugarten, 1961). Social engagement theory in gerontology (Havighurst et al., 1968) has related psychological well-being to activity patterns, social networks, and social roles. The widowhood literature holds various discussions of the impact of a spouse's death upon the social roles of the widow/widower (Barrett, 1977; Berardo, 1967; Gibbs, 1978; Kivett, 1978; Kline, 1975; Lopata, 1970). Role theory (Biddle and Thomas, 1966; Rosow, 1973) suggests that since the widowed have lost the role of spouse, they would be likely to replace this loss with new roles or relationships. Several studies have reported general support for this theory. Adults have been found to compensate for losses in one form of social activity by becoming increasingly active in other aspects of the social network (Heyman and Gianturco, 1973; Mutran and Reitzes, 1981; Palmore, 1968; Pihlblad and Adams, 1972). Some types of activity seem to be more strongly related to life satisfaction among the widowed, but there is no consensus as to which activity is the strongest predictor.

Friendships

Several questions regarding the nature of the respondents' friendships were posed, including number of friends, mode of contact with friends, and general attitudes toward friendships. Widows had an average of six close friends and 19 casual friends. The modal response for the length of knowing the closest friend was 41–50 years. This means that new friends were not defined as the closest. The longtime friend usually lived in another city, which is not surprising since the respondents had relocated out of state. The widows were also asked about the amount and type of contact with old friends. Almost all women indicated they had friends they hadn't seen in a long time. Visiting, correspondence, and telephone calls were all frequent modes of contact with old friends.

Activities and Organizational Membership

The respondents were asked how frequently they engaged in seven types of activities, ranging from working-for-pay to visiting with friends and neighbors. Table 4.3 shows a percentage breakdown of the amount of time the widows spent in the individual activities. There was greater involvement in informal activities (such as socializing, visiting with others, and solitary activities) than the more-structured activities, such as working, religious functions, or participating in social clubs. Visiting with friends and neighbors was a pastime for almost everyone. Volunteer work was also common. One-third of the widows indicated they did not participate in religious activities (although all but five described themselves as Jewish). Mean activity scores were created by summing the weighted responses to each of the activity items. The widows had a mean activity score of 11.9. This activity variable is related to the psychoemotional variables in a later section.

Study participants were asked to which of seven types of organizations or clubs they belonged (if any). The widows averaged 3.5 organizations. Table 4.4 shows the response frequencies for membership in each organization type. With no modal type dominating, widows were equally likely to belong to a homeowners' as to a charitable group. About one-third belonged to a formal religious group, and over one-fourth to a sports or recreational club. Another quarter belonged to senior-citizens groups. Finally, unions, professional, or retirement associations drew one-sixth of the widows as members.

Table 4.2 Close Friendships (in percentages).

How long have you known your closest friend?

Years	Widowed	Married
1	7	0
2–3	7	0
4–5	7	6
6–10	2	6
11–20	7	11
21–30	17	13
31–40	12	19
41–50	24	34
50+	15	11
	100*	100

Where does your closest friend live?

	Widowed	Married
Same building	14	23
Same neighborhood	19	23
Same city/area	12	17
Out of town	55	36
	100	100*

Have friendships become more important to you as you have grown older?

	Widowed	Married
Yes	76	73
No	4	0
No change	20	27
	100	100

*Totals do not always add up to 100 percent due to rounding.

Emotional Supports

Cross-sectional research on self-concept has yielded mixed results, although it appears that the elderly have a more negative self-image than younger people (Bennett and Eckman, 1973). It is not clear whether such a phenomenon is of a developmental nature, or whether it reflects the low socioeconomic status, poor health, or institutionalization of the individuals studied. In this study, data from younger persons was

Table 4.3 Amount of Time Spent in Various Activities (in percentages).

	Widowed	Married
Volunteer work		
None	38	33
Little	17	26
Some	21	31
Great deal	25	10
	100*	100
Religious activities		
None	35	57
Little	35	22
Some	27	19
Great deal	4	3
	100*	100*
Social clubs		
None	3	24
Little	23	18
Some	57	34
Great deal	17	24
	100	100
Informal social activities		
None	3	0
Little	8	2
Some	47	55
Great deal	42	43
	100	100
Visiting friends and neighbors		
None	2	0
Little	5	7
Some	52	51
Great deal	41	42
	100	100

Table 4.3 Continued.

	Widowed	Married
Solitary activities		
None	3	8
Little	13	3
Some	57	55
Great deal	27	35
	100	100*
Activities least involved in		
Work	68	74
Club	16	16
Leisure	16	11
	100	100*

*Totals do not always add up to 100 percent due to rounding.

not available for comparison. Self-concept was assessed with three items: intellectual ability, ability to get or hold a job, and general feelings about one's self as a person (see table 4.5).

Most widows had a positive self-concept. Half felt their intellectual abilities were above average, and almost all felt their ability to get or hold a job was either excellent or good, though virtually none did actually work. Finally, only five of the widowed women indicated that their feelings about themselves as a person "could be better." In order to develop a single self-concept variable for analysis of relationships among variables, the responses to these three items were summed together, yielding a three-item index with a high reliability.

Life satisfaction was measured with the 13-item LSI-Z from Wood et al. (1969). This scale is a subset of items originally used by Neugarten et al. (1961) to measure the construct of life satisfaction along five dimensions: zest, resolution and fortitude, congruence between desired and achieved goals, positive self-concept, and mood tone. An individual is at the positive end of the continuum of psychological well-being "to the extent that [she] (a) takes pleasure in the activities that constitute her daily life; (b) regards her life as meaningful and accepts that which her past life has been; (c) feels she has succeeded in achieving major goals; (d) holds a positive self-image; (e) maintains happy and optimistic attitudes and moods" (Neugarten et al., 1961). Life-satisfaction scores were created by dividing the total additive score by the total

Table 4.4 Organizational Memberships (in percentages).

	Widowed	Married
Senior citizens' groups		
None	75	67
1	21	29
2–3	4	4
	100	100
Fraternal, cultural, or political		
None	73	71
1	19	18
2–3	6	10
3	2	0
	100	100*
Union, professional, or retirement		
None	83	84
1	13	14
2–3	5	2
	100*	100
Homeowners/Block clubs		
None	48	47
1	46	43
2–3	6	10
	100	100
Charitable groups		
None	48	57
1	29	29
2–3	19	14
3	4	0
	100	100
Sports/Recreation		
None	73	69
1	19	29
2–3	8	2
	100	100

Table 4.4 Continued.

	Widowed	Married
Religious		
None	63	61
1	38	37
2–3	0	2
	100*	100

*Totals do not always add up to 100 percent due to rounding.

number of items answered. Widows had a mean life-satisfaction score of 1.55 (out of a possible 2.0), with a variance of 0.074.

Interrelationship of Social and Emotional Support Variables

The interrelationships of life satisfaction, self-concept, activity level, and organizational involvement were examined with correlation analysis. A correlation matrix of these variables for the widowed is presented in table 4.6.

Among the widowed, the emotional support variables of self-concept and life satisfaction were related to both informal activities and memberships in organizations. Specifically, life satisfaction was positively related with memberships and activity level. Self-concept was also associated with memberships and to activities. Some studies have found that organizational involvement, such as voluntary club or religious activity, is more highly related to morale than are informal relationships (Edwards and Klemmack, 1973). Pihlblad and Adams' (1972) study found a positive relationship between life satisfaction and social participation in organizations, friendships, and family contacts (in that order). Note that in the Deerfield Beach data, activity level is slightly more strongly related to life satisfaction than is the number of memberships.

Comparisons

Of the Recently and Long-Time Widowed

While the mean number of years widowed was nine, there was a wide range in the length of years widowed: one-tenth was widowed one

Table 4.5 Self-Concept (in percentages).

	Widowed	Married
Ability to get or hold a job		
Excellent	43	46
Good	51	39
Fair	6	4
Poor	0	11
	100	100
Feelings about self as a person		
Pretty good	80	79
Okay	11	6
Could be better	9	13
Not so good	0	2
	100	100
Perceived intellectual ability		
Very high	16	4
Pretty high	36	45
Average	48	43
Not very high	0	8
	100	100

$X^2 = 7.29$.
$df = 3$.
$p = 0.06$.

year or less, and two women were widowed between 25 and 34 years. In order to determine if length of widowhood was a significant factor in the responses to the social or psycho-emotional support items, two types of analyses were done. First, length of widowhood was correlated with the social support variables (activity level and memberships) and the emotional support variables (life satisfaction and self-concept), but it did not appear to be linearly related to these variables. In the second analysis, women widowed three years or less ($N = 15$) were compared to those widowed more than three years ($N = 33$). Three years was used as the criterion for differentiating the recently widowed from the longtime widowed because some authors (Glick et al., 1974) have noted that the typical recovery period following a spouse's death is approximately three years. T-tests of mean differences in these four

Table 4.6 Pearson Correlations of Widows' Social and Emotional Support.

	1.	2.	3.	4.
1. Life satisfaction	1.0	.37** (40)	.24** (40)	.25 (30)
2. Activity level		1.0	.59*** (48)	.37* (35)
3. Organization memberships			1.0	.35* (35)
4. Self-concept				1.0

* = $p<0.05$.
** = $p<0.01$.
*** = $p<0.001$.
Number in ( ) indicates *N* for that statistic.

variables revealed that the recently widowed had lower life satisfaction than the longtime widowed ($p<0.05$). Length of widowhood was not related to self-concept or to the social-support variables.

Of Married and Widowed Women

In the comparison sample of married women, the average years married was 34.7, and all but one of these women were living with their spouse. Two women were born in Eastern Europe and another two were born in Canada. The same proportion of married as widowed women completed high school, although fewer of the married women attended graduate school. Married women reported similar health status as that of the widowed (see table 4.1).

When asked about their financial status, over a half of the married women said they were comfortable, with "more than enough." The trend for the married women to have greater financial security than that of the widowed is also confirmed by U.S. Census (1978) data on income levels by marital status.

Most married women did not feel that living with others of the same group was advantageous, and they were less likely to support age segregation than were the widows. This difference may be the result of a greater desire by the widows to form new peer friendships, and may reflect the perception that close proximity to others of the same cohort increases the probability of forming new relationships. On the other age-segregation questions, the married women had similar responses to the widowed. That is, almost two-thirds stated they preferred living in an age-integrated environment, while one-third said they preferred age segregation. Regarding their preference for the age group with which they liked most to interact, half said they preferred activities with their own age group.

In terms of the advantages and disadvantages of life in the retirement community, the married group differed from the widows in their evaluation of the local transportation. Only a fourth of married women (compared to six in 10 of widows) reported that transportation was a disadvantage. This data, interpreted in conjunction with that of the superior financial status of the married women, suggests that they had more frequent access to an automobile than did the widowed. Transportation problems frequently contribute to social isolation, and while isolation is less of a problem for people living in congregate housing, the widows' negative evaluation of local transportation may be related to their more favorable evaluation of the age-segregated neighborhood, which reduces the need to travel for social interaction.

There were no other significant differences between married and widowed women on the advantages or disadvantages of climate, available activities, or medical care. While not statistically significant, there was a trend for fewer married women to endorse the community activities as an advantage. This suggests that outside activities may be less salient to the married individual as a result of time spent with the spouse.

When asked about the number and types of friendships they had, married women averaged 10 close friends (whereas widows averaged six close friends). The married women also reported more casual friends, although the difference was not significant. The finding that the widowed had fewer friends than those who were married lends indirect support to other studies in which widows reported that old and potential new friends avoided them as a result of their marital status (Berardo, 1968, 1970; Blau, 1961; Gibbs, 1978; Lopata, 1970). Other studies have reported that the widowed have fewer friends (Berardo, 1967, 1970; Blau, 1961; Bock and Webber, 1972; Booth, 1972). However, some studies have failed to find the widowed at a social disadvantage (Ferraro et al., 1984; Kohen, 1983; Lowenthal and Haven, 1968; Petrowsky, 1976). The diversity of findings in this area may be related to intervening variables such as length of widowhood, education, financial status, and race. The relationship of friends with marital status reported here is strengthened by the homogeneity of the widowed and married women on these potentially confounding variables.

There were no significant differences between married and widowed women in the frequency or type of contact with their friends. However, making new friends posed less of an adjustment for the married women, which may reflect the greater perceived need of the widowed to make new friends, or perhaps the difficulty faced by a single woman in a community comprised predominately of couples.

The theory that those who experience the most successful adjustment to widowhood compensate for the role loss by developing new roles or relations was the basis for the hypothesis that friendship networks would be more important for the widow than for the married woman, especially when other family contacts are infrequent, as would be common in this sample of widows who have migrated away from the region of origin. This hypothesis was not supported, as most women (married and widowed) indicated that friendships had become more important as they aged.

The mean activity score (14.5) of married women was significantly higher than that of the widows. The married women averaged 3.2 organizational memberships, which was not different from that of the widows. Thus, on two out of the three measures of social networks (activities and friendships) the married women in the retirement community were involved with more-extensive social networks than were the widowed. Note that the widows were not inactive, only less active in this activity-oriented environment. This difference in social networks by marital status cannot be accounted for by between-group variance in health or social isolation. Furthermore, it is unlikely that the group differences in financial adequacy or transportation would account for the less-extensive social networks of the widows, as most of the activities were available at no cost in the community.

Among the three items that measured different components of self-concept, married women differed from the widowed on only one. Married women rated their intellectual ability somewhat lower than did the widowed. One explanation for this would be that self-esteem increases among some women after widowhood as a result of greater self-reliance.

The mean life satisfaction score for married respondents was 1.71, with a variance of 0.047; this was significantly higher than that of the widowed. A number of studies have also reported that the widowed have lower life satisfaction or morale than the married (Beck and Leviton,

1976; Larson, 1978). Such a relationship is not surprising when one considers factors such as role loss, loneliness, low income, and the poor mental and physical health that are also experienced to a greater extent by widowed persons (Berardo, 1968; 1970; Harvey and Bahr, 1974). Other research has found that when income, employment status, and family-interaction variables are held constant, there is no difference in the morale of the married compared to the widowed (Morgan, 1976). In the Deerfield Beach study, health and age were found to interact with morale. That is, widows who were older or in better health had higher morale than the married, which is also what Blau (1961) found in her study of morale among widows.

The correlation matrix of the same social- and emotional-support variables for the married respondents is shown in table 4.7. It is of particular interest that the association between these variables was stronger for the widowed than for the married. Among the married, self-concept is only related to life satisfaction, another psychoemotional variable, rather than to either of the social-support variables. Table 4.6 indicates that, for the widows, self-concept is related to both memberships and activity level. For the married, life satisfaction was related to organizational memberships, but not activities, whereas life satisfaction is related to both social variables among the widowed. Even though it was previously demonstrated that the married were somewhat more active than the widowed, the correlation of life satisfaction with activity level only among the widowed women suggests that the relationship with the spouse may make such activities less important for those married.

Research on the widowed has generally detailed the ways in which their lives and psychological status change following the spouses' death. In this study, comparisons of the married and widowed women living in the retirement community indicated fewer resource differences than other researchers have reported. The similarities of the widowed and married Century Village women on many of the social, economic, and emotional support items may be the result of the homogeneous environment of the retirement community, where variation in race, income, religion, health, and environmental variables is minimal (Bultena and Wood, 1969; Longino and Lipman, 1981).

The widowed respondents at Century Village differed from their married neighbors in two major ways. First, widows had lower life satisfaction than married women, and this relationship cannot be attrib-

Table 4.7 Pearson Correlations of Married Women's Social and Emotional Support.

	1.	2.	3.	4.
1. Life satisfaction	1.0	.07 (46)	.35** (42)	.25* (43)
2. Activity level		1.0	.48*** (48)	.21 (45)
3. Organization memberships			1.0	.09 (45)
4. Self-concept				1.0

* = $p<0.05$.
** = $p<0.01$.
*** = $p<0.001$.
Number in ( ) indicates N for that statistic.

uted to poor health or poverty, variables that have confounded the interpretation of the low life satisfaction of the widowed in previous research.

One of the most interesting discoveries of this research was that social engagement was more strongly related to psycho-emotional well-being among the widowed than among the married, even though married women indicated a more developed social network than did widows. In reflecting on the meaning of the differential strength of the intercorrelations for widowed and married women, one is reminded that the t-test analysis of the differences between groups found only two significant differences: widows were lower on both activity level and life satisfaction. The discovery that the study variables were more strongly interrelated among the widowed suggests that psycho-emotional status is more dependent upon social engagement for the widow. This, then, does lend support to the role-theory perspective that the widow has a potential social void to fill. She may not become exceedingly active in the outside world, but social engagement is closely connected with emotional well-being. Perhaps the adjustment of those widows who are able to establish new activities or involvements is enhanced with such an "instrumental" coping response. Such outside contacts may be less important to the married women, as their life-style and self-concept have not been forcibly altered by the external events that have confronted the widow.

With Other Migrants

A number of studies have examined the characteristics of individuals who, after retirement, migrate to a different region of the United States. Biggar et al. (1980) reported that most migrants to Florida are married and that elderly interstate migrants are more highly educated than the national average. Patrick (1980) noted that interstate retirement migrants were above average in health status.

The Deerfield Beach respondents have demographic characteristics that are similar to those reported by Biggar (1980) and Patrick (1980). The large proportion of individuals who responded to the questionnaire were married, suggesting that retirement communities attract more married couples than single people. Thus, while they overrepresent married couples in the general U.S. population, the Century Village residents appear to have a marital status profile typical of elderly migrants. In addition, their high education level and good health status also appears similar to that of elderly interstate migrants.

With Other Retirement Community Studies

The literature on residential relocation contains many examples of its adverse impact on the elderly (Boursetom and Pastalan, 1981). However, the stress of such relocation appears to be alleviated when the move is a voluntarily planned one (Carp, 1978; Kahana et al., 1980; Schultz and Brenner, 1977), as would be the case with the retiree who moves from a northern urban home to a southern retirement village. Such an individual is presumably attempting a greater match between personal resources and environmental opportunities (Bultena and Wood, 1969). Shely (1974) has pointed out that the abundance and growth of various types of retirement housing increase the chances of residents finding a community or location to suit their needs and preferences. A community selected because of its perceived congruence with the individual's needs may reinforce a feeling of belonging that relieves any negative feelings associated with retirement (Carp, 1978). When such a relocation is desired, it is less likely that there would be the stressful effects of continuity breaks, removal of neighborhood social-support systems, or increased mortality risks.

The average number of organizational memberships held by Century Village residents was 3.5, which is higher than the 2.2 reported by Babchuk et al. (1979) from a survey of voluntary association memberships among the elderly in a Midwestern community of 35,000. The relatively high number of memberships in this study may be the result of the large number of opportunities that exist within the retirement community. Or perhaps the good health or warm climate enjoyed by residents was a factor in their formal activities.

Longino and Lipman (1981) found that widowed women in a retirement community had fewer primary relations but more secondary ones (analogous to casual friends) than did those who were married. The widows in Century Village had fewer friends, both close and casual, although only the difference in close friends reached statistical significance.

With the Chicago Widows

Lopata's (1979) research on Chicago-area widows documented a group of women with great diversity in background, support systems, and life-style. By contrast, the widows in the Deerfield Beach study are quite homogeneous. They are a white, Jewish, middle-income group, with a high education level, all of whom live in the same age-segregated retirement community. These background and neighborhood differences, along with Lopata's more comprehensive questionnaire, make it difficult to compare the two groups. However, some comparisons in the areas of activities, friendships, life satisfaction, and self-esteem can still be made.

The Century Village widows appear to participate in more social activities and formal organizations than does the Chicago group. This would be expected because of the greater accessibility of social opportunities in the retirement community. In addition, socially oriented individuals with financial means would be likely to select an environment that would meet such needs. Although the Century Village widows were socially active relative to the Chicago widows, they were less active than their married neighbors. This finding provides indirect support for the work of Lopata (1970) and Blau (1961), both of whom suggested that widows' social activity decreases following the death of the spouse. As Century Village is predominately composed of married couples, the widows may have been excluded from many activities, or perhaps they felt uncomfortable in social situations with other couples and voluntarily withdrew.

In some areas the Century Village widows had a similar profile to that of the Chicago-area widows. The Chicago women had been widowed for an average of 10 years, whereas the mean was nine years for the widows in Century Village. Both studies found a relatively low level of life satisfaction among widows. In the area of self-concept the Chicago study found that, after widowhood, some women developed more competence, independence, and self-sufficiency. While the data is not exactly comparable, the Century Village widows indicated greater self-confidence in their intellectual skills than did the married. It appears that in spite of the many negative consequences of widowhood, for some women the necessity of greater self-reliance leads to enhanced self-esteem.

Lopata (1979) reported that socializing with friends was largely a middle-class phenomenon. In her heterogeneous sample of Chicago widows, 16 percent said they had no friends. However, half of the friends reported were of a 20-year duration or more. The Century Village widows had an average of six close friends, and more than half had known their closest friends for at least 20 years. The Chicago widows said they were in contact with their old friends about once per month, although almost half saw this friend less often. The closest friend of the majority of Century Village widows lived out of town, so face-to-face contact was less than once per month. However, almost all were in contact with this friend through visits, letters, and telephone calls. Many widows had made new friends near their new home. Almost half said the closest friend lived in the same building (14 percent), in the same neighborhood (19 percent) or in the same city or area (12 percent). A third of the Chicago widows found new friends in their neighborhood or local clubs, and almost half said that they wished for more friends. Three out of four Century Village widows said that friendships had become more important over the years.

Conclusions

This study examined the relationship between psychological well-being and social networks among widowed and married Jewish women living in a Florida retirement community. Although the respondents were a self-selected sample of volunteers, their background variables were similar to those of all the residents who participated in a larger research project. This suggests that these data can be generalized to the widowed and married population at Century Village, Deerfield Beach, Florida.

The Century Village respondents also have a demographic profile similar to that of other interstate migrants. However, the study sample is probably more ethnically homogeneous than those who may have participated in other widowhood studies. In spite of this homogeneity, many of the relationships found are consistent with the literature on social networks and well-being among the widowed. Even though the married and widowed respondents were similar in background variables, the widows had lower life satisfaction and activity level. Many of the relationships reported, particularly in the area of friendships, are similar to what Lopata (1979) found among middle-class Chicago widows.

A fruitful approach for further research would be to examine feelings about being unattached in such activity-oriented settings as retirement communities, and how the perception of social support among those without immediate access to a family network is related to well-being. In addition, research on the social networks of residents in ethnically homogeneous communities compared to heterogeneous neighborhoods would clarify the cultural factors from those related to class or socioeconomic status. Finally, it would be interesting to know what variables influence the decision to relocate into a retirement community.

5 The Influence of Religion on the Subjective Well-Being of the Widowed

RUBYE WILKERSON BECK

As of 1980 there were over 10 million widows and over two million widowers in the United States (Lopata, 1980). This number is increasing each year. The death of a husband or wife, besides being a common experience, is emotionally devastating, sometimes ranked first on life-events scales, but usually ranked as the second most stressful event, with only the loss of a child ranked higher (Holmes and Rahe, 1967). Given these facts, it seems useful to examine factors that may influence the widowed person's experience in positive or negative ways.

The central focus of this chapter derives both from the symbolic interaction perspective and the sociological focus on culture and norms. Symbolic interactionists tell us that the way in which people define a situation affects their response to it, its meaning to them, and its effects on them. The bereaved individual's definition of the situation, in this case the situation of loss and widowhood, is heavily influenced by the culture of which the individual is a part. Culture provides a framework of interpretation, or meaning, for life's events and norms for how one should think, feel, and behave when confronted with particular events and in particular situations.

Many writers have discussed both the secularization of Western cultures and the lack of one clear view of the meaning of death. Some have suggested that there is a cultural "death denial" that leaves the bereaved person with a paucity of norms concerning how to grieve properly. Others have suggested that death is dealt with not by denial but by treating it as solely a rational-physical phenomenon, ignoring death's emotional and spiritual dimensions (Berardo, 1968; Becker, 1973; Feifel, 1977; Scheff, 1980; Jackson, 1979; Gorer, 1977; Dumont and Foss, 1972). Both approaches are seen by some as unhelpful to the bereaved. Berardo (1968) claims that bereaved spouses face "normative ambiguity" concerning how to behave when widowed. This normative ambiguity may elicit a great deal of uncertainty and anxiety. Religion, it seems, is the institution in society that deals most directly with death in all its cognitive, emotional, and spiritual aspects. Religion may provide both a framework of meaning in which individuals can come to understand their loss and consequent norms concerning how they should feel, think, and behave when bereaved. Religious organizations may also serve as sources of social support and interaction for the bereaved. Based on these assumptions, religion is used in this study as a way to explore how bereaved individuals view death, God, the afterlife, and so on, and whether their beliefs have any bearing on their subjective well-being. Involvement in religious organizations is also viewed as a possible source of social support and interaction.

Review of the Literature

Some studies have focused on the relationship between religiousness and fear of death. It has been found that fear of death is least strong among both the deeply religious and the deeply irreligious. People who are uncertain in their religious beliefs show the greatest anxiety and fear (Kalish, 1981). Kalish claims that it is those people with strong inner beliefs who probably find more meaning in life, regardless of whether or not those beliefs are traditional.

There is some evidence that certain religious beliefs may be life-preserving. Stack (1983), in a study of suicide rates in 25 nations, found that a high level of commitment to a few life-preserving religious beliefs, values, and practices lowered suicide levels. Examples of life-preserving beliefs include a focus on an afterlife, belief in a responsive God, and an eternal perspective. Examples of the latter would be seeing earthly suffering as a mere short moment in the context of eternity, or a belief in role models for suffering from religious literature that gives suffering a positive meaning, such as the Book of Job in the Old Testament.

A few researchers have found an association between certain aspects of religion and life satisfaction. Hunsberger (1985) found a moderate positive relationship between degree of religiosity and life satisfaction in a study of 85 elderly persons. Gray and Moberg (1977) claim that both religious behavior and belief are causal factors in the life satisfaction of older people.

Research has shown that religious organizations serve as social support systems for many of their members (Glock et al., 1967; Hadaway and Roof, 1978). Additionally, religious participation may bring the bereaved into contact with others who may reinforce his or her beliefs and provide normative guidelines for "appropriate" grieving behavior. Participation in religious organizations may also contribute to the subjective well-being of widowed individuals by increasing their degree of social participation and social integration.

Studies Specifically Concerning Religion and Bereavement

Certain religious beliefs and types of participation may facilitate resolution of grief. Bryer (1979:257), discussing her observational study of the Amish way of death, notes that the Amish view death as the "final rite of passage into a new and better life" and are socialized throughout life into a calm acceptance of death. They also have specific rituals and customs concerning death and bereavement. Certain families are assigned to the newly bereaved for at least one year to offer comfort and support. She saw no evidence of protracted or abnormal grief among this group. Amish religion provides both a "source of meaning" and a "sense of belonging" (Wuthnow et al., 1980), both important aspects of the ways in which religion may address the needs of grieving persons. Glick et al. (1974) suggested that religious beliefs sustain morale and are a major source of comfort to the newly bereaved. Harvey and Bahr (1980) found that for the widows in their study, perception of self as very religious and participating in church activities both had positive effects on perceived quality of life and overall happiness.

Religion as a Source of Meaning

Several authors have discussed the provision of meaning as one of the important functions of religion for the bereaved. In delineating the functions of religion, O'Dea (1966) includes the idea that religion can provide individuals and groups with a sense of the meaningfulness of life, which may help them find support and consolation for the difficult experiences that they encounter. Religion puts the many sorrows and tragedies of human existence in an understandable context; it "explains" them. In addition, religion provides a relationship to the transcendental realm, which can lead to a feeling of security and worth. Having a reference point beyond the present life can give people the belief that there is an order to life beyond what appears to them in the present. In particular, belief in an afterlife may ameliorate the sense of meaninglessness or unfairness of losing loved ones through death or of facing one's own death. Religious faith may enable the widowed person to explain and account for his or her loss, to give it meaning (Simpson, 1979; Jackson, 1979). Frankl (1963) has stated that the ability to find meaning in one's life is the most important task in attaining subjective well-being. This task is made more difficult for persons experiencing the pain of grief, a situation that may render some previously acceptable structures of meaning irrelevant or impossible. For Frankl (1963:xi), "to live is to suffer, to survive is to find meaning in the suffering. If there is a purpose in life at all, there must be a purpose in suffering and in dying." Frankl writes from the perspective of a psychologist who himself was a prisoner in a Nazi concentration camp. He observed that fellow prisoners who were able to find some source of meaning in their tortured lives were more likely to survive than those who "gave up," who found no meaning in their lives at that point, or who had no hope for the future. The situation of concentration camp prisoners, while different from that of widowed persons, shares the characteristics of extreme loss and the potential for hopelessness. This seems particularly relevant for the current study since one issue is whether or not attributing some non-negative meaning to suffering and death is associated with the subjective well-being of the widowed.

Wuthnow et al. (1980), in formulating a conceptual framework for viewing the relationship between religion and bereavement, discuss the effects of specific types of religious beliefs on the subjective well-being of bereaved persons. These include the ideas that believing that God can bring good from evil (in this case suffering and death) will be associated with subjective well-being and believing that something good for the self (such as greater understanding of God's love) can come from bereavement will be positively associated with subjective well-being and that fatalistic conceptions of death will be negatively associated with subjective well-being. Wuthnow and associates point out that the relationships between religion and bereavement are likely to vary by religious tradition. Some religious traditions more than others advocate beliefs that may contribute to the subjective well-being of the bereaved. Religious groups may also vary in the kinds of social support provided to members. In other words, the relationship between religion and subjective well-being varies according to religious group as well as to individual religious characteristics such as strength of commitment to religious beliefs and degree of involvement in the church organization.

According to Batson and Ventis (1982:247) "how one is religious does indeed have a dramatic effect on the relationship between religion and mental health." In other words, the consequences of religion for mental health, or subjective well-being, will vary according to the way in which a person is religious. Batson and Ventis, for example, discuss three types of religion, each of which may have quite different consequences for well-being. Religion may be a "means" to something else, such as gaining respect in the community, making friends, or improving one's business contacts. This type of religion, or religiosity, has also been termed "extrinsic." It probably does not offer the adherent a set framework of meaning that would provide comfort in bereavement. It may, however, provide the bereaved with a ready-made network of caring others who will provide social support and social interaction. The second type is religion as an end in itself or "intrinsic" religiosity. Intrinsically religious people view their faith as the central, integrating value in their lives. They often strongly adhere to an orthodox and absolute set of beliefs that provide them with certainty concerning spiritual matters. It may be these people for whom religion is most likely to offer the assurance that, for example, their loved ones are in heaven and that they will be someday reunited. The intrinsically religious may be most likely to have a firmness of faith that, although perhaps challenged by the death of the spouse, will remain essentially intact. According to Batson and Ventis, however, this category of the religious may also include those who are fanatical and inflexible, which may be viewed as mentally unhealthy or as detracting from well-being. The third type of religion is termed the "quest." Those whose religiosity falls into this category place a high value on thinking about and questioning religious values. Complexity, doubt, tentativeness, flexibility, and tolerance of the beliefs of others often characterize their religious views. The "quest" type of faith may not offer the same type of certainty and comfort as the intrinsic, but those who fit into this category may exhibit a self-directedness and self-reliance that could be a source of strength to them in bereavement. On the other hand, uncertainty may be a source of pain and worry for the bereaved.

In sum, there seem to be two aspects of religion that may contribute to the subjective well-being of the widowed: a belief system that gives meaning to their losses, and the availability of an organization containing like-minded others who may enhance the degree of social integration of the bereaved. Different types of religiosity may provide these in varying degrees or, in some cases, perhaps not at all.

Methods

Sample

The data in this study were obtained from in-person interviews with a sample of middle-aged and older, white, predominantly middle-class widowed persons living in a Southeastern university town. The sample included 44 widows and 16 widowers. The study was designed to explore various factors associated with the subjective well-being of widowed men and women beyond the first year of bereavement. The mean age of the respondents was 68.8 years, with a range of 41 to 88 years of age. The mean educational attainment of the respondents was 12.4 years. The religious affiliations of the sample members include one Congregationalist, four Episcopalians, one Disciple of Christ member, 11 United Methodists, 10 Presbyterians, six Catholics, one American Baptist, 14 Southern Baptists, eight sectarians (such as Jehovah's Witnesses, Apostolic, Holiness, etc.), and three who claimed to have no religious affiliation. One man refused to answer this question. This distribution is typical of religious affiliations in the South, which is dominated mainly by Southern Baptists and Methodists (Hill et al., 1972).

Methods of Data Analysis

This sample of 60 widowed persons is a nonprobability sample. In this analysis, appropriate measures of association—Kendall's Tau-C and Pearson's r—are used as well as cross-tabulation tables. However, because this is a nonprobability sample, no significance tests are conducted. Although it is not appropriate to generalize the results of statistical analysis beyond this sample, tentative conclusions may be drawn about factors affecting the subjective well-being of this sample.

In addition, "case study" examples and quotes from respondents will be used to complement, support, and challenge the findings from statistical analysis.

Focus of Analysis

This research is concerned with the relationships among various aspects of the religious beliefs and participation of respondents and their subjective well-being. Subjective well-being of the respondents was measured with two commonly used single items that assess happiness and life satisfaction. The life satisfaction question read: "In general, how satisfying do you find the way you're spending your life these days? Would you call it completely satisfying, pretty satisfying, or not very satisfying?" The happiness question read: "Taking all things together, how would you say things are these days? Would you say you are very happy, pretty happy, not too happy or very unhappy?" (Not too happy and very unhappy were collapsed into the one category of unhappy due to the small number of respondents in the very unhappy category.) The aspects of religion examined include frequency of church attendance, personal importance of religion, belief in an afterlife, belief in reunion with the spouse in the afterlife, religion as a comfort, and an open-ended question ascertaining whether or not the respondents' religious beliefs provided them with an explanation of the meaning of suffering and death.

Church attendance is included as a measure of religious participation. Thirty-six respondents attended weekly or more often, six attended one to three times a month, three a few times a year, four once a year or less, and eleven never attended. It was hypothesized that church attendance would be positively associated with subjective well-being.

Personal importance of religion was used as an assessment of religiosity. It was hypothesized that personal importance of religion would be positively associated with subjective well-being. People for whom religion is personally important can probably fall back on their faith as a source of strength and comfort in the experience of bereavement.

Belief in an afterlife and in reunion with the spouse in the afterlife was also assessed. Thirty-three respondents believed that there was an afterlife, eighteen were unsure (some of these saying "I hope so"), and nine definitely did not think there was any kind of afterlife. Twenty believed that they would be reunited with their spouses in the afterlife, 24 were unsure, and 14 thought this would definitely not be the case. It was hypothesized that believing in an afterlife would be positively associated with subjective well-being as this belief would ameliorate the supposed total annihilation of the loved one. It may be comforting to believe that the deceased still exists in spiritual form. It was also hypothesized that believing in postdeath reunion with the spouse would be positively associated with subjective well-being since this belief defines the separation from the spouse as temporary rather than permanent. Another important question was whether or not the respondents' religion had been a comfort to them in their grief and if so in what way. Two-thirds said that it had been a comfort. In some cases it was a comfort by promising an afterlife, in others by making widowed persons feel less lonely because they felt God's presence. Still others were comforted simply by the belief that there was a God who was "in charge" and had a plan, so that life and death were meaningful even if inexplicable to human beings. A few people found religion anything but comforting, feeling that if there was a God, He was terribly "unfair" in taking their spouse, who "deserved" to have lived longer or to have suffered less. One woman, who felt that suffering and death were a "punishment for killing Jesus," had particularly strong feelings concerning the unfairness of her husband's death. It was hypothesized that those who said their religion was a comfort would have higher subjective well-being than those who did not find their religion comforting.

The open-ended question concerning the meaning of suffering and death yielded the following results. Twenty-one of the respondents gave non-negative answers, while 39 gave either no answer or negative answers. It was hypothesized that those who attributed non-negative meanings to suffering and death would have higher subjective well-being. This is expected since being able to understand and give meaning to one's loss is important in working through the grief process. Those who can, in particular, find something positive in an overwhelmingly negative experience will be better able to cope.

Results and Discussion

It was found that attending church did have a positive effect on the well-being of respondents. The more frequently respondents attended church, the higher was their life satisfaction (r = .30) and the greater their happiness (r = .23). A number of respondents mentioned their fellow church members as sources of support and as good friends. Church attendance provided many people an opportunity to interact with like-minded and sympathetic others. One 45-year-old woman said, "Church is the only place I go. It feels good to go to church." For her, and for others, church attendance provided one of the main opportunities for social interaction outside the family. Petrowsky (1976) has even suggested that churches may serve as surrogate families for some people. In one instance in the current study, for example, a widower who was a Jehovah's Witness spent part of nearly every day with other church members and claimed them as his best friends. A case could be made that his church was for him a surrogate family.

It was hypothesized that those widowed persons who considered their religion to be more personally important would exhibit greater well-being. Those for whom religion was the most personally important were somewhat happier (tau-c = .18) and more satisfied with their lives (tau-c = .22).

A cross-tabulation analyzing the relationship between personal importance of religion and happiness adds further clarity (see table 5.1). The cross-tabulation shows that of those who said religion was extremely important to them personally, 24 percent were very happy, 56 percent were pretty happy, and only 20 percent were unhappy. Of those who said religion was not important, by contrast, 75 percent were unhappy, 25 percent were pretty happy, and not one person was very happy. Believing that religion is important is associated with happiness for this sample.

It was expected that believing in an afterlife would be associated with greater levels of subjective well-being. This hypothesis is only slightly supported. Having such a belief contributes only a little to life satisfaction (tau-c = .10) and happiness (tau-c = .11). Several writers on grief have said that anxiety and fear are greatly increased with the loss of a loved one, partly because of the increased fear of vulnerability to death one may feel, having been so close to another's death. A belief in an afterlife may reduce this anxiety by making death seem less threatening. The associations are probably no stronger because some of the respondents' beliefs included a belief in "hell" or some form of final punishment. A few feared that their spouses would be in such a place or state. Others were vague about what an afterlife would be like but seemed to fear some type of judgment. Still others gave an explicit

Table 5.1 Cross-Tabulations of Happiness by Personal Importance of Religion and Meaning of Suffering and Death.

	Happiness	
Personal importance of religion	Very happy	Pretty happy
Extremely important	8 (24%)	19 (56%)
Important	5 (28%)	9 (50%)
Not important	0 (0%)	2 (25%)
Meaning of suffering and death		
No or a negative meaning	6 (15%)	19 (49%)
Non-negative meaning	7 (33%)	11 (52%)

and very positive description of "heaven," making it seem that they had little to fear from death.

It was also expected that a belief that one would be reunited with one's spouse after death would be associated with higher levels of subjective well-being. Surprisingly, the statistical data do not bear this out. The qualitative data do, nonetheless, suggest that this belief is quite important to some of the respondents. For example, one 63-year-old man described the afterlife as a state of being "joined with loved ones . . . no worries" and said that "knowing she (his wife) is in Heaven and I'm going to see her again someday" was a comfort to him. One woman believed her husband "is with his sister, brother and mother; they're comforting each other," and believed she would eventually join them. One 76-year-old woman said of her deceased husband, "I know he's waiting for me . . . (this belief) has sustained me." One 74-year-old man said he'd been "thinking about it a lot. I won't remarry because of my first wife." One 83-year-old man said his religion was a comfort because he would "be able to be with her in the afterlife. I'd like to be with her again." For some people, it seems, believing in reunion with the spouse is sustaining and helpful. A large number of people were uncertain on this belief, most saying "I hope so." One 71-year-old woman said on this question "I would like to believe. It would be a comfort." Most of the uncertain people expressed a wish to be certain. Being uncertain seemed to be in some ways worse than being an emphatic unbeliever. This uncertainty may be one drawback of the "quest" type of religiosity.

It was hypothesized that those who claimed their religion had been a comfort to them in their bereavement would score higher on subjective well-being. The quantitative data do not support this hypothesis. Comments from respondents seem to suggest, however, that the comfort offered by religion is an important factor in the subjective well-being of some respondents. A 72-year-old widow said "I would have gone to pieces without it (her faith)." A 74-year-old widow said religion "gives me strength to overcome grief, loneliness, and loss." A 64-year-old woman said her religion was a comfort in that it helped her not feel alone since she believed her husband still existed in an afterlife. A 55-year-old woman said she could "feel Jesus' arms around me, helping me to cope the night he (her husband) died." A 68-year-old man said his religion comforted him "just to know someone (God) still thinks about me." A 77-year-old woman said "I talk to God and ask for guidance. Every day I receive help." Although it is clear from these statements that religion was helpful and important to these people, it did not guarantee they would be happier or more satisfied. It may be the case that those people who are least happy and satisfied turn to religion as a comfort as much or more than those who are better off psychologically. Alternately, one or more other variables that are not apparent at this time may be involved in this relationship.

It was expected that those widowed persons who were able to give a non-negative meaning to suffering and death would have higher subjective well-being than those giving either no meaning or a negative meaning. It was found that those who gave non-negative responses to the question on the meaning of suffering and death were happier (tau-c = .26) and more satisfied with their lives (tau-c = .18).

The cross-tabulation for this comparison makes this even clearer (see table 5.1). Of those who gave a negative meaning or no meaning, 36 percent were unhappy. Of those who gave a non-negative meaning, only 14 percent were unhappy. It appears that lack of a coherent explanation for suffering and death or attributing a negative meaning to them is associated with greater unhappiness. It also appears that respondents' life satisfaction is similarly affected (no table given). Of those giving no meaning or a negative meaning, 33 percent were unsatisfied, whereas of those giving a non-negative meaning, only 14 percent were unsatisfied.

Some examples that may help illustrate the findings follow. Mrs. Y., 83 years old, saw suffering as "punishment for wrongdoing" and death as having "no meaning, it's just the end of everything." She was "not too happy" and found her life "not very satisfying." She felt she had "nothing to look forward to." Mrs. X., age 61, who also was "not too happy," found her life "not very satisfying," and saw death as a "release from suffering." In her case, it was not so much that she saw death as negative but that she saw her life as negative and death primarily as an escape from it. Mr. W., who seemed lonely and bitter and was hostile during the interview, also had very low scores on happiness and life satisfaction. He said death and suffering had no meaning. Moreover, all his answers on the religion questions were in the negative, such as that religion was unimportant and that the questions were "stupid."

Mrs. V., who claimed to be very happy and completely satisfied, believed that death and suffering may "bring families closer to God," or may "save their souls," and that suffering is used by God to win others. In other words, Mrs. V. attributed a positive meaning to death and suffering. She also claimed that she "lives for the Lord." It would seem that religion gave a sense of meaning and purpose to her life. Mr. S., age 74, a Jehovah's Witness, was completely immersed in his religion. He was "very happy" and "completely satisfied," seeing death as the way to be resurrected and join with Jesus as a positive transition. Mrs. V. and Mr. S. seem to represent Batson and Ventis's (1982) "intrinsic" or "ends" type of religiosity. This type of religiosity is a major part of the adherents' lives and gives them certainty and comfort in that certainty. Mr. R., age 68, said "I wish I did know" what the meaning of suffering and death were. Mr. R. was "not too happy" and "not very satisfied." Mr. R. may represent the "quest" type of religiosity, which has the disadvantage of not offering absolute certainty. There were several other respondents who indicated that they had given some thought to the meaning of suffering and death but had not yet reached any definitive conclusion.

Mrs. Q., age 76, who was "pretty happy" and "pretty satisfied," described death as a "graduation." She said "God meets us in death and leads us across the border . . . a reunion." Mrs. U., age 73, was "pretty happy" and "completely satisfied." She said that "God made man perfect. Suffering is not His fault." In other words, the "blame" for negative events is on people rather than on God. This leads to an issue that came up fairly often in the interviews, although not asked: that is, the fairness of God or the fairness of death.

Some examples will illustrate the fairness, or "divine justice," issue. Mrs. P., age 58, said "it just isn't fair the good die young" and claimed her husband's death had reduced her religious faith since she now saw the universe, and consequently God, as unfair. Mrs. O., age 70, felt at first when her husband died that God had "forsaken" her. Mrs. N., age 51, who attempted suicide soon after her husband's death, "saw no reason for his dying. It turned me off religion when he died . . . he was so good, why him?" Mrs. M., age 73, and Mrs. N., age 86, by contrast, saw their husbands' deaths as "fair." Mrs. M. said she "knows it was time for his death . . . it was God's will, according to plan." Mrs. N., in a similar vein, said it was the "appropriate time that God took him (at age 94) to relieve his suffering. (It was the) right thing." Apparently a lot of people had specific ideas concerning what was fair and unfair in God's deciding who should die and when. If the spouse was relatively young or if he or she was seen as particularly "good," then death might be viewed as unfair. If the spouse was older or had suffered for a long time, death might be viewed as fair, appropriate, or even a blessing. Those who saw the loss of their spouses as unfair were generally unhappy and unsatisfied, and often bitter. The work of Hill et al. (1972:130) seems to offer some insight into the "fairness" issue. According to them, meaningful events such as death "are explained by the two fundamental principles of the [fundamentalist Christian] belief system: supernatural justice and fate. Supernatural justice, an eminently moral principle, . . . affirms that conformity to social norms is rewarded while deviance is punished . . . In contrast, fate is an eminently amoral principle. Bad people sometimes enjoy the best things in life while good people suffer misfortunes." According to "supernatural justice," it is unfair that "good" people suffer and die young. Apparently, the belief system of some members of this sample encompassed "supernatural justice" but not "fate." The belief in "fate," or something like it, may be a necessary corollary to "supernatural justice" if one is to maintain one's religious faith when "unfair" events occur. This may help to explain why some respondents' faiths were shaken by the death of their spouses while the faiths of others remained unchanged or in some cases were even strengthened. It may also partially help to explain why religion is more of a comfort to some people than to others. The fairness of death issue would be a good one to explore in future research.

Summary

This analysis has shown that religion is a complex factor with mixed effects on the subjective well-being of the widowed. One important finding is that those respondents who were able to attribute a non-negative meaning to suffering and death, based on their religious beliefs, were more likely to be happy and satisfied than those who attributed negative meanings or who were unable to answer. It seems that being able to put death and suffering, undisputedly negative experiences, in a non-negative context is a contributor to subjective well-being. An intriguing issue that came up during the interviews was the "fairness" of death. Some respondents' beliefs in "divine" or "supernatural" justice were challenged by what they saw as "unfair" treatment by God in allowing their "too good" or "too young" spouses to die. Others' faith was reaffirmed by "fair" treatment such as the one 88-year-old widow who thought it was kind of God to take her 94-year-old ailing husband. A general statement might be that just being religious is not enough; it is the nature of one's beliefs that either contributes to or diminishes subjective well-being.

Other findings from the statistical analysis were that believing in an afterlife had less of a positive effect on the subjective well-being of the widowed persons in this sample than had been expected, and that believing in a reunion with the spouse in the afterlife had virtually no effect on subjective well-being. Nonetheless, "case study" examples show that such beliefs were very helpful to some respondents. The same thing applied for the religion as a comfort variable, no statistical association with subjective well-being was found, but a few "case study" examples show this to have important effects for some respondents.

Personal importance of religion was found to be positively associated with life satisfaction and happiness. Those for whom religion was the most personally important were the happiest and most satisfied.

Clearly, then, the relationship between the religious beliefs and participation of the respondents and their subjective well-being is not a simple one. The relationships between the religion and the well-being of the widowed persons interviewed in this study varied according to the types of beliefs held and the importance of religion to each respondent. One may conclude from this research that certain types of religious beliefs and some aspects of religion are important factors in coping with bereavement for some widowed persons.

6 Widows in Urban Nebraska: Their Informal Support Systems

TRUDY B. ANDERSON

Older women's informal support systems are composed of individuals who serve as resources by providing assistance, companionship, and comfort on a daily basis and in emergencies (Longino and Lipman, 1982; 1985). These support systems "are dynamic since they are negotiated by individuals" (Longino and Lipman, 1985:230); over time they shift, with resources being added or dropped as the life situations of women change (Bell, 1981; Longino and Lipman, 1985). One such life situation is the loss of a spouse through death (Lopata, 1979).

This chapter examines how older women's informal support systems are affected by the end of marriage, when this occurs through death. Specifically, it compares the supports that older widows receive from their primary relatives and friends with those of their married counterparts.

All of the women in the study lived in a midwestern metropolitan community. The city in which women reside is important because it may facilitate social contacts and the use of informal support systems (Lopata, 1979).

Location

Omaha, with its population of 314,255, is the central city in the largest Standard Metropolitan Statistical Area in the state of Nebraska (U.S.

Appreciation is expressed to the Midwest Council for Social Research on Aging for its support.

Bureau of the Census, 1981). This metropolitan community offers many opportunities and settings for socializing and for engaging in activities with family and friends. There are numerous churches representing a variety of religions, each with its own calendar of activities for members. The city also has abundant clubs, service groups, and voluntary organizations. Like other urban places in the Snow Belt, the weather during the long winter months is often cold and snowy, which restricts social contact for many older women. Sometimes the bad weather necessitates canceling planned senior citizen and other social events.

Of particular interest is that section of the city where all of the women surveyed for this study lived. The Dundee area is located in the older, north-central section of the city and is predominately white. There were no blacks living in the area in 1978, and less than 1 percent of the residents were members of other minority groups (Omaha, City Planning Department, 1978). The area has a heavy concentration of elderly individuals; in 1978, the Dundee area had 60 percent more persons aged 65 and older than did the Omaha area as a whole (Omaha, City Planning Department, 1978).

While the tract has a high density of elderly, not all of its neighborhoods can be characterized as elderly (60 years of age and over). Some neighborhoods are age-integrated, with an even mix of older and younger residents. In still others, the resident life-style is dominated by the needs of middle-aged and younger families. The Dundee area, in fact, is experiencing some shift in its age composition as a consequence of, first, older persons moving to a nearby health-care center or other institutionalized facilities, and, second, a high death rate (U.S. National Center for Health Statistics, 1985).

The area is a little community, with its own central business district to which many people walk in nice weather. Traveling on foot to the merchants, however, can be hazardous as many of the sidewalks are in need of repair. The bus service to other sections of the city seems to be adequate; yet, relatively few of the older women surveyed (7 percent) use the bus system as a regular means of transportation. Most had access to an automobile and either drove themselves (37 percent) or depended on someone else (43 percent). The majority of the women in this study (88 percent) had some way of getting to neighborhoods outside the Dundee area.

Wives

Most women eventually marry. In 1981, 94 percent of the women over age 64 had at some time been married (U.S. Bureau of the Census, 1984). When women marry, their kin matrix expands to include a new set of relatives; in later life, it consists of spouse, in-laws (e.g., parents-in-law, siblings-in-law, and extended relatives-in-law) as well as one's own blood relatives (e.g., parents, adult children, siblings, aunts, uncles, cousins, nieces, and nephews).

Wives have traditionally been the "kin keepers" to whom the tasks of maintaining contact with relatives and of arranging family get-togethers have been assigned (Longino and Lipman, 1982; Troll et al., 1979). Because older women, particularly the married, have been responsible for remembering birthdays, anniversaries, and other special occasions, and for coordinating and planning family activities on holidays, their network is composed mainly of other female relatives, especially daughters, daughters-in-law, and sisters (Lopata, 1979; Longino and Lipman, 1985; Troll et al., 1979). It appears that "kin keeping" has been advantageous for married women. Longino and Lipman (1982) report that among the residents of two life-care communities, married women received more emotional, social, and instrumental support from primary family members, including spouse, than did widows and other formerly married women. These researchers (Longino and Lipman, 1982) contend that married women advanced in age have more family resources than either widowed or divorced women.

Marriage not only expands the kin matrix but also brings about a realignment of the friendship matrix. While married women have, as they did in the previous life-cycle stages, some friendships with other women as individuals, such friendships are not encouraged by American society. Same-sex friendships are viewed as competing with the marital relationship (Lopata, 1975). Among married couples, the husband–wife dyad constitutes the basic friendship unit. This is particularly true for middle-class couples (Babchuk, 1965; Bell, 1981). Couple-oriented friends participate in a variety of activities including card parties, dinner parties, and sport activities (such as golfing) (Babchuk and Bates, 1963; Lopata, 1975). In many cases, the sources of attraction between couple-companionate friends are between the two wives and the two husbands rather than the cross-sex relations in that particular network (Bell, 1981).

Just as being married affects the friendship and kinship matrices, the end of marriage brings about shifts and adjustments in kin and nonkin networks. Moreover, the informal support systems that can assist older women in adjusting to widowhood often themselves become "disorganized" (Lopata, 1979). The gerontological issue is which support resources, if any, step in to provide the services and companionship formerly performed by the deceased husband.

Omaha Women and Their Support Systems

The individuals most likely to provide companionship and assistance in daily life and crisis situations are the relatives and friends with whom women have developed very close or intimate (primary) ties; therefore, primary resources are roughly analogous to the informal support system. An informal support system, thus, is defined in this chapter as consisting of all relatives and friends who are primary relations of a woman.

Support Systems

Cantor (1979) has devised the hierarchical compensatory model to describe the nature of older persons' support systems. The model posits a hierarchical ordering of informal support based upon the "primacy of the relationship of the support giver to the elderly recipient" (p. 453). Kin, particularly children, are the preferred support element, followed by friends and neighbors. When kin are unavailable, elderly persons compensate by turning to nonkin. This model has received empirical support (see Peters and Kaiser, 1975).

The family support network has been conceptualized by Shanas (1979a) as operating on the "principle of substitution." According to this principle, family members are available in serial order. Married women rely on their husbands (Johnson, 1983; Shanas, 1979b) and widowed women turn to their children (Lopata, 1979). When spouses or children are unavailable, siblings and other relatives enter women's informal support systems. Indeed, for some widowed elderly, siblings assume the responsibilities formerly performed by deceased husbands (Johnson, 1983; Shanas, 1979a). Extended family members, particularly nieces and nephews, become important resources for the childless elderly (Shanas, 1979a). The family support system, however, may not always follow the substitution principle. In fact, Lopata (1978; 1979) has argued that the importance of siblings and extended kin has been overstated. She found that kin outside the family of procreation infrequently provide any type of support to Chicago-area widows. Lopata (1970) also has noted that widows lose contact with in-laws. Once the connecting link between families is dead, there is little reason to maintain contact, especially if the in-law relationship has been characterized by conflict and hostility.

Overall, the family literature suggests two counterbalancing trends: children and siblings appear more often in women's support systems after the spouse's death, while extended kin only occasionally furnish any type of support. The extant research findings, as well as the hierarchical compensatory model and the "principle of family substitution," suggest several hypotheses. Specifically, it is hypothesized that widowed women will prefer (a) children as support resources, followed by (b) siblings, (c) friends, and with (d), extended kin, selected last.

Sample

The population from which the sample individuals were drawn consisted of noninstitutionalized, white elderly women who live in a single census tract in Omaha, Nebraska. The tract was selected using race as well as density and proportion of aged as criteria. This mode of selection enabled the researcher to control for race/ethnicity by nonvariance.

Block statistics (U.S. Bureau of the Census, 1970) were used to determine which blocks were to be sampled; eligible households in these blocks were then obtained from the City Directory. A systematic procedure was used to obtain a representative sample.

Of the 249 households contacted with eligible respondents, 132 potential respondents agreed to be interviewed. This represented 53 percent of the eligible women. Twenty-one (18 percent) of the refusals were women unable to participate because of poor health or physical disability. The interviews were conducted in the respondents' homes between November 1980 and January 1981.

Forty-three percent ($N = 57$) of the respondents were married and 57 percent ($N = 75$) were widowed. The proportion of married and widowed older women surveyed approximated their representation in the general population. Ages ranged from 65 to 98, with a mean of 73.5.

There were only a few background characteristics on which the widowed and the married differed significantly (t-tests of the difference between means, $p<.10$). The widowed were significantly older and more likely to have restricted mobility and problems with hearing. These health differences were not surprising given the age differences between the widowed and the married. On the other hand, married women had a greater annual income and, although not significant, were more apt to state that their income was enough or more than enough to live on comfortably. Since married and widowed women differed significantly on several characteristics, health and income each are introduced as control variables in the analysis. The only exception is yearly income. Because many (35 percent) refused to answer this item, the subjective evaluation of the adequacy of income was used as a control variable. Husband's (whether living or deceased) principal lifetime occupation additionally was introduced as a control variable. Widowed and married women did not differ significantly on this background characteristic: 49 percent of the widowed women's husbands had been employed in white-collar occupations, compared with 40 percent of the married women's husbands. The rationale for using spouse's occupational status as a control was that an objective measure of socioeconomic status was needed. Spouse's occupational status, rather than either the woman's educational or occupational status, was selected because these older women have lived most of their lives during a historical period in which women depended upon spouses for economic support and social identity. All control variables in the present study are treated as covariates in the Multiple Classification Analysis (MCA) (SPSS, Inc., 1982).

Measures

Primary relations. Primary kinship was measured by having each woman enumerate all of her relatives. She was then asked to identify all relatives (excluding spouse) to whom she felt very close. These were designated as primary kin. Other questions focused on the relational status, geographical location, and other characteristics of these relatives.

A parallel procedure was used with respect to friends. After each woman reported the approximate number of her acquaintances and friends, she was asked to identify those persons to whom she felt very close. These were designated primary friends. The woman was then asked to provide information on the residence of these friends as well as some other characteristics, such as sex and marital status.

Types of support. Supportive activities were divided into three categories: social, instrumental, and emotional. Social support was measured by asking women whether they had (a) played games, (b) gone to movies and plays, (c) celebrated holidays, or (d) dined with each primary relative and friend. Having turned to a primary resource when (a) ill or (b) short of money were indicators of instrumental support. Emotional support was operationalized in terms of reliance on a primary relative or friend when (a) worried, or (b) depressed. Others (e.g., Babchuk and Ballweg, 1972; Cantor, 1979; Lopata, 1979) have used similar items in their research. A primary resource might provide support in all, any, or none of the support categories. In order to determine whether the support was reciprocal, women were asked whether each primary resource had turned to them when needing instrumental or emotional support.

Primary Resources

More women reported not having a single relative to whom they felt very close than claimed not to have an intimate friend: one-fifth of the women did not have a primary relative, while fewer than one in 10 (8 percent) did not have a primary friend. In addition, the primary friendship networks of these women included more individuals than did their primary kinship networks: the maximum number of friends was 15, with a mean 5.69, compared with a maximum of nine and a mean of 1.82 for kin. Overall, these older women had more nonkin than kin resources available to them.

Perhaps the critical theoretical issue is whether older women have *at least one primary resource*. Only four of the respondents (3 percent) were without a very close interpersonal tie: three of the married and only one of the widowed. Thus, an overwhelming majority of the women had one or more primary resource.

Children as resources. Children are an important part of women's kinship networks and a resource available to most older women. The majority of both widowed and married women in this Omaha study had at least one living child: 84 and 86 percent, respectively. Nationally, the corresponding figure for white women aged 65 and over was 80 percent in 1970 (U.S. Bureau of the Census, 1984).

Although most of the women were parents, a large proportion of them (68 percent) reported not feeling particularly close to any of their children. That only about one-third claimed to be on intimate terms with offspring illustrates the selective nature of primary (intimate) kinship ties (Anderson, 1984). Widows did not differ from the married in this regard.

Surprisingly, the women named more sons than daughters as part of their primary kinship network: 36 percent of the women named a son as primary, compared with 32 percent who named a daughter. It appears that more women developed primary ties with sons because of their greater availability. The number of living sons is significantly related to the number of sons named as primary ($t = 2.266, p<.001$), as is the number of living daughters to the number of primary daughters ($t = 2.314, p<.001$). Consequently, a greater proportion of the widowed and the married would have felt particularly close to daughters if they had any living daughters (Anderson, 1984).

Older women do not necessarily live in the same community as their children. Yet, living in close proximity facilitates social contact and the exchange of social, instrumental, and emotional support. Twenty-six percent of the women had at least one child in their primary kinship network living in the Omaha metropolitan area. Widows were slightly more likely to have a primary son or daughter in geographical proximity to them than were their married counterparts: 29 and 23 percent, respectively. Conversely, married women were slightly more likely to report that the children to whom they felt very close resided outside the Omaha metropolitan area.

Other relatives as resources. Besides children, siblings and extended kin are individuals who may serve as resources in older women's support networks. Brothers and sisters were generally available for inclusion in the support systems of the Omaha women. Over four-fifths (84 percent) of both the widowed and the married had at least one living brother or sister; yet, most (65 percent) of the women stated that they were not on intimate terms with any of their siblings. That just over one-third (35 percent) of the women reported primary relations with siblings once again illustrates the selective nature of primary ties with kin.

A similar proportion of the respondents (31 percent) selected extended relatives as primary kin, namely, nieces, nephews, aunts, cousins, grandchildren, and in-laws. Nieces were the only distant kin that were named as primary by at least 10 percent of the women. Relatives not cited as primary were great grandchildren, brothers-in-law, and uncles (Anderson, 1984).

The data (Anderson, 1984) suggest that the women in this study had been involved in "kin keeping," for they claimed to have primary relations with sisters (42 percent) rather than brothers (15 percent) and nieces (11 percent) rather than nephews (5 percent). It appears that the "principle of female linkages" that has been observed in the parent–child relationship (Lopata, 1979; Troll et al., 1979) also operates among siblings and other blood relatives.

Compared with children, fewer primary siblings and extended relatives lived within the greater Omaha area. Approximately a quarter (26 percent) of the women had a primary child in the urban community while less than a fifth (19 percent) had a primary sibling in the area. An even smaller proportion of the extended kin who served as primary resources lived in the city.

Friends as resources. Almost all of the women (90 percent) had at least one primary friend who lived in the metropolitan area. Over half of these women (58 percent) had restricted their primary friendships to persons who resided in the larger Omaha community.

Residential propinquity proved to be an important structural variable since the neighborhood provided the setting in which many friendships were formed. Over half of the women (57 percent) reported meeting one or more of their current primary friends in this way; 20 percent of the women reported continuing friendships with former neighbors. Thus, some neighbors are converted into primary friends who can serve as supports.

Individuals ordinarily seek close interpersonal ties with others who are similar to themselves (Bell, 1981). For example, most persons, particularly women, develop primary ties with individuals of the same sex (Booth and Hess, 1974; Powers and Bultena, 1976). The women in this study were typical in this respect. Of the 750 friends named as primary, 665 were female; over 90 percent of the women had a female friend to whom they felt very close. In contrast, only a fifth of them reported primary ties with individuals of the opposite sex. A minority of the women (12 percent) claimed to have two or more male primary friends, with the maximum being seven.

Support Systems of Married Women

Social supports. Table 6.1 summarizes the social supports that women with spouses received from their various primary resources. Primary children enter married women's social support systems mainly when

Table 6.1 Children, Siblings, Extended Kin, and Friends Serving as Social Supports

	Children Marital status			Siblings Marital status		
Activity	Widowed	Married		Widowed	Married	
Games						
Percentage sharing activity with a primary resource	15	12		23	14	
Mean number of primary resources						
Unadjusted	.15	.13		.23	.14	
Adjusted[b]	.18	.09		.29	.06	
Eta			.04			.11
Beta			.12 $p = .087$			.28 $p = .0$
Multiple R^2			.08			.14
Movies and plays						
Percentage sharing activity with a primary resource	16	4		15	7	
Mean number of primary resources						
Unadjusted	.17	.04		.14	.07	
Adjusted[b]	.17	.03		.18	.02	
Eta			.20 $p = .021$			.12
Beta			.22 $p = .056$			.26 $p = .$
Multiple R^2			.09			.13
Holidays						
Percentage sharing activity with a primary resource	29	26		24	19	
Mean number of primary resources						
Unadjusted	.29	.26		.24	.19	
Adjusted[b]	.31	.24		.29	.13	
Eta			.04			.06
Beta			.07 $p =$ ns			.19 $p =$
Multiple R^2			.08			.12

Extended kin Marital status			Friends[a] Marital status		
Widowed	Married		Widowed	Married	
15	10		49	46	
.15	.11		1.47	1.54	
.18	.07		1.64	1.32	
		.06			.02
		.15 $p = .002$			.07
		.15			.08
13	2		33	21	
.13	.01		.80	.34	
.13	.01		.93	.17	
		.21 $p = .017$			.16 $p = .054$
		.23 $p = .000$			.27 $p = .000$
		.19			.24
20	12		27	23	
.20	.12		.58	.53	
.21	.11		.60	.51	
		.11			.02
		.13 $p = .002$			.03 $p =$ ns
		.16			.05

Table 6.1 Continued.

	Children Marital status			Siblings Marital status		
Activity	Widowed	Married		Widowed	Married	
Dining						
Percentage sharing activity with a primary resource	29	28		33	28	
Mean number of primary resources						
Unadjusted	.30	.28		.33	.28	
Adjusted[b]	.31	.26		.40	.19	
Eta			.02			.06
Beta			.05 $p = .019$			.22 p = .0
Multiple R^2			.11			.14
N	75	57		75	57	

[a] Differences in the percentage of widowed and married engaging in social activities with frie are not significant.

[b] MCA controlling age, health (mobility, hearing problems), and socioeconomic status (spou

sharing meals and celebrating holidays; they are less apt to appear in this support category when the activities are playing cards, Scrabble, and the like, and going to movies and plays.

Like children, siblings are more likely to appear as social supports in connection with dining and holidays than when the activity is movies and plays. The married, in fact, were just as dependent on sisters and brothers as on daughters and sons for companionship. Holidays was the only activity that more of the married shared with children than with siblings.

Generally, extended kin are less likely to serve as social supports for married women than are children and siblings. However, distant relatives were like consanguineous kin in that they were more apt to appear as social supports when the activity was dining. Extended kin appeared less frequently as companions for the married when celebrating holidays or playing cards and board games; they were rarely companions at public events, such as movies and plays.

Although friends, compared with kin, are less evenly involved in social activities, friends are at the core of older married women's social support networks. The greatest proportion of the women with spouses shared lunches and dinners with friends; many played cards and other games with nonkin. Fewer of those with husbands mentioned

Extended kin Marital status			Friends[a] Marital status		
Widowed	Married		Widowed	Married	
28	23		79	68	
.28	.23		3.54	2.71	
.29	.22		3.77	2.42	
		.06			.12
		.07 $p = .018$			.20 $p = .005$
		.12			.14
75	57		75	57	

upation, subjective income). There was incomplete information on subjective income for one he widowed respondents.

friends as companions when attending public functions, such as movies and plays, or when celebrating holidays.

Instrumental supports. Table 6.2 examines the distribution of the extent to which married women relied on their primary resources for instrumental support. Slightly over a quarter of the married turned to offspring in the event of illness; less than 10 percent of them turned to their children for financial assistance. These findings suggest that women with spouses are more likely to depend on daughters and sons for service support than for economic support.

Sisters and brothers also appear in the instrumental support systems of these married women. Again, siblings parallel children inasmuch as they are more likely to be relied upon when she is ill (service support) than when she is short of money (economic support). Eighteen percent of the married turned to the family of orientation for sick-care help; only 2 percent turned to siblings for financial help.

As with social supports, fewer married women turned to their primary extended kin for assistance when needing instrumental support. Only 10 percent of the married relied on relatives outside the families of procreation and orientation for help when experiencing health problems; less than 5 percent turned to them when experiencing financial problems.

Table 6.2 Respondents' Reliance on Various Primary Resources for Instrumental Support.

	Children Marital status			Siblings Marital status		
Situation	Widowed	Married		Widowed	Married	
When ill						
Percentage turning to a primary resource	27	26		24	18	
Mean number of primary resources						
Unadjusted	.27	.27		.24	.17	
Adjusted[b]	.28	.26		.29	.11	
Eta			.01			.08
Beta			.02 $p = \text{ns}$			.22 $p = .0$
Multiple R^2			.07			.13
When short of money						
Percentage turning to a primary resource	8	9		11	2	
Mean number of primary resources						
Unadjusted	.08	.09		.11	.02	
Adjusted[b]	.09	.08		.12	.00	
Eta			.01			.18
Beta			.01 $p = \text{ns}$			.23 $p = .0$
Multiple R^2			.12			.09
N	75	57		75	57	

[a] Differences in the percentage of widowed and married turning to friends are not significan

[b] MCA controlling age, health (mobility, hearing problems), and socioeconomic status (spou

Finally, nonkin occasionally enter the instrumental support systems of married women who are advanced in age. While they seldom relied on nonkin for help with economic problems, these women with husbands were particularly likely to have relied on friends for assistance during an illness. A greater proportion of the married, in fact, turned to nonkin than to kin for help when experiencing health problems.

Emotional supports. The extent to which the married women relied on their primary resources for emotional support is summarized in table 6.3. Less than a fifth of the married confided in their offspring when worried or depressed. These data indicate that children are more likely to provide their married mothers with service support, such as sick care, than with emotional support.

Extended kin Marital status			Friends[a] Marital status		
Widowed	Married		Widowed	Married	
21	10		51	37	
.22	.11		1.27	.76	
.24	.08		1.44	.54	
		.15			.16 $p = .084$
		.20 $p = .002$			.27 $p = .000$
		.15			.18
5	4		4	2	
.06	.04		.06	.02	
.06	.03		.06	.01	
		.04			.08
		.07 $p = \text{ns}$			.13 $p = \text{ns}$
		.07			.04
75	57		75	57	

upation, subjective income). There was incomplete information on subjective income for one he widowed respondents.

Siblings are found to appear on occasion in the emotional support systems of older married women. Less than a fifth of the married turned to sisters and brothers when worried or depressed. Siblings, then, were just as likely as children to enter the emotional support systems of these married women.

Relatives outside the families of procreation and orientation are neither excluded from the emotional support systems of the married women nor are they the preferred resource for this type of support. Just over 10 percent of these married women confided in extended kin when feeling anxious or gloomy.

Friends also provide married women with emotional support. Approximately two-fifths of the married confided in nonkin when

Table 6.3 Respondents' Reliance on Various Primary Resources for Emotional Support

	Children Marital status			Siblings Marital status		
Situation	Widowed	Married		Widowed	Married	
When worried						
Percentage turning to a primary resource	28	19		27	16	
Mean number of primary resources						
Unadjusted	.28	.19		.27	.16	
Adjusted[a]	.30	.17		.30	.12	
Eta			.10			.13
Beta			.15 $p = .007$			.22 $p =$ n
Multiple R^2			.13			.07
When depressed						
Percentage turning to a primary resource	20	16		27	14	
Mean number of primary resources						
Unadjusted	.20	.15		.27	.14	
Adjusted[a]	.20	.16		.30	.09	
Eta			.06			.16 $p = .0$
Beta			.07 $p = .001$			.26 $p = .0$
Multiple R^2			.20			.15
N	75	57		75	57	

[a] MCA controlling age, health (mobility, hearing problems), and socioeconomic status (spou occupation, subjective income). There was incomplete information on subjective income

worried; a third confided in friends when depressed. As was the case with instrumental support, a greater proportion of women with spouses relied on friends for emotional support than relied on kin.

Reciprocity of support. The norm of reciprocity implies that the flow of support is a two-way exchange with an individual both giving to and receiving from the resources in her support network (Longino and Lipman, 1985). Twenty-eight percent of the women with husbands claimed that a primary daughter or son had turned to them for instrumental or emotional support (table 6.4). Thus, all but 4 percent of the married women who reported primary ties with children also perceived the relationship as being reciprocal.

The flow of support between siblings tends to be reciprocal, as it is

Extended kin Marital status			Friends Marital status		
Widowed	Married		Widowed	Married	
20	14		60	44	$p = .066$
.21	.14		2.19	1.55	
.22	.13		2.46	1.19	
		.08			.12
		.11 $p = .015$			.24 $p = .000$
		.12			.22
15	12		60	32	$p = .001$
.15	.13		1.84	.90	
.17	.10		2.06	.62	
		.04			.22 $p = .015$
		.10 $p = .012$			.33 $p = .000$
		.12			.21
	75	57		75	57

of the widowed respondents.

between parents and their adult children. Fully a quarter of the married stated that a primary sibling had turned to them for support. Only a few married women (8 percent) with a primary sister or brother did not consider the relationship mutually supportive.

Because of their rather uncommon involvement in the support systems, extended kin are less likely than children and siblings to seek comfort and aid from these older married women. Only about 20 percent of the married reported that primary extended relatives had relied upon them for support; yet, merely a handful (6 percent) did not consider their relationships with distant relatives as involving mutual exchange.

The majority of the married women (61 percent) viewed their rela-

Table 6.4 Primary Resources' Reliance on Respondents

Primary resource	Marital status: Widowed	Married	
Children			
Percentage having a child rely on them	26.67%	28.07%	
Mean number of children			
Unadjusted	.27	.28	
Adjusted[a]	.28	.26	
Eta			.01
Beta			.02 $p = .025$
Multiple R^2			.11
Siblings			
Percentage having a sibling rely on them	30.67%	24.56%	
Mean number of siblings			
Unadjusted	.31	.24	
Adjusted[a]	.37	.17	
Eta			.07
Beta			.22 $p = .014$
Multiple R^2			.12
Extended Kin			
Percentage having an extended kin rely on them	21.33%	19.30%	
Mean number of extended kin			
Unadjusted	.22	.20	
Adjusted[a]	.24	.16	
Eta			.03
Beta			.10 $p = \text{ns}$
Multiple R^2			.07
Friends			
Percentage having a friend rely on them[b]	73.33%	61.40%	
Mean number of friends			
Unadjusted	2.82	2.17	
Adjusted[a]	3.08	1.84	
Eta			.11
Beta			.21 $p = .000$
Multiple R^2			.19
N	75	57	

[a] MCA controlling age, health (mobility, hearing problems), and socioeconomic status (spouse's occupation, subjective income). There was incomplete information on subjective income for one of the widowed respondents.
[b] Difference in the percentage of friends relying on the widowed and the married is not significant.

tionships with friends to be mutually supportive. But this is not too surprising given the fact that these women had more nonkin than kin resources available to them.

These data indicate that older women with spouses provide as well as receive support. Married women, then, are generally involved in interdependent systems, exchanging instrumental or emotional support.

Support Systems of Widowed Women

The end of marriage brings about shifts and adjustments in kin and nonkin networks. In this section, the support systems of widowed women are examined.

Social supports. Primary children engage in social activities with their widowed mothers. Daughters and sons enter spouseless women's social support systems chiefly as companions at mealtime and on holidays; they are less likely to serve as companions when the activities are movies, plays, and card games (table 6.1).

Siblings are an integral part of widowed women's social support systems. Sisters and brothers are like daughters and sons in that they are less likely to appear as companions when the activity is movies and plays. Siblings, however, are more likely than children to share the activity of games with widowed women: 23 percent of the widowed played card games with sisters and brothers compared with 15 percent who did so with daughters and sons.

Extended kin usually enter the social systems of widowed women less frequently than other kin; yet, distant relatives parallel children and siblings in the activities for which they serve as social supports. Specifically, relatives outside the families of procreation and orientation were most apt to function as companions at mealtime or on holidays; they were less likely to serve in this capacity at public activities, such as movies and plays, or when playing card and board games.

Friends are more involved in the social support systems of widowed women than are kin. Nevertheless, participation of nonkin in this support system is less uniform. An overwhelming majority of the widowed shared meals with friends; nearly half of them played card and other nonathletic games with nonkin. A smaller proportion of these spouseless women attended movies and plays or celebrated holidays with nonfamily.

Instrumental supports. Offspring are a source of instrumental support for widowed women. A greater proportion of the widowed stated that they depended on daughters and sons for assistance when needing sick care than when needing financial help: 27 percent and 8 percent, respectively (table 6.2).

Widowed women also receive instrumental support from siblings. As with children, spouseless women depend more on siblings for service than for economic support: about a quarter of the widowed relied on sisters and brothers for help when experiencing health problems compared with 11 percent who relied on siblings for help when experiencing financial problems.

Distant blood relatives and in-laws occasionally provide widowed family members with instrumental support. Just over a fifth of the widowed relied on extended kin for assistance when ill; only 5 percent relied on these relatives for assistance when short of money. Although the widowed relied less on extended kin than other relatives for help when experiencing financial problems, they depended on these distant family members just as much as other kin for assistance when experiencing health problems. These data indicate that extended kin are an important resource for the widowed who need service supports, such as sick care.

Nonfamily are also included in the instrumental support systems of women who have lost their husbands. While less than 5 percent relied on nonkin for help when short of money, roughly half of the widowed turned to friends when ill. Compared with kin, friends, in fact, were more likely to provide assistance when the widowed needed this type of support.

Emotional supports. Daughters and sons often serve as emotional supports for spouseless women. Nearly a third of the widowed relied on children for comfort when worried; fully a fifth turned to offspring for solace when depressed (table 6.3). These findings suggest that children are an important source of emotional support for widowed women that should not be overlooked.

Siblings too enter the emotional support systems of their widowed sisters. Twenty-seven percent of the widowed women relied upon sisters and brothers for comfort when worried or depressed. These data indicate that the widowed are just as likely to turn to siblings as children when needing solace during periods of worry or depression.

Relatives besides children and siblings are now and then sources of emotional support for women who have lost a spouse through death. A fifth of the widowed confided in extended kin when worried; 15 percent confided in these kin when depressed. These findings reveal that some widowed women depend on distant family members for emotional support.

Friends appear more as emotional than instrumental supports for widowed women. Nearly two-thirds of these spouseless women confided in nonfamily when worried or depressed. As in the case of service supports, friends are more involved in the emotional subsystem than are family.

Reciprocity of support. Reciprocity characterizes the relationship between widowed women and their daughters and sons. Twenty-seven percent of the formerly married reported that a primary child had relied upon them for instrumental or emotional support (table 6.4). Thus, the majority (84 percent) of the widowed who reported primary ties with adult offspring also perceived the relationship as mutually supportive.

Widowed women also tend to be involved in a two-way flow of support with their siblings. A third of the widowed claimed that a primary sister or brother had depended on them for aid or comfort. Thus, all but 4 percent of the widowed with primary siblings viewed the relationship as being reciprocal.

Compared with their relationships with children and siblings, widowed women are less likely to perceive relationships with extended kin as mutually supportive. Fourteen percent of the widowed did not consider their relationships with extended kin as reciprocal, although a fifth of them stated that their primary distant relatives had relied on them for some type of support.

The principle of exchange is the norm for widowed women and their primary friends. Roughly three-fourths of the widowed reported that their friends had relied upon them for support. Many widowed women, therefore, provide aid or comfort to their friends.

Comparison of Support Systems

The number of similarities between the support systems of the married and widowed is striking. First, in the area of social supports, kin and nonkin alike serve as companions for both groups of women chiefly when the activity is dining. Holidays are the province of relatives, not friends. On the other hand, card and board games and movies and plays are activities that married and widowed women share mainly with friends.

Second, there are parallels within the instrumental and emotional subsystems. The married and formerly married depended more on family and friends for help when ill, a service support, than when short of money, an economic support. Surprisingly, friends are the preferred resources for both groups of women, while extended kin are relied upon least. Friends too are singled out by married and widowed women for the sharing of confidences when worried or depressed. These older women also often confide in children and siblings when feeling anxious or gloomy.

Finally, the support systems of both the married and widowed are characterized by reciprocity. This is especially true of relationships with friends, children, and siblings. Distant relatives relied less on these older women for instrumental or emotional support.

Multiple classification analysis. Despite the parallels in the support systems of married and widowed women, a greater proportion of the widowed depended on family and friends for all types of support. There were, of course, some exceptions. For example, the married were just as likely as the widowed to have turned to offspring when needing financial assistance. In order to determine whether this greater reliance on primary resources by the widowed was due to marital status or the differences in age, health, and socioeconomic status, Multiple Classification Analysis was performed.

The results of the multiple classification analysis reveal that controlling for the covariates (age, health, and socioeconomic status) strengthens the relationship between marital status and social support from adult offspring (table 6.1). The Etas summarize the relationship between marital status and primary children providing social support. For example, an Eta of .04 for games indicates that there is a weak relationship between marital status and children entering women's social support systems by playing games. The Betas are adjusted Etas—that is, adjusted for the effects of the control variables; they may be viewed as a standardized partial regression coefficient (SPSS, Inc., 1982). The Betas in table 6.1 indicate that there is a relationship between a woman's marital status and offspring serving as social supports even after the effects of the control variables are held constant. Moreover, the values of the Betas are significant, with the exception of the Beta for spending holidays with children.

Marital status, then, is important for whether older women receive social support from adult offspring. Specifically, widowed women are more likely than married women to engage in social activities with their primary children. The Multiple R^2s reveal that marital status and the control variables (age, health, and socioeconomic status) explain between 8 and 11 percent of the variance in children serving as social supports.

The difference between the widowed and the married in their sharing of social activities with relatives outside the family of procreation also became significant when the important background variables were controlled. Therefore, the marital status of these women was found to be a significant factor in whether siblings and extended kin served as social supports. Specifically, widowed women are more likely than their married counterparts to turn to distant relatives as well as sisters and brothers for fellowship when participating in social activities. Siblings and extended kin, then, become social substitutes for women whose marriages have been ended by death.

For friends, the relationship between marital status and social supports is more complex. After controlling for age, health, and socioeconomic status, the relationship between marital status and social supports from friends is reversed for games. Specifically, the widowed women would have shared the activity of games with more, rather than fewer, friends if they had been younger and healthier and had a more adequate income. The data also indicate that friends are more likely to appear in widowed women's social networks in connection with meals or public activities. Widowed women were more likely than married women to share fellowship with friends at mealtime or at social outings. The only activity that was not affected by a woman's marital status was holidays. The sharing of holidays is primarily reserved for kin; celebrating festive occasions with friends generally occurs when kin are unavailable (Lopata, 1979).

The marital status of the women in this study was less important for the instrumental support system. First, there was no difference between widowed and married women in the extent to which they depended on assistance from children in times of need; the relationship between marital status and women's reliance on children for instrumental support remained essentially the same when the important social and demographic variables were controlled (table 6.2). These findings suggest that primary children are not more likely to appear in older women's instrumental support systems after they have lost a spouse through death. Children, then, do not assume the sick care and financial responsibilities formerly performed by the deceased husband. These data clearly support the argument that there is some role specialization among support resources (Longino and Lipman, 1982).

As with daughters and sons, being widowed was not found to be an important factor in whether an older woman received economic assistance from extended kin and friends when short of money. Marital status, however, became a significant factor in reliance on distant family and friends when needing help during an illness after the important background variables were held constant. Specifically, widowed women, compared to the married, are more likely to turn to extended kin and friends when experiencing health problems. These data indicate that there is some selectivity in relying on primary extended kin and friends for instrumental support and that widowed women are more likely to turn to distant relatives and friends when needing help during an illness.

The relationship between marital status and reliance on siblings for instrumental support proved to be significant after the effects of the important social and demographic variables had been held constant. Thus, these data indicate that widowed women are more likely to rely on their families of orientation for instrumental support than are their married counterparts. Siblings, therefore, appear to replace the deceased husband as a support resource when older spouseless women are faced with health and financial problems.

Marital status was found to be a more important factor in the emotional than instrumental subsystem. When the important variables of age, health, and socioeconomic status were controlled, the marital status of these women became a significant factor in whether or not they received emotional support from their primary children (table 6.3). These data indicate that women who have outlived their husbands are likely to rely on their primary children when worried or depressed. Therefore, the findings are consistent with other research on informal support from offspring. These inquiries (e.g., Longino and Lipman, 1982; Lopata, 1979) also report that children are significant support resources for widowed women who need comfort when emotionally troubled.

In contrast with offspring, the marital status of these women remained an insignificant factor in an older woman's reliance on siblings for comfort when worried. However, as with children, there was found to be a relationship between a woman's marital status and confiding in sisters and brothers when experiencing melancholy. Thus, when feeling depressed, widowed women are more likely than their married counterparts to turn to siblings for emotional support. These findings suggest that, among formerly married women, there is some selectivity in confiding in siblings.

As in the case of children, marital status was found to be a significant factor in an older woman's reliance on extended kin for emotional support. Widowed women are more likely than are married women to turn to kin outside the families of procreation and orientation when worried or depressed. Distant relatives, therefore, appear to be latent emotional support resources for older women.

There were significant differences between widowed and married women in confiding in nonfamily; the marital status of these women remained a factor in whether or not an older woman relied on friends for emotional support after the important background variables were controlled. Compared with the married, widowed women are more apt to depend on nonkin when worried or depressed. Being widowed, then, is related to friends entering older women's emotional support systems.

Finally, marital status was found to be a significant factor in the reciprocity of support with primary resources. There is a relationship between a woman's marital status and children's reliance on her when the important social and demographic variables have been held constant (table 6.4). Specifically, widowed women are more likely to view their relationships with adult offspring as involving mutual exchange. This finding is consistent with other research on the reciprocity of aid with kin (e.g., Adams, 1968; Lopata, 1979). Children, particularly daughters, receive aid, often in the form of baby-sitting, from their widowed mothers.

The marital status of these women was also found to be a significant factor in siblings' and friends' reliance on them. Explicitly, widowed women are more likely than their married counterparts to be involved in mutually supportive relationships with sisters and brothers as well as with nonfamily. Lopata (1979) has reported that widowed women generally exchange services, such as sick care, with siblings and friends.

In contrast with friends and other relatives, there was no relationship between marital status and the reciprocity of support with extended kin. Widowed women are no more likely to provide assistance to relatives other than children and siblings than are married women. Therefore, the absence of a spouse does not increase the likelihood of an older woman dispensing aid to distant blood relatives and in-laws. Lopata (1979) also has reported that extended kin, excluding grandchildren, rarely receive economic and service support from widowed women.

Summary

This chapter has examined the informal support systems of the widowed and the married living in urban Nebraska. The findings shed light on those individuals who serve as older women's supports. There appears to be some continuity in support networks for persons in later life inasmuch as children do not increase their participation in the instrumental support category after their mothers have been widowed. Daughters and sons, however, become important resources in the social and emotional subsystems. The one exception was holidays. Widowed women were no more apt to celebrate festive occasions with children than were their married counterparts.

Relationships with siblings, particularly sisters, and other relatives take on an added significance for women after they have lost a spouse through death. These findings provide support for the "principle of family substitution," which states that widowed women rely first on their children, and when offspring are unavailable, they turn to their family of orientation and other relatives for assistance, companionship, and comfort.

Friends also become significant resources after the death of a spouse. These data, however, indicate that friends do not compensate for unavailable kin; rather, they function as a separate support network—a greater proportion of the widowed women had relied upon friends rather than kin for all types of support. The two exceptions were sharing holidays and borrowing money.

Most of the women reported that the various persons who were part of their support systems in turn had relied upon them. These findings dispel the view that widows are only receivers of support. When called upon and able, widowed women provide assistance and comfort to others. Widowed women, therefore, are givers as well as receivers of instrumental and emotional support.

Omaha Widows Versus Chicago Widows

In assessing how these research findings contribute to our understanding of older women's support networks, it is useful to compare the widows in this study to the Chicago-area widows studied by Lopata (1978; 1979). Several similarities are observed. First, friends are important support resources for both Omaha and Chicago widows. They are particularly likely to enter the social system as companions for lunch and dinner or when attending public functions, such as movies. These nonkin furnish widowed women with emotional support by comforting them when worried or depressed. While neither Omaha nor Chicago widows rely on friends for economic support, the two groups of widows differ in the service support they receive from friends: 51 percent of the Omaha widows reported that friends provided help when sick compared with only 8 percent of the Chicago widows.

Second, children are also important contributors to widowed women's support systems. Omaha and Chicago widows reported that children function as social support by accompanying them to movie theaters and other public places and by sharing meals. Both groups of widows discuss their problems and seek solace from offspring. Once again, Omaha and Chicago widows differ with respect to instrumental support. The formerly married Omaha women did not obtain much instrumental assistance from their adult offspring, while the Chicago widows received a considerable amount of economic and service support from these same kin.

The biggest disparity between the women in the two studies centers on kin outside the family of procreation as contributors to support systems. Lopata's Chicago widows infrequently mentioned siblings and other relatives as furnishing any type of support. In contrast, the widows in the Omaha study claimed that siblings, particularly sisters, and extended kin become important support resources.

Differences in sampling and methodology may explain, at least in part, why the family of orientation and more distant relatives appear as important resources in one study and not the other. First, the Chicago study included nonwhites as well as whites, while the Omaha study surveyed only whites. Second, in the Chicago study, each woman could list up to three persons as contributors of each support activity in each support system. In contrast, the women in the Omaha study could list up to as many as 15 primary friends and 15 primary kin. Each such friend and relative could provide all, any, or none of the various types of support.

Part II
Comparisons and Contrasts

7 Support Systems for American Black Wives and Widows

JESSYNA M. MCDONALD

Introduction

Three strikes . . . and you are out!
Strike one . . . you are widowed,
Strike two . . . you are elderly,
Strike three . . . you are black.
Like a black widow spider . . .
In a web . . . Sucked in a vacuum,
Hidden in pockets of poverty . . .
In the mainstream of do-nothings.
Who know the price of everything . . .
and the value of nothing . . .

While it appears that the strikes are against them, many American black wives and widows have managed to overcome various barriers to occupational and social mobility. Despite the vestiges of historical occupational oppression and discrimination, many black wives and widows have not only survived but have made significant contributions to their families, communities, and professions. Historically, American black wives and widows have managed various familial, occupational, and social roles with limited resources. In many instances, however, the only source of support was "emotional strength" (Hooks, 1981; Lopata, 1979; Myers, 1980).

Since slavery, the black woman has worked in the American labor force, performing laborious, and often demeaning tasks for the survival of her family. From dawn to dusk, she labored in the fields beside her husband, or in the plantation house—cooking and cleaning—or rearing someone else's children. From dusk to dawn, she performed the same tasks in her own home in addition to "expressive functions." These expressive functions included nurturing her spouse and family from the dehumanizing effects of slavery, by promoting a sense of belonging, self-worth, and dignity within the family unit. However, as black women assumed various roles and functions, there was limited support for them (Billingsley, 1968).

In a speech before the second annual convention on women's rights in Akron, Ohio, in 1852, Sojourner Truth, a former slave, described the various occupational and familial roles she assumed, with limited resources and support (Hooks, 1981:160). In response to a male heckler, she stated:

> Dat man ober day say dat women needs to be helped into carriages, and lifted ober ditches, and to have de best places . . . and ain't I a woman? Look at me! Look at my arm! . . . I have plowed, and planted, and gathered into barns, and no man could head me—and ain't I a woman? I could work as much as any man (when I could get it), and bear de lash as well—and ain't I a woman? I have borne five children and seen 'em mos all sold off into slavery, and when I cried out with a mother's grief, none but Jesus hear—and ain't I a woman?

Over a century later, in an interview with the *New York Post* on September 29, 1969, Lena Horne described the unique strength of American black wives (Staples, 1973). She stated:

> I think Negro wives, no matter what their age or background or even their understanding of the problem, have to be terribly strong—much stronger than their white counterparts. They cannot relax, they cannot simply be loving wives waiting for the man of the house to come home. They have to be spiritual sponges, absorbing the racially inflicted hurts of their men. . . .

Many black wives and widows have felt the need to compensate for those "racially inflicted hurts" by providing additional support for their spouse and/or families. However, as they assumed this nurturing or care-giving role, what types of support systems and networks were available to them? Upon the death of a spouse, to what extent were supports, social engagements, social roles, and/or social relations modified? It has been recognized that the extent to which widows are integrated into the community is contingent upon the access and availability of various support systems, interactional sequences, and social relations (Lopata, 1979).

The effects of race, class, and gender proscriptions have placed the black female in one of the most vulnerable positions in American society. When compared to other ethnic American women, black women are more likely to be overrepresented at the bottom of the economic and social hierarchy (Powers, 1984). While married, these effects are somewhat mitigated by the emotional and economic supports of the spouse. However, the death or loss of a spouse may be among the most devastating events for a black woman. For, in many instances, the husband provided a major source of economic support.

While there has been a proliferation of research conducted on wives and widows, little research has been conducted on black wives and widows. Existing literature on black women reveals a broad spectrum of views, ranging from "the dominating superwoman" to "the passive inferior female" (Rodgers-Ross, 1980). Whether myths or realities, the needs and experiences of black wives and widows warrant further investigation.

How do American black wives and widows cope with various conditions? Are black wives and widows who reside in urban areas similar to wives and widows in other areas? To what extent do black wives and widows utilize various informal and formal support systems and networks? Are existing support systems effective and/or efficient mechanisms for enhancing the quality of life among American black wives in urban areas? These are a few of the many questions that will be addressed in this chapter.

The purpose of this chapter is to present various sociodemographic characteristics of American black wives and widows as well as a concurrent analysis of various support systems and networks utilized by each group. A comparison of perceptions toward and utilization patterns of various support systems will also be presented, along with an analysis of special circumstances complicating support systems.

Blacks in America: Demographic Characteristics

Despite various legislative mandates enacted to extirpate the effects of slavery and discrimination, disparities continue to exist between black and white Americans. While there is considerable debate concerning the effects of ascribed factors on class variations, race and gender appear to be primary determinants of occupational and social mobility (Davis, 1981). In comparison to other ethnic groups in America, blacks are more likely to be disadvantaged and impoverished.

According to the United States Bureau of the Census, in 1982 there were over 26 million black Americans, or a little over 11 percent of the total population. The greatest percentage of blacks live in the south and north-central regions of the country, with 53 percent and 20 percent, respectively. These data reflect a trend toward the "second great migration" of blacks. After emancipation, blacks migrated from the South to the North. Over a century later, there appears to be a trend of black migration back to the South. The migration of millions of blacks back to the South may be attributed to declining economic and employment opportunities in many northern cities.

In 1982, 33 percent of black families lived below the poverty level, as compared to approximately 9 percent of white families and 27 percent of Hispanic families. The median income for black families was 59 percent of the median family income for the total population—i.e., a median income of $13,267 for black families compared to $22,388 for the total population. While over 48 percent of blacks were employed in 1982, almost half of the black population was reported as unemployed, or not in the labor force.

Between 1960 and 1982 the percentage of black families with female householders doubled, from over 20 percent to over 40 percent. In 1982, 48 percent of black children lived below the poverty level, as compared to approximately 17 percent of their white counterparts (U.S. Bureau of Census, 1982).

Black Women in America

Recent trends reflect a growing concern over the "feminization of poverty" in America. While women, in general, are more likely to be economically disadvantaged than their male counterparts, race continues to be an overriding factor. In comparison to white females, black women are more likely to be impoverished. The effects of class, race, and gender oppression have placed the black female in "triple jeopardy" (Williams, 1979).

Relative to the effects of race, on class variations among American women, Powers (1984:32) contends that:

> We should not, however, underestimate the continued differences in black and white women's economic positions. Black women are still considerably more likely to be in service occupations than white women; . . . Unemployment rates for black women are twice those for white women and black women are considerably more likely than white women to live in poverty, especially if they are raising children alone. . . .

In comparison to other females, black females are also less likely to marry or remarry. In 1982, slightly over 29 percent of black females were single, compared with 17 percent of the total population. Less than half (49 percent) of black females were married.

Between 1970 and 1982, the percentage of married black females decreased from a little over 61 percent to 47 percent. While the number of divorced black females almost doubled, from 5 percent in 1970 to over 9 percent in 1982, the percentage of widowed black females dropped to slightly over 13 percent by 1982 (U.S. Bureau of the Census, 1982).

Relative to differences in income among black and white females, black females earned almost half the income of their white female counterparts. In 1981, the per capita income for white females, with husbands present, was $9,678, as compared to $5,191 for their black female counterparts. Black widows earned less than half the per capita income of white females, $3,174 and $7,009, respectively (U.S. Bureau of the Census, 1982).

The effects of class and race appear to be significant indices of differentials in income and status between black and white females. On the whole, black females were more likely to be single heads of households and earn less than their white female counterparts.

The Black Family, Marriage, and Mate Selection

In order to establish a theoretical framework for the examination of factors influencing support systems for American black wives and widows, it is necessary to understand the unique and diversified nature of American black families. It has been recognized that the extent to which wives and widows receive various supports depends upon several factors. These include: (a) the organizational structure of the family unit; (b) the reciprocal exchange of roles, duties, and rights among family members; and, (c) the availability of financial, social, and emotional supports (Lopata, 1979; Scanzoni, 1976). Given the effects of historical occupational oppression coupled with race and class discrimination, the black family has undergone various changes for its survival. Concurrent roles, duties, and rights of wives and widows within black families have also changed.

Recent socioeconomic trends and projections reflect a decline of the traditional black nuclear family and the resurgence of the black extended family, particularly in urban areas. Martin and Martin (1978:1) described the black extended family as:

> a multigenerational, interdependent kinship system which is welded together by a sense of obligation to relatives; is organized around a "familybase" household; is generally guided by a "dominant family figure"; extends across geographical boundaries to connect family units to an extended family network; and has a built-in mutual aid system for the welfare of its members and the maintenance of the family as a whole.

This "built-in mutual aid system" found in black families is a major survival component, which may be traced back to Africa and to slavery in America.

The traditional African family served as an economic, political, and religious unit that was highly structured, with designated roles, rights, and duties for individual family members. Marriage was not merely a ritual between two individuals, but a union between two families. The African family was also viewed as an autonomous social system in which there was high regard for the sanctity of family members (Ladner, 1981).

African women held economic, political, and social power within the family. The "Queen Mother" or "Queen Sister" was afforded power, status, and authority with her role in the family. The African family was an extended patriarchy that was based on mutual respect for elders and parents (Ladner, 1981).

The effects of slavery were devastating to American black families. Alienated from familial and cultural ties, coupled with the various legal restrictions placed on slaves, the black family began to deteriorate. Black slaves were severely punished for trying to protect and defend their wives and children. Parents were denied rights of authority over children. The subsequent roles, rights, and duties of the father were denied.

Slave marriages were not legally recognized. The selection of mates was usually done by the plantation owner for economic reasons, namely breeding of additional slaves for sale and distribution in the labor force. Bonds between husband and wife, and between parents and children, were discouraged and often broken due to the sale of various family members. Despite these constraints on the slave family, it was considerably difficult to destroy the bonds that existed among family members (Rodgers-Ross, 1980).

While there is considerable debate about the extent to which slavery impacts on the black family of today, there appears to be an association between the "adaptive capacities of the black family to slavery and urban poverty" (Gutman, 1976). Regarding the adaptive capacities of urban black families, Stack (1981:369) concluded: "To cope with everyday demands of ghetto life, these networks have evolved patterns of co-residence; elastic household boundaries; lifelong if intermittent bonds to three generation households, social constraints on the role of the husband-father within the mother's domestic group, and the domestic authority of women."

These findings have also been supported by other social scientists and historians who contend that, due to various economic and social factors, the traditional nuclear black family is being supplanted by the extended black family. It has also been observed that the black extended family provides various economic and emotional supports for its members. Major components of the black extended family include: an extended family base, which is controlled by a dominant figure; the subextended family; and the mutual aid system (Shimkin, Shimkin and Frate, 1978).

The black extended family has also been described as a source of protection and strength against societal pressures and social isolation. Additional functions of the black extended family include: care of the elderly and young, providing for kin on the move, and assistance during economic or family crisis. Financial aid usually flows along generational lines, from parents to children, or middle-aged to aged (McAdoo, 1980).

Interactions between husbands and wives are based upon a reciprocal exchange of duties, rights, and obligations. The traditional role of the husband in the dominant American culture is as the "provider," while the wife often assumes the role of the "expressive agent" (Scanzoni, 1971). In many black families, the duties and rights of the father are often mitigated due to various economic constraints placed upon the family. In comparison to white males, black males are more likely to be unemployed or underemployed. Under these circumstances, the role of provider becomes difficult, at best. The inability to perform the role expectations associated with the provider often results in marital discord within the black family.

When the husband loses his job, or receives a low income, his ability to provide for the family is impaired. This becomes a source of conflict and frustration between the couple. In many instances, the wife may have to assume the role of provider along with her expressive functions. This reversal of roles may also create additional tension, hostility, and/or stress within the household.

Staples (1982:115) found that external forces often contribute to problems among black males and females:

> The problems black men and women have in their relationships often are shaped by external forces. Many have been unable to form a monogamous family due to structural impediments. In a society where money is the measure of the man, many black males are excluded as potential mates because they lack the economic wherewithal to support a family in a reasonable manner.

Among the primary relations between husbands and wives are companionship, physical affection, and empathy. In a study of black families, Scanzoni (1971) concluded that black wives were less satisfied than their husbands in each of these areas. In the area of companionship, black husbands were more satisfied than their wives, with 78 percent of them reporting satisfaction, as compared to 50 percent of the wives. Black wives were slightly less satisfied with physical affection than were their husbands; 77 percent of the husbands were satisfied, compared to 60 percent of the wives.

Like most women, many black females have relatively the same ideals and standards for the selection of mates. However, given the shortage of eligible black males, some black females may compromise their ideals. In many instances, black women may overlook the shortcomings of potential mates for the sake of companionship (Staples, 1973).

Among the major factors influencing mate selection among blacks are: the low ratio of black males to black females, the tendency of black males to marry younger women and to date interracially, or die at an earlier age. These factors often limit the pool of eligible mates. For low-income black females, marriage is usually discouraged because of various regulations associated with the receipt of social benefits. Should the female marry or remarry, she may be subject to loss of benefits.

With respect to the formation of relationships between black males and females in poor urban areas, it was observed (Stack, 1980:356) that:

> Notwithstanding the emptiness and hopelessness of the job experience in the Black community, men and women fall in love and wager buoyant new relationships against the inexorable forces of poverty and racism. At the same time, in dealing with everyday life, Black women and men have developed a number of attitudes and strategies that appear to mitigate against the formation of long-term relationships. Even when a man and woman set up temporary housekeeping arrangements, they both maintain primary social ties with their kin. If other members of a kin network view a particular relationship as a drain on the network's resources, they will act in various and subtle ways to break up the relationship. . . .

In urban areas, black females are more likely to be single heads of household, being unmarried, separated, divorced, or widowed. Since the extent to which one obtains economic, emotional, and/or social supports is contingent upon the availability of resources within the family and community, it may be concluded that without relatively stable family ties, these supports are limited, if not nonexistent.

Black Widows

In comparison to widows of other ethnic backgrounds, black widows are the most vulnerable. Black widows are more likely to be heads of households, live below the poverty level, and are less likely to remarry. Among the primary indices of successful adjustment to widowhood is the access and availability of formal and informal supports. However, for black widows in urban areas, economic and formal supports are minimal, at best. Given the scarcity of economic resources, black widows are more likely to be isolated rather than reintegrated into new roles within the community. This isolation often leads to loneliness and depression, which are often associated with, and may extend the duration of, the grieving process.

While there has been some research conducted on widowhood and bereavement, there is only a paucity of information on black widows. A review of the literature reveals a general consensus that black widows, on the whole, receive fewer economic and formal supports than their counterparts. However, among the social supports utilized by black widows to cope are family, friends, religion, and emotional supports (Lopata, 1973; 1979).

Upon the death of her spouse, the black widow may experience the loss of various duties and rights that had been assigned to her as a wife. Confronted with the loss of economic and emotional supports, which were to some extent provided by her husband, the black widow may experience a reversal, if not a loss, of many roles. In addition, her social roles and relations may be disorganized and/or modified (Lopata, 1979).

The extent to which the black widow will be integrated within the family and community may depend upon several factors, which include access to and the availability of various informal and formal resources, such as educational, economic, political, religious, recreational, and family. While there is limited economic support for black widows, the major suppliers of support systems appear to be the family, religion, social supports, and personal emotional strength (Lopata, 1979; Myers, 1981; Stack, 1981).

Support Systems for Black Wives and Widows

Methodology

In the fall of 1984, an exploratory pilot study was conducted to determine the differences in the attitudes toward and utilization patterns of various support systems by black wives and widows. The purpose of the study was threefold: first, to determine the demographic characteristics of black wives and widows; second, to determine the utilization patterns of various economic, familial, social, and other institutional resources by black wives and widows; and, third, to determine differences in perceptions of the access and availability of various resources.

The study was limited to a convenience sample of black wives and widows in selected urban areas, including Detroit, Indianapolis, Los

Angeles, and Washington, D.C. Questionnaires were distributed to religious and social organizations in each city. Volunteers were solicited for participation in the study. A total of 140 questionnaires were disseminated (35 per city); 128 were returned, of which 85 were usable. The adjusted return rate was 60 percent.

The questionnaire was self-administered and consisted of two sections. The first part contained various demographic items; i.e., social and economic characteristics of the respondents and their families, as well as the utilization patterns of various support resources by wives and widows. Results of this study may be affected by the failure of respondents to answer certain items. Widows were more reluctant to black wives and widows toward various types of supports and their personal feelings. A five-point Likert scale was utilized to indicate responses. The range of responses included: 1 = strongly disagree, 2 = moderately disagree, 3 = does not apply to me, 4 = moderately agree, and, 5 = strongly agree. Data were analyzed using descriptive statistics. The chi square test of independence was utilized to determine significant differences in the responses between widows and wives.

Since this was an exploratory pilot study, subsequent findings may not be generalizable to the total population of American black wives and widows. Results of this study may be affected by the failure of respondents to answer certain items. Widows were more reluctant to participate in the study for fear of "losing social security benefits." In many instances, widows refused to respond to items that addressed supplemental sources of income. Wives, on the other hand, were more cooperative and willing to participate in the study. As a result, the sample consisted of more wives than widows.

Demographic Profiles

The sample consisted of 84 black females, 54 of whom were married and 30 widowed. In comparison to the widows, the wives were more likely to live in nuclear families, to be employed full-time, and to have higher educational and income levels. Black widows were more likely to live alone or in extended families and to be retired and on fixed incomes. In general, widows were older than wives, 80 percent of the widows being over the age of 60. The mean number of years that the widows reported being without a husband was 13.4 years.

Education

In general, black wives were more educated than black widows. Four in 10 of the wives had one or more years of college. However, over half of the widows had not completed high school. None of the widows had completed college.

The differences in educational levels between black wives and widows may be reflected in the significant differences in income levels. Due to lower educational levels, many of the widows may not have qualified for higher-status occupations. Subsequently, retirement benefits received by widows were probably based upon their occupational status at the time of retirement.

Family Characteristics

The majority of the wives lived in nuclear families, while the largest percentage of widows lived alone or in extended families. Two-thirds of the wives had one or more children living in the household, as compared to four in 10 of the widows. There was no difference in the number of parents living with wives and widows, with 10 percent and 9 percent, respectively. Presented in table 7.1 is a demographic profile of the sample.

In general, the respondents perceived themselves as having very close families. The majority of the widows indicated that they had close families. Relative to the frequency of communication with relatives and the family members, there was little difference between wives and widows. Three-fourths of the widows reported frequent communication with relatives. However, several widows reported that they never communicated with families.

Support Systems

Economic Supports

Formal support systems for black widows appeared to be limited, if present at all. Given recent increases in the costs of living, coupled with declines in federal age-related programs, many elderly black widows live in adverse economic and social conditions. One widow stated, "I have a choice between heat and food, and when I die I'll still be

Table 7.1 Demographic Profile of Respondents.

	Wives		Widows		Total	
	N	%	*N*	%	*N*	%
Age						
20–29	2	4	0	0	2	2
30–39	15	28	0	0	15	18
40–49	12	22	3	10	15	18
50–59	18	33	3	10	21	25
60–69	5	9	6	20	11	13
70–79	2	4	12	40	14	17
80–89	0	0	6	7	6	7
Total *N*	54		30		84	100
Income						
Below $6,000	2	4	18	69	20	26
$6–10,000	8	11	3	11	11	14
$11–14,000	10	20	4	15	14	18
$15–19,000	15	29	0	0	15	20
$20–24,000	7	14	1	4	8	10
$25–29,000	4	8	0	0	4	5
Over $30,000	5	10	0	0	5	7
Total *N*	51		26		77	100
Employment status						
Full-time	44	83	5	18	49	61
Part-time	3	6	4	14	7	9
Two positions	0	0	1	4	1	1
Unemployed	0	0	2	7	2	3
Retired	6	11	16	57	22	28
Total *N*	53		28		81	100
Years of schooling						
Elementary						
0–8 years	0	0	8	28	8	
High school						
1–3 years	2	4	8	28	10	
4 years	16	30	8	28	24	
College						
1–3 years	21	40	4	14	25	
4 years	7	14	0	0	7	

cold." Over half of the widows indicated that the lack of money and adequate income was a major problem. Additional problems included inadequate housing and poor medical care. One widow, who was a former nurse, indicated that "the black elderly who are on Medicaid were often mistreated and misdiagnosed in community clinics." She further stated that, "If you are old, black, and on Medicaid, don't get sick." Similarly, another black widow observed that many of her friends, who were widows and lived alone, were afraid to go to the hospital or physician. They feared that they would be sent to a nursing home if they were too ill to take care of themselves. These observations may explain the underutilization of health and medical services by the black elderly.

There was a significant difference in the income levels of black wives and widows. Wives were more likely to have moderate to middle incomes, while widows were heavily represented at the lower income levels. One-third of the wives earned over $20,000 per year, while almost two-thirds of the widows earned less than $6,000 per year. These disparities in the income levels of black wives and widows may be reflected in the economic support from husbands.

Wives were more likely to hold full-time positions. Eight in 10 of the wives held full-time positions, as opposed to less than one in 10 of the widows. Due to the low income levels, many widows reported the need to obtain additional sources of income in order "to make ends meet." Over half of the widows, and only 11 percent of the wives, were retired.

There appeared to be an association between economic support and family support. While the majority of respondents perceived themselves as having close families, both groups identified the lack of economic support as their major problem. These discrepancies between perceived and actual levels of support may be attributed to the availability of financial resources within the family unit. Since most of the widows lived alone or in extended families, they were less likely to receive support from their families.

In response to the statement, "If I had a better job, things would be different," there was a significant difference between wives and widows (chi square $= 0.428$; $p < .05$). Over one-half of the widows strongly agreed with the statement compared to less than half of the wives. The need for economic security appeared to supplant the peripheral needs for belonging and esteem among many black widows.

Both wives and widows indicated that their friends would assist them if needed. Eight in 10 of the wives and seven in 10 of the widows agreed with this statement. However, the widows were slightly less likely to call a friend if they needed help. One widow stated, "All I have is my pride, and I'd rather die than ask for help." Similarly, another widow stated, "I don't want my friends to know my business."

Remarriage As Resource for Support Systems

While both wives and widows indicated that they were satisfied with their husbands, both groups also expressed negative attitudes toward remarriage. Almost two-thirds of the widows and less than half of the wives indicated that they would never remarry. These findings are consistent with other studies that conclude that black females are less likely to remarry. However, these negative attitudes toward remarriage may be attributed to several factors. First, negative or positive attitudes toward the first marriage may be transferred to attitudes toward future mates. For example, if a wife or widow experienced an unpleasant first marriage, she may be skeptical about remarriage. Conversely, if the experience with the first mate was positive, the wife may feel that she would be unable to find a mate with similar characteristics. Secondly, due to the shortage of eligible black men in this age group, older black women may feel that their likelihood of finding a suitable mate is virtually impossible. Finally, many black widows associated remarriage with the loss of benefits.

Emotional Supports

Included among the primary support resources or coping mechanisms identified by black women is their own emotional strength. Not necessarily by choice, but rather by necessity, many black women have had to be intrinsically motivated in order to cope with diversified roles and with scarce resources. This perception of emotional strength was also found among respondents. Regarding emotional strength, one widow stated: "I don't have a choice . . . I have to be strong . . . to keep going. . . . I don't have anybody to fall back on . . . so if it gets done, I do it myself. . . ."

Black widows perceived themselves as having to be stronger than other women. In response to the statement: "Black women are stronger than white women," there was a significant difference in the perceptions of black wives and widows (chi square = .0319; $p < .05$). Over

Table 7.2 Perceptions of Black Wives and Widows (Chi-Square Test of Independence; in percentages).

Statements	Strongly agree		Moderately agree	
	Wives	Widows	Wives	Widows
Black women are stronger than white women.	38.0	66.9	36.0	7.4
If I needed help, I know I could depend on my family.	57.7	60.0	30.8	24.0
Most black women are jealous of me.	7.3	34.8	12.2	17.4
I feel guilty when I take time for myself.	6.4	25.9	12.8	22.2
Nothing bothers me.	6.5	28.0	4.3	20.0
When I'm alone I feel depressed.	6.8	38.5	6.8	11.5
If I had a better job, things would be different (economic).	42.9	59.1	23.8	22.7
Everything happens for the best.	37.5	57.7	29.2	38.5
No matter what I do, no one understands my problems.	4.7	18.2	7.0	27.3
If I get sick, I don't know how my family would survive.	18.4	9.5	8.2	38.1

two-thirds of the widows agreed with the statement compared to only one-third of the wives. Similarly, black widows perceived themselves as having to be stronger than black wives. In response to the statement: "I have to be strong to keep the family together," all but one of the widows agreed as compared to eight in 10 of the wives. While there was no significant difference between the groups, both black wives and widows indicated the need to be emotionally strong in order to support their families.

Relative to the respondents' perceptions of family support during periods of crisis, the majority felt that they could depend upon their families. However, in response to the statement: "If I needed help, I know I could depend upon my family," there was a significant difference between the wives and widows (chi square = .0494; $p < .05$). Widows perceived themselves as less likely to receive support from their families.

While emotional strength is identified as a major support among black wives and widows, there appeared to be an association between

Moderately disagree		Strongly disagree		
Wives	Widows	Wives	Widows	*p*
8.0	11.1	18.0	14.8	.032
1.9	16.0	9.6	0.0	.049
19.5	21.7	61.0	26.1	.015
21.3	3.7	59.6	48.1	.021
17.4	12.0	40.0	71.7	.006
25.0	15.4	61.4	34.6	.007
26.2	0.0	7.1	18.2	.043
18.8	0.0	14.6	3.8	.034
34.9	4.5	53.5	50.0	.001
20.4	23.8	53.1	28.6	.015

the perceived need to be emotionally strong and high levels of stress and anxiety among both groups. There was a significant difference between both groups in response to the statement: "Nothing bothers me" (chi square = .0063; $p<.05$). Almost three-fourths of the widows strongly disagreed with the statement, as compared to a small number of wives. This suggests that black widows, because of their lower socio-economic status, may be under more stress and anxiety. Since many of the widows live alone and on fixed incomes, there is limited support outside of their own emotional strength.

The differences in perceived levels of stress among black wives and widows may be attributed to the diversity of roles assumed by wives. Since the majority of black wives were also working mothers, not only did they have occupational roles but also various familial roles. One wife stated: "Coping with the kids, mate, and family, in addition to working outside, is causing too much stress . . . there are just too many roles, too many time constraints, and too little support."

Summary and Conclusions

> For those of us, who suffer in silent desperation.... In a web of economic deprivation ... entwined by social isolation.... Filled with deadly poisons from historical oppression and discrimination.... Supported by fragile threads of hope.... Praying silently for strength to cope.... For the rest of our lives.... Black widows and wives....

American black wives and widows in urban areas often face the "best of times" and the "worst of times." The best of times is characterized by the emotional and social support they receive from their families and friends. The worst of times is characterized by the limited economic and institutional supports received from society. Yet, as many black wives and widows continue to cope with the realities of urban life, there appears to be a "fragile thread of hope" that stems from an enormous emotional and religious strength.

This emotional and religious strength is, perhaps, the "thread of hope" that stretched from the fields of the plantation to the streets of the ghetto. While limited in financial resources and economic supports, they frequently utilized the unlimited resources of families, friends, kin, and their own inner strength. Whether perceived or actual supports, the mutual aid system found within the black community appears to be one of the major mechanisms for survival.

For the black widow, however, the "thread of hope" is often broken by the loss of a spouse, severed social ties, and decreased financial supports. Despite these losses, many widows appeared to be hopeful. One widow stated, "The only joy I have is the joy of hope, and that's the only thing the world can't take from me...."

The statement of one black widow best summarizes the status of support systems for American black wives and widows. When asked if she felt there were adequate support systems for black widows and wives, she smiled and replied, "What's a support system ... a girdle ... or pantyhose?" Her response, while humorous, raises serious questions about the status of formal/informal supports for black wives and widows.

Results of the study revealed an association between economic, family, and emotional supports for wives and widows. Wives tended to have more economic support, higher perceptions of family support, and lower needs for emotional strength. Conversely, widows had less economic support, lower perceptions of family support, and higher perceptions of emotional strength and religious support.

8 Comparison of the Needs and Support Systems of Remarried and Nonremarried Widows

MARGARET GENTRY, LINDA ROSENMAN, and ARTHUR D. SHULMAN

Widowhood and Remarriage

Research suggests that widowhood is a stressful life experience. This is apparent in the self reports of widowed individuals as well as from indicators of adjustment difficulty such as increases in depression, physical illness, and mortality in the widowed (Bunch, 1972; Clayton, 1974; Glick, Weiss, and Parkes, 1974; Lopata, 1979; Maddison and Viola, 1968; Parkes, 1972). Since many of the problems that women face arise from the difficulty of living in this society without a husband, one potential way to cope with these needs might be to enter into a new marital relationship. We know, however, that not all widowed individuals consider remarriage seriously, and fewer actually remarry (Lopata, 1979).

Widowed women are fairly unlikely to remarry, although women are more likely to be widowed than men. Depending upon age, a widower is two-to-six times more likely to remarry after a spouse's death than is a widow (Cleveland and Gianturco, 1976; Spanier and Glick, 1980). One factor that may explain this phenomenon is the longer life span of women and the tendency of women to marry men who are older and who usually predecease them. This results in a larger pool of potential spouses for widowers and may explain, in part, why widowers are more likely to remarry than widows. On the other hand, there is some evidence that males may suffer more from being widowed (Stroebe and Stroebe, 1983), and remarriage may be a way for males to cope with difficulties in widowhood.

The age of a person at the time of the spouse's death also has been found consistently to be related to probability of remarriage (Cleveland and Gianturco, 1976; Spanier and Glick, 1980). The older the individual, the less likely he or she is to remarry. This relationship exists for both males and females, although the probability of widowers remarrying remains fairly high even at older ages.

Age, however, has been a perennial puzzle as to the physical, psychological, or social construct it reflects. For example, age could reflect society's negative attitudes about the appropriateness of remarriage for the older widowed (McKain, 1969); the demographic imbalance between older men and women; cohort-related differences in past marital experiences or attitudes about marriage; specific age-related concerns such as health, losing pensions, alienating adult children; or, it could represent numerous other possibilities. Whatever age represents, it is significantly related to decisions regarding remarriage and must be taken into account in studies of remarriage decisions.

The purpose of this chapter is to examine the similarities and differences in needs and support systems of three groups of women —widows who have remarried, widows who have considered remarriage but have not remarried, and widows who have not considered remarriage. Although there is a growing body of research on the needs and support systems of widows, we know much less about the concerns and support systems of remarried widows. This lack of research might be because of the assumption that, once a widow has remarried, she no longer has as many problems to cope with, or that she has a built-in support for dealing with problems—that is, her new husband. There is, furthermore, very little research that examines the issues surrounding remarriage in a systematic way. In fact, most research on remarriage has bypassed the widowed woman in order to focus on the experiences of divorced women. There are marked differences between widows and divorcées in such things as the degree of choice involved in ending the marriage, the stigma attached to divorce, and the attitudes toward remarriage of widows and divorcées. These differences are substantial enough that the work on divorce sheds limited light on the factors involved in widows' decisions about remarriage (Berardo, 1982; Kitson et al., 1980; Schwartz and Kaslow, 1985).

There are some studies on remarriage that directly examine either the adjustment of widows to remarriage or the similarities and differences between the two marriages (e.g., Bernard, 1956; McKain, 1972; Schlesinger and Macrae, 1971; Vinick, 1978). In general, these studies report satisfaction with remarriage and successful adjustment by both partners and children. They do not, however, directly compare the needs and support systems experienced in widowhood to those of remarriage. The purpose of this chapter is to make such a comparison.

Method

This study was part of an extensive research program investigating the needs, resources, and coping strategies of widowed women across the life span that was carried out in St. Louis in 1979–80. Although the primary focus of the larger project was on widows, a smaller subsample of women who had remarried after being widowed was also studied. Participants were selected through stratified random sampling of their spouse's name from the State of Missouri death records for married men. The sample was stratified by age, using the following categories: (a) under 39; (b) 40–49; (c) 50–59; (d) 60–69; and (e) 70 and over. The sample was also stratified by time since the spouse's death, using the following categories: (a) 6–18 months; (b) 19–36 months; and (c) 37–60 months.

Participants were initially contacted by a letter that described the project, asked for their participation, and contained a stamped postcard for their reply. Women who did not reply received follow-up telephone calls requesting their participation. Trained research assistants arranged interviews with participants and used a structured interview schedule, usually in the woman's home. The interviews took two and one-half hours, on the average, to complete. Participants were compensated for their time.

For the purposes of this research, participants were classified into the following three groups: (a) 39 women who had been widowed and had remarried; (b) 192 women who were widowed, had reported that they had at some point in their widowhood considered remarriage but had not done so at the time of the interview; and, (c) 410 women who were widowed and did not consider remarriage as an option for themselves.

Description of the Three Groups

Widows Not Considering Remarriage

The widows who had not considered remarriage were, on the average, 59 years old, with ages ranging from 24 to 88. The median length of time they had been widowed was 23 months, with a range of four months to five years. They had, on the average, three children, and the average age of the youngest child was 27.29 years. Forty-one percent of the widows who had not considered remarriage were currently employed, and an additional 24 percent had previously been employed but were now retired. When the widows who were currently employed were asked why they were working, the major reasons given were as follows: money (80 percent), companionship (49 percent), to use their training (41 percent), and because they were bored at home (30 percent). (The percentages of reasons for working and not working exceed 100 percent because most women gave more than one answer.) The unemployed widows in this group gave the following reasons for not working: (a) they did not want to (48 percent); (b) they were retired (41 percent); (c) their health was poor (25 percent); (d) they had responsibilities at home (17 percent); (e) they were unable to find a job (16 percent) or child care (15 percent); and, (f) they wanted to stay home with their children (8 percent). The median yearly income of this group was $7,362, and they reported an average of 11 years of formal education.

Widows Considering Remarriage

The widows who had considered remarriage were 10 years younger, on the average, than the widows who had not considered remarriage. The range of ages in this group was from 22 to 77 years, with an average of 49 years of age. The median length of widowhood was 30 months and ranged from six months to five years. These widows also averaged three children; however, the average age of their youngest child was 20.12, which is younger than that of the other group of widows. Sixty-two percent of the widows in this group were currently employed, and 9 percent were retired. The major reasons the employed women gave for working were the same as those for widows who had not considered remarriage—money (84 percent), companionship (54 percent), using their training (37 percent), and boredom (37 percent). The reasons the unemployed women cited for not working were as follows: (a) not wanting to (50 percent); (b) staying home with children (32 percent); (c) retirement (24 percent); (d) unable to find job (21 percent) or child care (13 percent); (e) responsibilities at home (21 percent); and, (f) poor health (17 percent). The major differences between the two groups of widows in reasons for not working appear to be age-related. The older group of widows, those not considering remarriage, were more likely to be retired and less likely to want to stay home with their children, probably because their children are older and less likely to be at home or to need supervision. The average level of education for widows who had considered remarriage was 12 years, and the median yearly income was $11,060. This is significantly higher than the income of the other group of widows and may reflect the differences in current employment levels and education.

Remarried Widows

The remarried women were very similar in age and life-stage characteristics to the widows who had considered remarriage. The average age of remarried widows was 49.5 years, and it ranged from 24 to 73. They also had an average of three children, with the average age of the youngest child being 20.75 years. The median length of time the remarried women had been widowed was 35 months, and they had been remarried an average of two years. Fifty-eight percent of the remarried widows were currently employed and 9 percent were retired. The remarried women who were employed were working for the same reasons as did the other two groups—money (79 percent), companionship (47 percent), using their training (47 percent), and boredom (16 percent). The unemployed remarried widows cited the following reasons for not working: (a) other home responsibilities (63 percent); (b) not wanting to work (53 percent); (c) wanted to stay home with children (47 percent); (d) retirement (26 percent); (e) poor health (16 percent); and, (f) couldn't find child care (5 percent). No remarried woman reported not being able to find a job. It is possible that if a married woman cannot find a job, she redefines herself as a housewife with family and other responsibilities at home. Widowed women, however, may need to stay in the job market even if they can't find a job for financial reasons, for companionship, or because they have less to do at home, etc. The remarried women reported a median annual family income of $16,460 and an average of 12 years of education.

Reasons for Remarrying or Not

What are some of the factors that widows take into account when considering remarriage? The widows in this sample were asked to give reasons why or why not they had considered remarriage. There were two major reasons that the widows who had not considered remarriage gave to explain their decision. Thirty-eight percent of these widows like being unmarried and enjoyed the independence it gave them; 37 percent said they would never be able to find someone as nice as their deceased spouse. Other reasons cited were as follows: still mourning husband (8 percent); too old (7 percent); economic reasons (3 percent); not enough men (2 percent); children's disapproval (1 percent); and other miscellaneous reasons (4 percent). It appears from these results that age and scarcity of men do not figure prominently as reasons for widows not remarrying. If one interprets not finding a man as nice as the deceased spouse as a rationalization for the scarcity of males rather than as an idealization of the spouse, it increases somewhat the support for the demographic explanations for widows' low rates of remarriage. It is, however, unclear if this is an appropriate interpretation of these findings. The fact that a third of the widows liked being unmarried, and the independence and freedom it brings, suggests that not remarrying is for many women a freely chosen alternative to marriage and not a consequence of the demographic realities.

The widows who had considered remarriage gave reasons either why they wanted to remarry, or why they had not yet done so. The primary reason given for wishing to remarry was for love and companionship; this was cited by 42 percent of the women. Other reasons were that they liked married life (12 percent), that they wanted to have more children or to provide a father for the children they currently had (6 percent), economic reasons (2 percent), safety (1 percent), and decision sharing (1 percent). Reasons for not having remarried were cited less frequently. The ones reported were: not having met the right man (14 percent), liking their independence (3 percent), and being too old (1 percent).

Those widows who had remarried were asked to recall the time when they were considering remarriage to their current spouse. Sixty-nine percent of the remarried women reported thinking at that time that remarriage would solve problems for them. The most frequently reported problem they thought would be solved was loneliness or a need for companionship (45 percent). Obtaining emotional support was cited by 13 percent; solving financial problems was also reported by 13 percent; 7 percent cited obtaining assistance in problems with children; and resolving problems with living independently and sexuality were reported by an additional 3 percent. Fifty-two percent of the remarried women reported conflicts over their decisions to remarry. The only two conflicts reported with any consistency were with children (47 percent) and other family members (16 percent).

In summary, it appears that the primary reasons for considering remarriage, or for remarrying, are for companionship and love. Financial concerns and children are also involved in the decision. The primary reasons for not considering remarriage are enjoying the independence of the single life and not having met an appropriate potential spouse.

Differences Between Concerns of Remarried and Widowed Women

It is reasonable to expect that the kinds of problems faced by remarried widows would be different from those experienced by women who were still widowed. The women in the study were asked to discuss concerns that they were experiencing in 23 different areas. They were asked to detail specifically what they wished to see happen to resolve the problem and what resources they had drawn upon to try to meet this need. The 23 need areas were generated from a content analysis of tape-recorded, nonstructured interviews with a pilot sample of 90 widows. Analysis of the responses to the 23 areas found them to be relatively independent from one another. Therefore, a measure of the total number of concerns was constructed for each woman in the study.

There were similarities in, and differences between, the needs of the three groups in terms of both the number and the nature of the needs reported. An analysis of covariance, controlling for age, was done on the total number of needs and indicated significant differences between the three groups. The remarried widows reported the fewest concerns ($M = 3.26$), followed by the widows not considering remarriage ($M = 4.56$), and finally those widows considering remarriage ($M = 5.46$). This suggests that remarried widows *do* experience fewer difficulties than those still widowed. There are two interpretations of the finding that those widows who have decided against remarriage also experience significantly fewer concerns than widows who have considered remarriage. One possibility is that they have found alternative resources to deal with the problems. Alternatively, they may have had fewer problems to begin with and so did not need to consider remarriage in order to cope.

Despite the differences in number of needs, no differences in self reports of stress between the three groups were found. Although remarried widows do experience fewer specific needs than nonremarried widows, they apparently see themselves as experiencing similar amounts of stress. The lack of significant differences in the perceptions of stress levels of the three groups suggests that despite the fewer needs reported by the remarried women, they have some unique and stressful events to cope with. The analysis of differences in individual need areas will address this issue.

Table 8.1 presents the percentage of each group that reported experiencing the individual 23 need areas. The three groups—remarried widows, those interested in remarriage, and those not interested in remarriage—differed significantly from one another on 13 of the need areas reporting the need in terms of percentages. Before discussing how the groups differed from one another, it is useful to note their similarities. The groups did not differ in the percentage of each group reporting concerns with independence or dependence, funeral matters, transportation, husband's death, legal matters, medical or health problems, things to do, privacy, safety, or self-betterment. It is particularly interesting that the groups did not differ in terms of medical or health problems, or concerns about independence or dependence. One would have expected the widows who had not considered remarriage to report more concerns with health because of their age, and for there to be differences in concerns with independence or dependence because of differences in marital status.

Both groups of nonremarried widows were more likely to report concerns with loneliness, housing, home maintenance, and finances than were the remarried group. In fact, loneliness was the number one concern for those still widowed, while it ranked twelfth for the remarried widows. Given that one reason for remarrying is companionship, these results are not surprising. Housing or home maintenance is the second or third most frequently occurring need for the widows, while it is eighth for the remarried women. Again, a new spouse may help resolve home maintenance problems by sharing in decision making, by reducing costs, or by doing some of the maintenance tasks. Despite the larger percentage of widows reporting concerns about finances,

Table 8.1 Percentage Within Each Group Reporting Concern in Current Time Period.

Concern	Remarried	Considering remarriage	Not considering remarriage	X^2
Career	21	40	27	13.13**
Children	41	35	19	38.05***
Independence	23	26	19	4.28
Emotional support	21	35	24	8.63*
Female friend	5	15	8	9.58*
Finances	26	43	36	20.81***
Funeral matters	0	6	4	2.53
Getting along with people	10	7	2	9.85*
Getting around	13	11	14	1.34
Housing	21	46	38	9.13*
Husband's death	5	10	8	1.58
Legal matters	21	18	14	2.00
Loneliness	18	60	52	22.64***
Male friendships	15	34	11	42.62***
Medical issues	18	26	28	1.98
More free time	26	21	13	8.51*
Things to do	8	19	16	2.94
Future plans	38	55	31	31.68***
Privacy	13	9	6	3.34
Safety	18	16	18	.18
Self-betterment	31	44	35	5.22
Sex	10	20	3	44.30***
Family concerns	3	2	2	15.63*

*$p < .01$. **$p < .001$. ***$p < .0001$.

the rank ordering of financial matters across the three groups is very similar (3 for those not considering remarriage, 4.5 for the remarried women, and 5 for those considering remarriage).

The remarried women's primary concern was their children. Although a very similar percentage of the widows who had considered remarriage also reported this concern, it was only the seventh most frequently mentioned concern for them. The similarity in percentages of remarried widows and those who had considered remarriage who reported concerns about children may be partially a function of their ages. Generally, both groups were at similar points in the life course and had younger children who needed more daily care and support.

In addition, the remarried women must deal with their children's adjustment to a new family situation, one involving a stepfather. The widows not considering remarriage were older, and their children were more likely to be adults and in need of less day-to-day care.

Similarly, the two younger groups of women were more likely to report a need for more free time than were the older widows who had not considered remarriage. This may be related in part to the demands of raising younger children. The need for more free time was rated as more important by remarried women than by either the widows who had considered remarriage or those who had not. It may be that having a spouse means having to juggle his demands in addition to the children's and one's own. While not necessarily a *problem*, it was an issue for the remarried widows.

The widows who had considered remarriage were the group with the largest number of needs. Over one-third of these women reported concerns with loneliness, planning for the future, housing or home maintenance, self-betterment, finances, career or employment, children, emotional support, and male friendships. With the exception of needs relating to children and the addition of female friendships and sex, a much larger percentage of the widows who had considered remarriage reported having unmet needs than either of the other two groups. This paints a picture of this group that suggests that they were experiencing considerably more problems than the other two groups.

There are several possible explanations for why the widows who have considered remarriage report more total problems in a wide variety of areas. It may be that because of their stage in the life course that they are facing a particularly difficult set of circumstances. Although this may explain some of the differences between this group and the older group of widows in such concerns as worries about children, not enough free time, or career concerns, it does not account for the differences between the widows who had considered remarriage and the remarried group. Given that these two groups were similar in age and stage of the life course, the differences in needs may perhaps be more directly attributed to difference in marital status. The nature of some of the needs expressed points this out—such as these widows' concerns about male friendships, need for emotional support, worries about sexual matters, difficulties with housing or home maintenance, and loneliness. A spouse would be one obvious resource for meeting these needs.

Other alternative explanations for the more difficult situations apparently faced by widows who had considered remarriage are that they may not be as adept at coping with problems as those widows not interested in remarriage or that they have fewer resources to draw upon for help in handling the needs. And so, they think of a man as the best, or only, solution.

Resources for Meeting Needs

One of the possible interpretations of these data is that many widowed women view remarriage as a solution to problems they experience with widowhood. It is therefore interesting to know how they deal with problems that arise while they are widowed. In this study, women were also asked who or what they used as a resource for dealing with the problems mentioned. The most frequently cited resource for dealing with all of the needs—except for sexual matters, legal issues, and medical issues—was the widow herself. Both those widows who wanted to remarry and those who did not were fairly similar in the percentages reporting using themselves as resources for most of the needs. The exceptions were that the widows not considering remarriage were less likely to report themselves as resources for dealing with problems with children (47 percent versus 57 percent) and were also less likely to rely on themselves as resources for self-betterment (35 percent versus 76 percent). In the case of concerns about children, the widows who had not considered remarriage also relied upon their families (15 percent) and professionals such as psychologists, physicians, or ministers (20 percent). In the case of concerns about self-betterment, they relied on educational resources (14 percent) and jobs (9 percent) more than the other widows.

The other resources that were most frequently used for dealing with emotional or psychological concerns such as independence or dependence, emotional support, and loneliness were: (1) social organizations, such as social clubs, church groups, widow-to-widow groups, singles clubs, etc.; (2) female friends; (3) family; and (4) professionals, in that order. Social organizations were also the most frequently mentioned resources for dealing with problems related to female and male friendship for both groups of widows and concerns about sex for the widows who had considered remarriage. Education and job-related resources were mentioned in connection with employment concerns and planning for the future for both groups of widows.

In addition, the widows who had not considered remarriage used education and job-related resources to help cope with self-betterment concerns. Jobs were also the most frequently mentioned resource for dealing with financial concerns. Economic resources such as savings, pensions, owning a home, etc., were mentioned as resources for financial problems; and for the widows who had not considered remarriage, it was mentioned in relation to planning for the future. Repairpersons were the most mentioned resources for housing and home maintenance concerns, followed by family, and female friends.

The remarried widows had fewer concerns and needs. As would be expected, they also had a somewhat different patterning of resources and support networks than did the nonremarried widows. It is interesting, however, that for the majority of the needs mentioned, remarried women saw themselves as the major resource for dealing with the problem. A second resource mentioned for dealing with concerns related to personal independence, financial problems, and self-betterment was gaining or improving her own educational qualifications. Surprisingly, remarriage, or the new husband, was frequently mentioned as a resource for only two concerns: those about the children—particularly concern for the children's future—and the need of a father figure for the children. The second concern was in terms of a need for independence and giving a sense of direction to life. Even with these needs, however, the remarried widows were more likely to view themselves rather than their new husbands as a resource.

It appears that the major differences in resources between the three groups were that the new husband replaced the secondary or tertiary resources such as family, friends, or social groups, which were likely to be used by those still widowed. The remarried widowed women were as likely as those not remarried to see themselves as the primary resource for dealing with problems.

There are several possible explanations for this. One is that the remarried widows had resolved many of their problems through remarriage. Therefore, those problems that were mentioned were most likely to be personal concerns for which a new husband was not the solution. A second is that, possibly as a result of being widowed, these women had learned to be self reliant and so did not see their new husbands as being the solution to every problem that arose. Without a comparison sample of married women whose lives have not been changed by marital disruption through death or divorce, it is not easy to test this hypothesis.

Summary and Conclusions

Remarriage appears to be an effective way of dealing with many of the needs that women in our society face upon the death of a spouse, including such personal problems as loneliness and planning for one's own life, financial problems, and practical problems such as housing and house maintenance. But, remarriage also apparently gives rise to other concerns, particularly concerns relating to children and lack of free time. Younger widows were more likely to see remarriage as a way of coping with their problems than were older widowed women. Those who wished to remarry were also likely to report many more problems than either remarried widows or those not interested in remarriage.

Remarriage reduced, or eliminated, many of the problems of widowhood. The new husband, however, was not a resource for everything. Those problems that remained, or surfaced after remarriage, were likely to be those that the widows saw themselves as having to cope with rather than using their new husbands as resources for.

Remarriage is not a solution to all problems for widows, nor is it a desired path for many. Close to 40 percent of the unremarried widows reported that they did not wish to remarry because, despite the difficulties, they enjoyed the independence that life without a spouse gave them. These findings challenge the societal stereotype that the vast majority of widowed women want to remarry but are unable to do so because of the shortage of available men.

9 Widowhood as the Next Stage in the Life Course

PHYLLIS SILVERMAN

Introduction

Widowhood is not generally viewed as a stage in the life cycle. In looking at what are the characteristics of a new life-cycle phase, widowhood meets these criteria. A new stage in the life cycle is often introduced by a change in life circumstances that requires an alteration in the way the individual relates not only to him or herself but to others as well, thus leading to a new identity. Adolescence is the most commonly mentioned as such a period of identity transformation. This phase of the life cycle is closely associated with the individual's biological age. In adults, development and change are not closely associated with age so much as with other changes that take place in their situation, as for example when people marry, get divorced, or are widowed. The critical period that occurs after the death of a spouse involves a loss of identity and can similarly be understood as a temporary stage in identity reconstruction (Lopata, 1975). When widowhood is seen as a stage in the life cycle, then it can also be understood not only as an ending but as a beginning as well.

Hummon (1986), quoting Berger and Luckmann (1967), describes identity as: "a person's sense of self: the self is the reflexive answer to that ongoing inescapable and quintessentially human question 'who am I?' As such it involves a 'positioning' of self in reality, a symbolic placement that situates the person in the world. . . . We identify ourselves as people of a certain type, quality or value—we also identify ourselves with others or significant objects forging a sense of belonging and attachment."

G. H. Mead (1934) notes that self can only develop in relationship to another, that we can only know ourselves as we know others. Nonetheless, in most contemporary theories of psychological development, reflected in social practice, autonomy and individuation are prized and are considered to be the optimal goals of development (Mahler et al., 1975; Ericson, 1968). In this view of the world, women are criticized for failing to achieve the same degree of self-sufficiency as men do (Miller, 1976, 1986; Gilligan, 1982). Women, Miller and Gilligan both observe, seem to be more related to the side of development that is concerned with relationships and maintaining connectedness to others. With men they note that the focus is on developing as separate individuals. Gilligan, using the metaphor of voice, suggests that men and women speak in different voices. Gilligan (1982) suggests that women's self is formed out of a sense of responsibility to others. Women's development, she suggests, moves along a continuum from a point where they do not recognize their own needs, but act on others' behalf, to a point where they can recognize the legitimacy of their own as well as other people's needs. A new mutuality and interdependence then occurs. Men seem to focus more on self-sufficiency and getting the job done.

Marriage is one social institution where the self in relationship is readily apparent. Marriage provides each partner with a way of framing and focusing their daily life, with a personal identity and a place in society (Berger and Kellner, 1974). When a spouse dies the survivor loses not only the marriage but the sense of self defined by the marital relationship.

From the perspective described by Gilligan and Miller, marriage would have different meanings to each of the partners (Silverman, 1981). Women would be more concerned with the caretaking role, with maintaining the connections between family members. Widows reflecting on their role as wife recall: "I was always Mrs. Joseph Smith or Jimmy's mother." "Whatever I did was with my family in mind. They came first."

A 65-year-old English widow reflected on her life as a wife: "Before N died I would always do what he wanted because I thought the husband had the final word, so I had no real identity of my own." It was not that she had no identity but that she knew herself through her caring for and connectedness to her husband.

Men, more concerned with the economic and physical well-being of their families, spend their energy on maintaining them as viable and separate units. Widowers, while they talked about themselves as "just a husband or father," did not talk of the marriage as providing them with the same sense of identity. They were more concrete when referring to themselves. They used such adjectives as breadwinner and provider; they did not see themselves as the person who held the marriage together. They talked about their wives as: "the port in the storm" or "the glue that held the family together." They understood her role as the caring, nurturing member of the couple. If their sense of self was different in the marriage, then we might expect that the nature of the transformation of self for the widowed after the death of a spouse might be different.

We are assuming, then, that to live successfully with their changed life circumstances requires a transformation in the widowed person's sense of self. We propose that this transformation may have different consequences for men and for women. Lund et al. (1986) and Arens (1982), in studies of widows and widowers, found no difference between them when measuring self-esteem or sense of well-being. However, they did not look at the concept of self. It is very difficult to identify the variables that would reflect change in self. Kegan (1982) suggests that the development of self changes over the life cycle as the individual develops new capacities and perspectives for making meaning out of their relationship to self and others. They move from, for example, an embeddedness in others who give them guidance and direction for their actions to a mutuality in which they can negotiate to arrive at joint decisions. One dimension for describing self might be to look at the part people see others playing in their lives and how this changes given different life circumstances. Using Gilligan's metaphor of voice, can changes in the way people talk about self and others be captured from a time before they were widowed to after they were widowed?

The purpose of this chapter is to see if it is possible to identify the variety of voices with which widowed people speak about themselves, to see if these voices reflect a transformation, and to see if widows and widowers speak in different voices. This chapter will look in greater detail at the nature of the change. The next section of the chapter will describe the way this data was gathered and the population who responded. The third section of the chapter is devoted to reporting on the patterns of change.

Methodology

The data are drawn from responses to a paper-and-pencil questionnaire administered to members of several mutual-help organizations for the widowed. In a preliminary analysis of change reflected in this data I noted two trends: women seem to become more decisive and self-reliant and the men more caring (Silverman, 1987a).

These mutual-help organizations are voluntary organizations run by the widowed for the widowed. They provide their members with many kinds of assistance, including outreach shortly after they are widowed, one-to-one informal counseling, group discussions, and social activities. Helpers in these groups are the widowed themselves. Respondents to the questionnaires came from all over the United States, Canada, Great Britain, and parts of Western Europe. The questionnaire was distributed at national and international meetings of these widowed organizations. Elsewhere I describe in detail the methodology I used in this study (Silverman, 1987b). A total of 233 questionnaires were returned; of these, 30 were from men—all but one of whom were from the United States. Some 207 of the responses were from women, one-third of whom were from outside the United States. Forty-four percent of the population were between the ages of 61 and 70, the oldest respondent, a woman, was 83. The youngest, also a woman, was 25. The men were more likely to be university graduates, 30 percent as opposed to 18 percent of the women, and more likely to be working or have worked in executive positions. The women were most likely to be working in clerical positions or sales. About one-third of the population were retired. In comparing the population from Europe with that of Canada and the United States in terms of age distribution, income, work history, and length of time widowed, there seemed to be no apparent differences. A fourth of the women were widowed 10 years or longer, two-thirds of them were widowed more than three years. Several men were widowed as long as 10 years, but the distribution was more even across time with the newest widower having been widowed for three months at the time he responded to the questionnaire.

This population is not seen as representative of all widowed people.

These are people who joined and remained involved in mutual-help programs. We know very little about how these people are different from the larger widowed populations. It is possible that the outcomes identified here are a result of their special experience in these organizations for the widowed. This cannot be demonstrated from this data alone. The data is used to simply explore one aspect of the widowed experience to see, without identifying cause, if widowed people experience a change in identity and, if so, in what direction the change goes.

The questionnaire was a set of open-ended questions designed to allow the widowed respondents to answer in their own words how they viewed the experience of widowhood, if they had changed as a result of their being widowed, and in what way they had changed. There were also questions about their affiliation with their particular mutual-help program to see how, in their view, it was helpful in their accommodating to their widowhood. The answers to the questions about what was most difficult when they were first widowed, what was easiest, what was still difficult, and what became easiest, and how they had changed as a result of their widowhood were particularly relevant to the current analysis of change. Other relevant questions were those asking them to describe themselves to themselves as they are now and to describe themselves as they were when they were married. I also asked them if they felt they had lost their voice when they were widowed, and if they had gained a voice after they were widowed. Voice was described as speaking up, speaking out, listening, being heard, saying what you think and feel, thinking and feeling what you are saying, and being able to share thoughts and feelings with others. Taking these responses together it was possible to get a sense of change and the direction it took.

A Typology

Each of the headings that follow describe a different trajectory. The titles are quotations from people in the identified group. The distinction between men and women is apparent at the extreme. There were some categories, however, in which some men had reactions similar to those of the women.

Happiness Was Being Married

Most people, when they are widowed, feel that their life changed for the worse. For some, this perception does not change, and no matter how much time has passed they can see little good in their present situation. They use the past as their reference point against which to measure their current satisfaction or dissatisfaction: then it was good and now it is not. In the population being discussed in this chapter, only three people fall into this category—one man and two women. The man was widowed for 11 years and, at the age of 71, he now describes himself as: "gregarious and extroverted when I am with others. I'm depressed when I'm alone. In contrast, before my wife died, I was the happy-go-lucky type, rarely depressed. I had a full, enjoyable life spotted with problems but none so overwhelming because they were shared with my wife. I was happy, contented, complacent." Being alone seems to be his biggest problem. In similar words, a 57-year-old woman from Ireland said: "It hurts to say this. I am always lonely. I love company and hate to be alone. I can't lean on my children too much. I was a very happily married lady with a lovely marriage—for which I am grateful. Life was good—love was all with my dear husband and children." They don't seem to find pleasure in themselves or receive satisfaction from their own company. A 64-year-old woman from England, widowed 21 years, talked about it not getting any easier. Even being with others did not bring her respite. She has developed an appropriate sense of independence and determination to care for herself but it gives her no satisfaction: "Since being involved with the National Association for the Widowed, I have had more upsets than hitherto, but now I have got harder and say what I think. But I do not like myself quite as much for this outlook." Her concept of appropriate behavior seemed acceptable for a married woman who deferred to her husband. She could not accept in herself (in contrast to women described later) the qualities of independence and being able to take care of oneself required for a woman or a man to survive alone. The widower said that he was being treated for depression. While the women did not use this word, they too seemed excessively sad. While they felt better when with others they were not consoled by people. The widower said: "When my wife first died I was unable to speak. My throat contracted. My lower jaw moved, but no sound came out. I am less aggressive in conversation now. I have a greater fear of being criticized. I am convinced that people do not want to hear my opinions. I am often squelched when I do speak." The widows expressed the futility of speaking. "In a way I did lose my voice when my husband died to keep myself from getting too upset about things. I can speak, but now I feel that nobody wants to hear anymore. Seven years have passed. I always try to smile in public—the illusion is that all is well now and 'you must be over it.'" The second widow said: "You can't burden others with your grief. They don't understand unless they've been widowed themselves. One can only say that it doesn't get any easier."

People may not be listening because all these widowed people can talk about is their sadness and their pining for a time past, which they cannot recapture, when things were "better." These are people who are still invested in their marriage and can only understand their current life as deprivation compared to what they had in the past. They seem to be skirting a confrontation with the loss they have experienced. In the words of the widower: "I have too much time for myself and problems to be faced alone." While they live socially in the present, psychologically they seem invested in the past. They have not found a way of redefining how they see themselves and their place in their world. This is in contrast to a group of newly widowed people, who express similar qualities but who are struggling with what it means to be widowed.

Alone and Frightened: Can I Really Stand on My Own Two Feet?

A sense of malaise and pessimism is appropriate in people who are newly widowed. The concept of new widow in most research refers to someone widowed less than six months, at most, a year (Osterweis, 1984). Here we find a group of widows (approximately 10) who have been widowed on the average of two years. The pain of the loss is still very real. They are still finding their way. It would seem that when your identity has been shattered it takes a long time to assemble a new one. Many of these women had never lived alone in their lives, and now they weren't yet sure that "life was worth living." An American widow, aged 67 at one year, writes: "Now I am lonely and frightened. I'm confused—but trying to stand on my own two feet. I used to be sure of myself, independent, active, alert, moving all the time. Now I have nothing left." Not only are they cut off from themselves, but, to compound the injury, they feel cut off from their community, from their place in society. Marriage framed and focused their lives, making it easy to act. A 52-year-old woman widowed for two years wrote: "I feel as if as part of a couple I was included. Now I am an afterthought." While they recognize that their world has crumbled, and they sense there is a need to change, they don't have a sense of having arrived there yet. They talk about "trying to stand on my own two feet" but not always making it. A 54-year-old widow of two years with three dependent children at home: "I could do anything and was very secure in knowing that I could do anything. After his death I felt beat down, defeated, things beyond my control had happened, and for the first time in my life there was nothing I could do about it." Not only are these women close to their pain but to the sense of helplessness that many widowed people feel shortly after their spouse's death. In groping for ways in which they might have moderated this pain by their own deeds this same woman recommended: "Develop an independent life while you are married. In that way you hope you can function alone although you hope you never have to." She was not able to recognize how able she had been and still was. After her husband's death she described how she worked out her budget, paid bills, and managed her investments. While he was alive they had a relationship in which: "We each took a turn at being leader or follower depending on how strongly we felt on the subject." She had no experience doing things completely on her own. She was in reality as prepared as anyone could be to manage her own life, but she was not yet ready to acknowledge this in herself. The language these widows use is the same as that used by people who were living in the past; however, it is not their solution but a stage in the process of making an accommodation. They don't like being alone, and, in many ways at this stage in time, they are still their husbands' wives.

> I was a wife, mother for 47 years. Now I am always on the run. I hate to be alone but am afraid to take anyone in my house. My husband was a very strong man, and I lived as he wanted even though I am a strong person myself, but we made a happy medium. I can't seem to care—it is so lonely. I feel as if half of me has been totally taken away and I am just a half. I have lost my self-confidence—worry about the future. I can't understand why I was not more prepared—and even now—more so than at the beginning. I fret that I didn't say more to my husband that last week when he was on a respirator but I realize now—it never

> occurred to me that he would not get better. How I could have deceived myself is not understandable to me now.

These women seem to be reflecting on their situation. They are touching the pain and trying to understand it. They begin to recognize their own naiveté. They seem not to have been in touch with real dangers that exist in the world, and as they get in touch with the reality of their lives they try to alert others to the fact that they need to be aware that: "the worst can happen—their spouse can die." It is as if they are emerging from a sheltered cocoon. The process is slow and torturous. They must struggle with making the fact of their husband's death real. They are struggling to find out what being a widow means because in many ways they still live as their husbands wanted and feel that when they were married there was a place for them in society. A 56-year-old Irish woman said: "I am very aware of my aloneness, very sensitive when in mixed company. I think of myself now as an actress on stage alone when the leading man has given a good performance and I am left to carry the play along until the final curtain comes down. Before, I guess the picture or play would have been a success with myself and my leading man supporting each other." When they were married they felt good about themselves and felt whole. They were a success. They feel lost but are not despairing of finding their way again.

> My sense of humor serves me well.
>
> I've gained a new voice—only in spending money or saving it. Financially I have to make my own decisions and I am doing it.
>
> Everyone of the family wants to take over. There is a fine line between help and taking over. After too much taking over you find yourself stripped of everything—material things as well as self-will. Then suddenly you are on the road. I am trying to keep as much of this (self-will) as I can. I am still trying, as you say, to find my voice.

They are learning to be comfortable with the need to take charge of their lives. "I have taken control of my financial affairs. I must be self-reliant, whereas it was so comfortable to lean on my husband. I'm learning." They are not yet sure of what the future will look like, or that life will be good again. They are very aware that they cannot go back again. "I am an outgoing independent woman. Hurt at my loss and made to travel in different circles. I do not feel fulfilled or that I am fulfilling any need. I am not always sad, but never really satisfied. I feel like I am acting all the time. There is such an emptiness in my everyday living. Though it is full with my family needs and a great job now, but still there is that void." This is a void that may always be there, for there may never be a replacement for the type of relationship in which there is the kind of mutual regard this woman was accustomed to receiving and giving. However, with time, other selves and other relationships emerge that bring other satisfactions.

I Was Just a "Wife": People Don't Recognize Me as the Same Person

For many women being married meant that others always came first, before their own needs were fulfilled. They defined themselves in terms of the role they filled as caretaker to others as described by Gilligan (1982) and by Kegan (1982) as a stage in the development of self. An American woman reflected: "I had no plans for my self as a person. I was just a wife and mother. My future was based on his retirement, during which I felt I would be taking care of him." Family life was based on their husband being in charge and his needs setting the tone.

> My husband was a gift and I was grateful to have him for 35 years. He did not care for a social life and that restricted my activities some.
>
> The children and my husband came first. I never dreamed anything bad could happen.
>
> I was very dependent on my husband for most all decisions.

These are women who, in looking back at their marriages, felt that they did not speak out. Their husbands' and children's needs took precedent. If this arrangement was unsatisfactory, it was not a critical issue in how they viewed their lives then. A 54-year-old woman from Ireland who had been widowed for three and a half years recalled: "I didn't have any worries. I was happy-go-lucky, loved my life and family, loved cooking. I felt a bit tied, lots of things I wanted to do but couldn't. I gave all my time to my husband and family." A 67-year-old woman from Portugal who had been widowed for 13 years recalled: "Before I was widowed I had to submerge my personality in order not to hurt my husband." Several women from both sides of the Atlantic Ocean reflected that speaking out could be disruptive. They feared that they would hurt someone or be rejected. One woman went so far as to say that she: "didn't want to lose my family or friends by saying the wrong thing." Their energies were devoted to maintaining their connections to others and to keeping their family together. A 70-year-old American woman, widowed three years, describes herself before she was widowed: "I was strong but apt to want to *keep peace* in the family at any cost. I was intolerant to a certain extent, very stubborn and not very flexible. I liked to maintain the status quo. I had spiritual values but I was reluctant to mention them for *fear of being ridiculed*." As they considered the metaphor of voice many reflected that they did not have a voice to lose. "As you put it, I didn't have a voice to lose. I found a voice. I can now say, 'what about me?'"

Following the analysis in the earlier section of this paper, I anticipated that the majority of the women would have described themselves in words that would put them in Gilligan's stage one of women's morale development. For women at this stage, maintaining relationships was dominant because they understood and valued themselves primarily through these relationships. Only one-third of the women in this sample described themselves as the caretakers and peacemakers in the family and saw themselves as having no identity of their own. All of the people in this group moved from this point of denying self to a place where they can say: "I am a different person than I was 14 years ago." This 72-year-old English widow went on to say: "I am an independent feminist rather than someone's wife (lovely as he was). I feel I have learned to face up to things (most of the time), and to stand on my own two feet." Their being widowed led all the people in this group to redefine who they were so that they related to themselves and others in a totally different manner. A 65-year-old woman from Canada said: "Instead of being concerned with how he thought and felt . . . it is now me alone. I have learned to say no, before it was maybe." It was now acceptable to put themselves in the center of the picture. "If I don't speak out now, I am nothing." Another widow said: "My friends, values, interests, understanding have all changed. I've developed a complete new way of life." Changes were profound and affected most aspects of their lives. They began by getting confidence in themselves. "Over time I returned to work. My record there gave me confidence. I became a person in my own right. I had to make decisions. I soon learned other people's advice was unreliable and detrimental to the family as a whole." A widower reported: "As I developed self-confidence I could consider myself first in most cases." One widow noted how important it was to talk up for yourself: "I am getting more confidence in myself, standing up to tradesmen. I think that many women are bullied by the menfolk but not me anymore." The woman who earlier feared ridicule if she spoke out describes herself now: "I am a strong, dependable individual who champions the underdog and am constantly wrestling injustice in my life. I am reserved but loving and a constant friend, tolerant, more aggressive, flexible, more spiritual and not afraid to say so." These women have gained a "voice." "I am a sociable individual, not easily rebuffed, although still shy underneath my bravado. I rebel at things I don't want to do but that others expect me to do. I have progressed in making my wants known. I have learned to say no and not feel guilty." They are still involved with others, but they are relating differently. They are no longer only taking their cues from others to do their bidding; they are taking their cues from within themselves as well. They take pleasure in thinking about themselves, in taking care of themselves, and in themselves.

> I am my own person. I make my own decisions. I changed my job to have more time for myself. When my husband was alive he felt home and children came first.
>
> I appreciate the freedom to please myself in whatever I do.
>
> I am a young widow, though not age-wise. I am independent, alone but happy. Now I think and I decide.

Since they no longer see themselves only in relationship to others, even the label widow is not acceptable. "I like to be treated as an individual rather than as a widowed woman." A 68-year-old woman who has been widowed for 23 years wrote:

> I never thought much about widows. I always felt uncomfortable in their presence. I was completely absorbed in my own domestic life and family. I now marvel at how smug I was, never dreaming any such tragedy could happen to shatter our family, and, in a way, I have a slight contempt for my former attitude. I think I am now a much more developed personality.
>
> I was an echo of my husband's voice when he was alive. Now I see things with my own eyes, have my own opinions, live through my own senses. My identity is now my own.

Not all widows begin their widowhood without a voice.

I Always Could Speak Out but Now It Is Very Different

> My marriage offered recognition of my "voice." I have now to "speak" in a different forum.

This group represents about a third of the study population. Since they seemed more able to speak for themselves, I thought that they might represent a younger group of women, who had greater exposure to the ideas of the women's movement and therefore would be less silent in their marriage. All of these women were over the age of 55 and seemed not different from the other widows from a demographic point of view. They did not think of themselves as assuming a submissive role in their marriage. Being involved in what they saw as egalitarian marriages was not an age-specific phenomenon. In their marriage they could speak out. This meant they shared ideas, thoughts, and feelings with their husbands. There was always an active exchange between them.

"My husband helped me make decisions. We really talked things over." While they saw themselves as "independent" this did not mean that they stood alone. "I was one-half of a couple, independent but still depending or leaning on my husband." Some leaned more on their husbands than others did. "I was always protected, coddled, taken care of. Decisions were almost always discussed. I deferred to what I believed were better decisions, because my husband was wise and experienced, had a lot of common sense, and his judgments were not based on emotions so much as reason. I always thought 'father knows best.'" While this woman did not act on her own, and she talks about not valuing her own judgments, she did not see herself as her husband's agent or as one with her husband. There was more a conscious division of labor. She made a choice and acted on it. This quality separates her from women described above who felt they had no voice before they were widowed. All the women in this population sometime set aside their own needs to care for others. This did not involve denying their own needs. "My husband had been sick and he was very dependent on me. I always considered his wishes before my own but I always had a voice." The main focus in their marriage was the interdependency. "My husband seemed to fill the interstices of my life where I had lacks. He had supported me in feeling like a solid unit. Without him I felt fragmented. But I am very articulate so I had no difficulty explaining how I felt." When they talked about what they lost, they said they missed the companionship, someone to share things with—someone to care about and to care for them, someone to love and be loved. They missed having someone to confide in and to share small things with. They felt a mutuality in their relationship. "The most difficult thing for me at the beginning was the absence of laughter and loving and the companionship. I discovered all the things my husband had done that I didn't even notice—car upkeep, fixing things in the house, and so forth. It was hard making decisions alone without having someone to consult." A 54-year-old widow of four years said: "I felt that I had no sounding board."

In their marriages, then, these women had a voice, but it was intertwined with that of their husband so that they felt supported and able to speak. Their relationship did not inhibit, rather it enhanced, their voice.

Many of these women felt that with the death of their husband, their voice was stilled or shattered. "I always had a good sense of who I was, but I was shaken for a while following the death." A 65-year-old widow of six years said: "Initially I could not sleep and I couldn't communicate . . . I simply could not talk. There was a dreadful numbness." A 53-year-old woman who had been widowed for 16 years recalled:

> In the beginning I had the feeling of being very vulnerable. I felt I was worthless because I had no husband. Before my husband died I could stand up for myself if insulted or rebuffed. I accepted insults and sexual advances from other people's husbands without fighting back.
>
> I would not do that now. I am even stronger than before my husband died (I gained a voice again).

Other women felt they lost their voice because people in their social network could not deal with the fact that they were now widowed. To have a voice meant there had to be someone to listen. "My friends dropped me. No one asked my opinion. I was ignored." A 70-year-old woman widowed for four years wrote: "I became a nonperson. I lost all privileges of a couple-oriented society: a curse, a bad thought of what might or will happen to my friends and acquaintances." These women did not simply regain their voice. Instead, they developed a new voice. One woman said she learned from work, from the approval of others, and from her own will to survive. Necessity, in part, propelled them forward.

> I've always been reasonably independent, but now I have to think for myself and my family to improve things for us.
>
> In my early widowhood I used to feel left out. This used to make me rebel in myself. I tried to come out of loneliness by going to courses, developing my interests, and finding my hidden capacities.

They had to learn to act on their own behalf in a way that they had not had to do before. A 76-year-old widow said: "How hasn't it changed? After 43 years of habits and sharing life with another—even your thinking changes." They can now put themselves into the center of their lives without apologizing or feeling selfish. The concept of selfishness is exemplified in the negative by the comment of a woman who became uncomfortable in the independence she was developing. She wrote about her decision to get married: "I have an incredible need to love and share and an incredible need to get out of what I consider a very selfish tendency to take care of myself." She did not see that she could move ahead to both consider herself as well as others in the relationship (Gilligan, 1982). Most women in this group did not have a conflict about meeting their own needs. In the words of a 57-year-old woman widowed for two years: "I am a person who takes charge of her life, makes decisions and accepts the consequences of these good or bad. I sometimes wish I didn't have to but that is the way it is." Another widow said: "Before I might have gone along with popular opinion but now I have to be true to myself and do what I feel is right." They could accept responsibility for themselves and find pleasure in it, but they were still very much involved with others. "I've developed my voice because I'm more attentive to others and I think more." They develop a new view of themselves. They become more reflective. As one woman noted: "My voice is quieter, more self-contained." They also develop a new view of others. "While I am still a very private person, I feel more sympathetic and understanding of others, more open-minded. I know that the decisions I make are mine, there is no one else to blame. I can do what I want when I want and I like that." They talk about freedom and self-reliance, but they also talk about responsibility and caring for others. "I am almost a whole person, independent, self-sufficient, helpful, liberal with money. I am very good at counseling. I am practical and grateful for good health and very compassionate for those who are ill. I have earned and keep wonderful friends. I have learned to live with loneliness and have complete responsibility." They see good in their lives and find pleasure in it:

> I have a freedom now I never had before.
>
> I am a happy single person, independent, and enjoying it.
>
> It's not so much that I gained a voice but I use my voice differently, to assist in speaking for causes or legislation. I felt I had an obligation to be of service to people any way I could. Widowed people need help with decision-making techniques. After 20 years I had developed my skills.

The change in these women is not as dramatic as it was for the women and men who were without a voice in their marriage. The change nonetheless is in a similar direction for both these groups. They both know themselves in different ways now and find pleasure and excitement in themselves and in their new relationships. What happens to men who had a whole different sense of self in their marriages?

I Was Much More Selfish: I Have Much More Time for Others Now

On the whole, men were much less articulate than were the women. Many men described themselves in words of one syllable. For example, in response to the question "describe yourself as you were before your wife died," some men said "independent." Many more said that there was no change. The sparseness of data makes it more difficult to characterize their experience. In addition, many men invited to fill out the questionnaire refused, so there are fewer respondents to draw upon. In this sense there was a dramatic difference between the men and the women. The men's pain was not less profound. One new widower was able to say: "I feel like nobody with no future and loneliness closing in on me." But on the whole, they were simply not able to articulate their feelings. As one man put it: "Widowers need to learn to cry, to let their feelings out. They need to learn to talk." Many of them said they did not change—saying so in the same breath as they said how different they were. A 56-year-old widower of four years said: "I now have a different kind of life. When she died I felt like half a person." Unlike the women, most men did not lose the ability to act on their own behalf. "I had confidence in my ability to make decisions." Another widower noted his ability to act was not impaired. He just seemed to put things off. Even new widowers did not seem to lose this ability. A 41-year-old widower of three months wrote: "I'm quiet, but very strong in coping and handling financial affairs, making decisions."

It was not that they were less caring or involved. Some men talked about their marriage in terms of the sharing they did.

> We were a team—we did things together and made decisions based on the ideas presented by each party.
>
> I had a gentle, understanding wife. We were devoted to each other. We didn't always have to say things to know what we were thinking.

Several men cared for their wives when they were ill and took over the role of caretaker in the family. Three of the men used language that showed how much of themselves was invested in the relationship. For example, one widower said: "I was invested in others, in caring for them. I give too much to my kids even now. I have to learn to say no." This widower changed and spoke in a different voice: "I can now say no and not think I will hurt someone."

For most men their sense of who they were was not as intimately tied to their role of husband. Most men talked about losing someone "to come home to" and one man said: "my home became a house." A 38-year-old widower, widowed for over three years, said: "I didn't lose my voice. I lost a person to confide in and a shoulder to lean on." In this view they lost someone who listened to them and who responded to their needs and who made their "house a home." Only after her death did they realize what their wives meant to them, and they became aware of how much their married lives had centered on meeting their own needs. A 66-year-old man widowed for two years described himself before as most concerned with himself: "I think I was more selfish in my thoughts. Only because I did not have any idea what I would have to go through when she died." The death caused a disruption in the way they lived their lives that they were not prepared for. The 38-year-old widower referred to earlier was raising three dependent children by himself. He did not see himself as changed, yet he wrote: "I am a person who has gone through a very traumatic experience and came through it having found an inner strength I never knew I had. I made up my mind to do a job and I did it (taking care of my children). It was difficult dealing with being both mother and father and with the death of their mother." He sees himself as more understanding now. Other men talked of working on being more understanding. The thrust of change for these men seemed to be in the way they saw their relationships to others. They moved from the place where they described themselves as: "more selfish with my time for others, less understanding and probably less independent," to where they are "more understanding, more generous with my time for others."

They seemed to be involved in a new mutuality and to recognize the importance of relationships in their lives and their responsibility in nurturing these relationships. "I think I am a decent human being, God-fearing, and sympathetic to others. I know what I am going through since the loss of my wife, and it seems to me that my goals are to help others who are in the same place as I am."

Many men talked about remarriage. Women rarely brought this up as an option for the future. Many women felt they enjoyed their "freedom" and would not remarry. However, the possibility of remarriage from a purely numerical point of view is not available to women. A common thought is that women mourn and men remarry. Only one man articulated his wish to remarry as the opportunity to recapture the past. This was the young widower of 38: "I want to get back to the way life used to be by getting married and being complete again. It will also be good for my children." He makes it sound as if women were replaceable. Since he, indeed, did change, he may be surprised to discover he cannot make a carbon copy of the marriage he lost. Most men, however, talked about the possibility of remarriage not as a way of recapturing past marriages but as a way of expressing their newfound abilities to be involved with others. One man of 70 said: "I want someone to share with—someone who needs me." Another man in his sixties wrote: "I want someone to make a life partnership—living for another person can insure my happiness."

Conclusions

From this data it is evident that there are differences between men and women in the way they accommodate to the death of their spouse. However, it is clear that we are not talking about invariable differences since there were also similarities in some widows and widowers. The construct of voice does seem to be a productive tool for elicitating these differences as well as for pointing to similarities. Differences emerged, then, not only based on gender but on what can be considered appropriate or inappropriate accommodations to changed circumstances. The group committed psychologically to the past can be considered to have made a problematic accommodation. Those people who affected a change in the way they related to themselves or others, and who felt satisfied with their lives, can be considered to have made a satisfactory adjustment. On the face of it, it would seem that women moved to positions of greater autonomy. They seemed to take pleasure and satisfaction from the freedom they experienced and from their newfound abilities to manage their own lives and assume responsibility for meeting their own needs. Making decisions on their own became easier with time, and speaking for themselves did not make them feel uncomfortable, nor did they see this as risking their connectedness to others. Autonomy may not be the best word to describe this experience. It is not that they now stood alone but rather that their connectedness to self and others took on different dimensions.

Men, in contrast, seemed to take more responsibility for their relationships, to understand the importance of being able to take the "role of the other" so that they saw more clearly that they had a personal responsibility for maintaining their connectedness to others. In many ways, this shift for men could be seen as bringing them closer to the way women saw themselves when they were married.

In part, both the men and the women seemed to develop another side of themselves. They are now more connected to themselves as well as to others. Their relationships take on a mutuality that didn't exist before. For women, it is not that they need people less, rather they include them in a different way. This new way involves listening to their own voice as well as the voice of others. These are the qualities needed to live successfully in this next stage of their life cycle. Men, in turn, recognize their need to be connected to others, and they learn to hear other people's voices as well as their own.

From this data we see that the study of the impact of widowhood has to extend beyond the first years of acute grief. Further, in studying outcome we cannot talk about recovery but of transformation. More research is also needed to understand the relationship of a sense of personal identity to changing life conditions. Many of these respondents, especially the women, expressed concern about being able to maintain their new life-styles as they continue to age, thereby becoming less able to care for themselves and less able to initiate and sustain their involvements with others.

The question needs to be asked about what facilitates the kind of changes described in this chapter. All the respondents in this study were members of mutual-help organizations. Lopata (1986) has suggested that the kind of change widowed women experience may be class-related. The men and women represented in this study population were from both working- and middle-class backgrounds. It may be that affiliation with a mutual-help organization facilitates the kind of accommodations described above regardless of social class and regardless of the positions the widowed held in their marriages. The mutual-help organizations to which these people belonged were free-standing organizations that were run by and for the members, all of whom are widowed. Here the widowed find new opportunities for what can be called linking relationships (Silverman, 1981). These relationships provide a bridge between the past and the future. In these relationships, participants do not develop new dependencies but interdependencies based on respect and mutuality. These people find others like themselves with whom they can identify. They find role models that facilitate their learning (Silverman, 1978, 1980, 1986). Hence, it may be easier to identify the type of change described in this chapter in this population of the widowed.

I want to thank my daughter, Nancy S. Tobi, B.A. in Sociology, who so ably organized these data. Without her assistance this work could not have gone forward.

10 Widowhood Among Low-Income Racial and Ethnic Groups in California

ANABEL O. PELHAM and WILLIAM F. CLARK

Introduction

Over half of all elderly women, or about eight million women, in the United States are widows (Bureau of the Census, 1980). As one would expect, this proportion increases with age. By the age of seventy-five, nearly 70 percent of women are widowed (Bureau of the Census, 1983a). Given the differences between male and female life expectancies and that the majority of younger women are married, widowhood is the most probable future for the majority of American women.

What do we know about these eight million widows? Unfortunately, for a social phenomenon of such magnitude, we know very little. Only in the last several decades have social scientists systematically begun to study widowhood.

To provide more specific and disaggregated information about widows, we present in this chapter our analyses of low-income widows in California. To raise the level of specificity, we focus on this group by asking whether race and ethnicity make a difference along various dimensions, which include demographics, functional status,

Support for research reported in this chapter was from HCFA Grant No. 11-P97553/9-04—MSSP. Statements contained in this chapter are solely those of the authors and do not necessarily reflect the views or policies of the Health Care Financing Administration or of the California Health and Welfare Agency. The authors would like to acknowledge the assistance of Diann S. Haines in preparation of this manuscript.

family structure and interaction, and use of both informal support (i.e., support provided by unpaid family and friends) and formal support services (i.e., paid or publicly funded social and medical services). We begin, however, with some historical background on California.

California: The Place and Its People

California has always been full of images as the end point for America's Manifest Destiny—the edge of the continent, the rim of the Pacific, and all of the mystique that goes along with that. California had, and continues to have, a reputation for the rough and ready, like Davy Crockett looking for breathing space and freedom.

Things began to boom in 1849 with the great gold rush, which attracted people from all over the United States and the world. Most of the foreign-born immigrants were Asian, mainly Chinese, who were first used as cheap labor in the mines and then later to help build the transcontinental railroad. The gold rush provided the impetus to separate from Mexico, and California became a state in 1850. Today, California leads the other states in agriculture, manufacturing, and population (every tenth U.S. resident is a Californian). The state's gross product, estimated at $312 billion in 1980, exceeds that of all but seven of the world's nations (National Geographic Society, 1981). The 1985–1986 state budget itself is about $35 billion.

Historically, the development of the state occurred on a north–south basis. The initial mineral wealth of the north became transformed into railroads and banks. Commerce was centered in San Francisco, which began a slow but steady growth until the early 1900s, when the great earthquake struck in 1906. The local economy did not really recover until World War I.

Meanwhile, in the south, Los Angeles slowly expanded from a cluster of *ranchos* to a metropolis of over a million people by 1930. The city achieved this growth by solving its energy, water, harbor, and labor problems. The harbor, by the 1920s, handled more tonnage than any other American port except New York, eclipsing the northern ports of San Francisco and Oakland (Romo, 1983). Also in the 1920s, oil was discovered on Signal Hill in Long Beach, south of Los Angeles, and thousands of wildcatters sprinted to the area, a type of "black gold rush." Even today you can see what are locally called "donkeys"—rigs moving up and down, up and down, removing the oil 24 hours a day (Morris, 1985).

In the 1930s the dust storms pushed souls out of the Midwest and into the rich valleys of California: the Central, the San Joaquin, and the Sacramento. Families mostly came as fruit pickers, and they are forever burned in our memories as John Steinbeck's "Okies." Decades later the California aqueduct project would irrigate these valleys and turn the entire central part of California into the richest agricultural area in the world, producing over 200 specialty crops.

In the late 1930s, as war clouds formed over Europe, shipbuilding began in earnest in the ports of San Francisco, Oakland, Los Angeles, Long Beach, and San Diego. This increased economic activity brought another wave of immigrants, particularly blacks from the southern states. As World War II progressed, the aircraft industry emerged in southern California; the aerospace industry presently plays a dominant economic role in the southland.

After World War II, the whole Los Angeles basin experienced a boom fueled by freeways and affordable housing. Today about a third of California's population lives south of the Santa Monica Freeway, a major east–west highway in Los Angeles. In the north, a steady growth continued after World War II, with an expansive growth in the 1970s in the San Jose area, south of San Francisco. This is the area known as the "Silicon Valley" because of the concentration of the computer industry there.

This brief historical synopsis illustrates that the influx of ethnic minorities occurred in episodic waves stimulated by economic opportunities. The first large group were the whites who invaded Mexican-owned California in the 1850s, followed by the Asians to work in the mines and on the railroads. The next large group was the blacks, almost a hundred years later during World War II. During and between both of these periods other ethnic groups also emigrated to California, always in search of one kind of freedom or another—religious (e.g., Russian Jews), political (e.g., Armenians), or economic (e.g., Irish). Although all of these ethnic and racial groups represented significant numbers, they were fewer than California's largest and fastest growing minority population, the Hispanics. Hispanic was the dominant culture until statehood (1850), but eventually the Hispanics lost their economic and social status to the Anglo minority-soon-to-become majority. During the last 20 years, Hispanics have begun to recuperate some of their lost status, but their present situation is still economically and socially precarious.

The overall effect of these immigration and demographic patterns is that it is estimated that by the year 2000 the majority of Californians will be what are today termed "minorities."

The California Senior Survey

Data reported here are from the California Senior Survey (CSS), the comparison group of the California Multipurpose Senior Services Project (MSSP), a research and demonstration project in community-based long-term care (California, 1984a). CSS sampling strategy mirrors the research needs of MSSP and, in accord with that strategy, contains three distinct subsamples defined by point of acquisition (i.e., community, hospital, and skilled-nursing facility) and was drawn from eight purposively chosen locations—i.e., in those areas of California where MSSP situated its demonstration projects.

Detailing the California Senior Survey sampling sites, Eureka in the farthest north is found along Humboldt Bay and near the redwood timberland. Eureka's economy is one suffering the fate of a decline in natural resource production—commercial fishing and timber harvesting have been embattled industries for decades. This small city (population 25,000) is economically depressed due to the effects of high unemployment rates in these extraction industries. Allegedly, a large underground and illegal economy centered on marijuana cultivation constitutes the most profitable industry in the area. The low-income widows, mostly white, in this area are either long-time residents who moved here initially with their husbands in search of work or are residents of the back country of the coastal mountain range who have moved to the county seat, Eureka, to be nearer the available urban amenities and services. Because of its cool and rainy climate, Eureka is not a retirement center.

San Francisco is the gateway to the Pacific and the most polyglot city in northern California. Among its 679,000 residents, San Francisco has the highest proportion of Asian, particularly Chinese, elderly in California. The Chinese population has been expanding since the gold rush days, although it suffered some slowdown during the twenties (e.g., the Quota Acts of 1921 and 1924) and the widespread internments during World War II. Many of the Chinese widows in the CSS sample are recent arrivals who were brought over by their children. San Francisco also has a sizable black population, which grew due to the shipbuilding activity during World War II and to the numerous military bases in the area.

Oakland, on the eastern shore of San Francisco Bay, is a sprawling city of 339,000, with blacks making up 47 percent of its inhabitants (Bureau of the Census, 1983b). The "Flatlands," next to the Bay, contain some of the worst crime and drug-ridden slums in California and are where most of the CSS respondents live. The topography rises eastward into the Oakland hills, where multimillion-dollar homes have spectacular views of the Bay, San Francisco, and the Golden Gate Bridge while overlooking the Flatlands. Somehow the city functions surprisingly well and even boasts one of the finest environmental museums in the country.

About a two-hour drive from the urban stresses of Oakland lies Santa Cruz next to the Pacific Ocean. This city of 42,000 had been for years a sleepy summer resort area and features a boardwalk and amusement park built around the turn of the century and modeled on Coney Island in New York. In the sixties the University of California established a new campus in Santa Cruz, which quickly established itself as the most nontraditional campus within the nine-campus system (e.g., no grades for undergraduates). The general real-estate boom of the seventies lifted Santa Cruz from a backwater summer resort and retirement area to a plush seaside city with a village and bohemian atmosphere. The 1,500-square-foot, 30-year-old stucco bungalow built in the fifties and selling at $10,000–$15,000 now sells for over $100,000. It is an irony of the modern welfare state that low-income elderly possess such assets but do not capitalize on them due to the lack of reliable and trustworthy financial counselors and affordable housing alternatives. The growth of the city and county during the last decades has been such that the U.S. Census in the seventies conferred upon it the designation as a "Standard Metropolitan Statistical Area." Santa Cruz is no longer a nonmetropolitan (i.e., "rural") area.

In the south, three sites are in Los Angeles county and one in San Diego. Within the Los Angeles basin of 7 million people, two sites are within the city limits: West Los Angeles and East Los Angeles. While the historic dividing line between east and west was the Los Angeles River, today cultural and language differences are more effective in separating geographical territories. The East Los Angeles area of about 110,000 people is presently made up of mainly Hispanics of Mexican ancestry, while West Los Angeles, particularly the Beverly-Fairfax CSS sampling area, is mostly Jewish, with a recent influx of Russian and Eastern-European émigrés. Separating the two, near the downtown central Civic Center area, is a growing Japantown. To the immediate south are black areas such as Watts and Compton. These areas are outside our sampling sites.

The third site in Los Angeles county is Long Beach, about 15 miles south of the Civic Center. Economically, Long Beach is supported by an active port, electrical generating plants, a modest oil industry left over from the boom times, defense and high-technology industries, tourism, and a large service sector. A priority for the service sector is the large elderly population in Long Beach, most of whom are retirees from the Midwest. In fact, Long Beach is known as "Iowa-by-the-sea" or "Nebraska-by-the-sea," depending on the pundit's origin.

The fourth site in the south, San Diego, is also a retirement center, although now limited to the more-affluent elderly. San Diego is another city profoundly affected by World War II in that its growth can be traced to the establishment and expansion of naval bases around San Diego Bay. In addition to defense-related industries, San Diego has a large commercial fishing fleet and a growing high-technology sector. Throughout San Diego county, total population 1,862,000, are also located some excellent research and educational centers such as the University of California, San Diego, the Scripps Institute, and San Diego State University. Tourism, with the world-famous San Diego Zoo as a focal point, is another important economic activity. Since San Diego county borders on Mexico, a large subpopulation of illegal aliens lives in the area.

CSS ended in June 1983, and MSSP has since become a state-wide program of case-managed, community-based long-term care. The total sample size of CSS is 2,567, and the sample reported here was randomly drawn from the community setting and has a total of 528 respondents. We have described the CSS sampling methodology and survey operations elsewhere (Pelham and Clark, forthcoming).

The survey questionnaire used was an adaptation of the MSSP psychosocial and health assessment questionnaire and responses were self-reports. A respondent's racial self-identification was recorded according to standard U.S. Census categories. After the racial item, respondents were then asked if they were of Spanish origin, once again following U.S. Census protocol. Proxy interviews were allowed only for the "objective" data (e.g., demographic and functional status), not for the subjective data items (e.g., mental status). Bilingual interviewers were used for most non-English-speaking respondents, although some interviews were done through translators who were not full-time CSS staff.

Definitional and Cross-Cultural Considerations

For our purposes "low-income" means recipients of Supplemental Security Income/State Supplemental Payment (SSI/SSP) and Medicaid enrollees (Medi-Cal in California). When we use the term "dependency" it means that personal assistance is required to perform an activity. A person who uses some type of assistive device in carrying out the task but no personal assistance is coded as "independent." Data are from the first interviews, which occurred between August 1980 and March 1981.

We have chosen to group the widows according to the U.S. Census' racial categories and to separate out widows of Spanish origin, who may be of any racial category and whom we refer to as Hispanic. Since we sometimes make references to all widows in the sample, we employ the somewhat awkward term "racial/ethnic" groups. Also, we reserve the use of the term "minority" for those groups (i.e., blacks, Asians, and Hispanics) who have been subjected to differential and injurious treatment by the dominant culture. Within this framework we aggregate all white widows, irrespective of their ancestries.

While grouping widows in the four racial/ethnic subsamples of white, black, Hispanic, and Asian, we were aware that this approach has several limitations, particularly when exploring for differences between these principal groups. A major limitation is that such an aggregation is too gross and hides differences attributable to intraracial or intraethnic factors. For example, how reasonable is it to expect that a white Jewish émigré widow behaves like a white widow born and raised in California; or a Chinese widow like a Japanese widow; or a widow born in Mexico or in El Salvador like a Hispanic widow born in New Mexico; or a black widow raised in a rural Southern environment to be like her counterpart who has never left Oakland. Obviously, such cultural differences exist and may affect our results. In the face of what might become irreducible pluralities of incommensurable behaviors and overwhelmed by relativistic analytic paralysis, we chose to proceed with the four groupings. Our expectation is that by ordering our observations in this manner, some light can be shed on the conditions of different ethnic widows who, by anyone's definition, may be vulnerable to the potential multiple jeopardy of age, poverty, widowhood, womanhood, and, in some cases, being a minority person. Whatever cross-cultural insensitivities we have committed, our decision was guided by Sir Francis Bacon's observation that truth is more likely to emerge from error than it is from confusion. As the growing literature from our more qualitatively oriented colleagues in the fields of ethnography and anthropology contributes a better understanding of the intraracial/ethnic subtleties, we can apply these insights to our own, more quantitatively oriented, analyses. Our hope is that melding these two orientations will produce a better overall understanding of these women's situations.

Formal Services

Because expenditures for formal, publicly funded services are of such interest during these times of retrenchment, and because California is "atypical" of the other states in regard to its programs for the elderly, we feel that the topic merits some descriptive discussion.

Programs and Organization

In California, formal, publicly funded services for low-income elderly may be divided into three types: medical, income transfer, and social services. The organizational structure for determining eligibility for income-tested programs is through the local Social Security Administration (SSA) offices and the 58 local county welfare departments that administer social services as well as monitor eligibility status. In addition, many private nonprofit agencies provide a wide range of services (e.g., transportation and meals). Quasi-public local agencies provide housing assistance in the form of rental subsidies and the operation of housing complexes for all ages. Medical services are delivered by private or nonprofit providers, who are reimbursed on a fee-for-service basis according to rates and fees negotiated with public and private insurers.

The principal medical insurance plan for the low-income elderly, as it is for all elderly 65 years and older, is Medicare. In addition, specifically for low-income persons of any age, Medicaid (known as "Medi-Cal" in California) exists. Together, these two medical insurance programs, authorized by Titles XVIII (Medicare) and XIX (Medicaid) of the Social Security Act of 1965, cover most of the medical, nursing, rehabilitative, and pharmaceutical services used by the low-income elderly. For California's low-income elderly population as a whole, it is estimated that, for 1982, the average monthly cost of services provided through Medicare was $390 per person, and for those provided through Medicaid it was $135 per person (Miller et al., 1986).

The income-transfer program for the low-income elderly, as well as for the blind and disabled, is Supplemental Security Income/State Supplemental Payment (SSI/SSP). The SSI portion is the federal program authorized by Title XVI of the Social Security Act and is meant to provide a minimum income level. In July 1983 this federal minimum was $3,652 for individuals and $5,477 for a couple (Schulz, 1985). An individual receives SSI if his or her Old Age and Survivor Insurance (OASI) payment from Social Security does not reach the minimum level or if the individual does not qualify for any OASI payment at all. For the purposes of this exposition we do not consider the OASI payment itself as a "formal, publicly funded" service since it is totally funded by a tax that can only be used for that purpose.

States have the option to add to the federal minimum established through SSI by means of the State Supplemental Payment (SSP) program, which is funded entirely through state monies. California not only has this program but its SSP payment levels are the highest in the nation. For payments to individuals it is three times as high as the second-place state (New York) and five times as high for payments to an aged couple. Some of the most populous states (e.g., Texas, Illinois, Florida, and Ohio) do not have any SSP program (Legislative Analyst Office, 1984).

For individuals in the CSS sample, for 1982 the average monthly SSI payment was $61, and the SSP portion was $129.

In terms of social services in California, the single largest social service used by low-income elderly, as well as by the disabled, is In-Home Supportive Services (IHSS). IHSS is funded through the federal Social Services Block grant (previously known as Title XX) of the Social Security Act and, in California, is supplemented with state and local monies to a degree unparalleled by other states. All told, the $0.3 billion IHSS program is split 60–40 between the federal government and the State of California, with the federal share the larger. At the local level, IHSS is administered by the county welfare departments and makes up the largest social-services program that the county provides to low-income elderly. Approximately 66,000 low-income elderly (about 23 percent of California's low-income elderly population) receive about 66 hours a month of IHSS. The actual service consists mostly of household chores, shopping, meal preparation, and personal-care tasks such as dressing and grooming that are provided by "unskilled" labor paid a minimum wage (California, 1984b).

In addition to these three major programs, many others exist that are funded and administered through other agencies (e.g., Area Agencies on Aging and cities' departments of social services). In fact, the plethora of programs and services for the elderly, of all income brackets, has given rise to "Silver Pages" supplements to the "Yellow Pages," as well as to locally produced resource guides. See Estes (1979) and Rich and Baum (1984) for more detailed reviews and analyses of programs for the elderly.

Program Priorities and Funding Sources

One way to gauge program priorities is to examine expenditure levels. For the CSS sample as a whole, medically related expenses accounted for 60 percent of the respondents' average monthly public service costs (Medicare was 45 percent of the total, while Medicaid was 15 percent). In 1982 dollars, this amounted to $525 per month per respondent.

The next largest category was income transfer, which accounted for 22 percent of the public costs of CSS respondents. This was made up of SSI (7 percent of the total) and SSP (15 percent of the total), for a total average monthly per respondent expenditure of $190. We estimate that the average monthly OASI payment was $269 per person, or a total annual income of $5,508 ($3,228 from OASI; $1,548 from SSP; and, $732 from SSI)—$459 per month in 1982. This does not include an additional $20 per month as a general exclusion that a person may or may not have.

The third and final category was social services, which accounted for 19 percent of the public costs. About 77 percent of these costs are for IHSS. All told, 29 different services were used by the CSS respondents, attesting to the service diversity present in California.

In sum, most of the public funds for the low-income noninstitutionalized elderly are spent for medical services and the remainder divided about equally between income payments and in-kind services.

Given the different funding ratios of the various programs for the noninstitutionalized elderly, the federal government pays about 74 percent of all types of services, and the state of California pays the remaining 26 percent. The federal share goes mostly for medical services, 71 percent, through Medicare and Medicaid. California's portion is mainly aimed at income transfers through the SSP program, which makes up 56 percent of its part.

Overall, the composite picture of California is a service-rich environment with a concentration on medical services and a *relatively* liberal income-transfer policy. On the other hand, even though the state's SSP program's award levels are the highest in the country, the prospect of living on a total of $459 a month (1982) is not inviting. Finally, although California has a rich array of services for the noninstitutionalized, the state also spends about $1 billion a year for nursing-home care for approximately 75,000 Medicaid (Medi-Cal) elderly (Legislative Analyst Office, 1984).

Baseline Demographic and Functional Data of the CSS Respondents

As table 10.1 shows, the majority of black widows are in the San Francisco Bay area (San Francisco and Oakland), as are the Asian widows. Hispanic widows are mostly in East Los Angeles. The most ethnically diverse area is San Francisco, while Santa Cruz and Eureka, our two smallest areas, are the most ethnically homogeneous. This distribution is to be expected, given the demographics of the localities—e.g., East Los Angeles is 94 percent Hispanic, and Oakland is 47 percent black (Bureau of the Census, 1983b).

Table 10.2 presents baseline demographic and functional status data of the widows. Mean ages reveal that all groups are in the category of the old-old, the frail elderly, the over-seventy-five group. At average age seventy-eight, they are all about four years older than their average counterparts in the U.S. general elderly population (Bureau of the Census, 1983c). Also, table 10.2 shows striking similarities of mean age between groups (no statistically significant difference at the $p \leqslant .05$ level using a chi square test). This lends credence to the notion of a crossover in mortality rates and that, after a certain age, longevity is not significantly affected by race. For example, the crossover of black and white age-specific mortality rates in the United States appears by the age seventy-five (Manton et al., 1979). Whatever enables these elders to survive high infant-mortality rates of minority groups and pass through the rigors of childhood and adolescence seems to have guaranteed them a "normal" life span, if the white widow is taken as the norm.

Table 10.1 Distribution of Noninstitutionalized Widows Among Sampling Sites (in percentages; $N = 528$).

		Groups			
		White	Black	Hispanic	Asian[a]
Site		(N=331) 63%	(N=102) 19%	(N=49) 9%	(N=46) 9%
	N				
Oakland	125	30	57	5	7
Santa Cruz	13	92	0	8	0
East Los Angeles	38	39	0	55	6
West Los Angeles	136	93	2	4	1
Long Beach	63	92	5	3	0
San Francisco	96	33	22	12	33
San Diego	41	83	10	7	0
Eureka	16	100	0	0	0

[a] "Asian" includes Chinese and Japanese only.

Educational levels begin to bring out some of the differences in life choices that minority widows faced or that were made for them. The most pronounced difference is that while over half of white widows achieved an educational level of high school or beyond, over half of the Asian widows (Chinese and Japanese) had no formal schooling.

In terms of literacy, there is a consensus that a basic literacy standard consists of five years of schooling (Newton and Ruiz, 1981). Given this standard, we see that Hispanic widows, again separate from the whites per se, are barely literate, while Asian widows are illiterate. Standard deviations of these mean years of schooling indicate that blacks also fall inside the range of illiteracy. For widows who are foreign born, we can assume that they are illiterate both in their native language as well as in English.

Educational achievement levels may explain marked differences in mental status scores. The index used to calculate these levels is the Short Portable Mental Status Questionnaire (Pfeiffer, 1975), which is a ten-item list that measures intellectual impairment and is adjusted by educational level and race. Its developers created the racial adjustment based on samples of white and black elders in Durham County, North Carolina, and we suspect the adjustment is not sufficiently sensitive for Asian and/or illiterate groups. Our suspicions are based on reports from our Chinese and Japanese research assistants, who feel that over three-quarters of their Asian respondents had an "intact"

Table 10.2 Baseline Demographic and Functional Status Data of Noninstitutionalized CSS Widows ($N=528$).

	Groups			
	White	Black	Hispanic	Asian[a]
Item	($N=331$)	($N=102$)	($N=49$)	($N=46$)
Percentage distribution				
Race/Ethnicity	63	19	9	9
Age				
65–79	11	15	6	11
60–74	21	28	31	20
75–79	22	25	20	24
80–84	24	15	27	26
85–89	12	10	10	9
90+	10	7	6	11
(Mean age)	(78.8)	(77.5)	(78.3)	(78.9)
(*SD*)	(7.5)	(7.5)	(7.3)	(7.3)
Education level				
None	9	9	20	52
Grade school	38	56	57	37
High school	43	25	16	7
High school+	16	11	6	6
(Mean years)	(9.4)	(7.5)	(5.0)	(3.1)
(*SD*)	(3.5)	(4.1)	(4.6)	(4.1)
Mental status				
Intact	84	75	75	49
Mild	10	13	21	35
Moderate	4	10	6	14
Severe	2	2	0	2
Number of activities of daily living dependencies				
0 (Most independent)	72	62	74	78
1–2	25	30	16	20
3–4	2	5	4	0
5–6 (Most dependent)	1	3	6	2

Table 10.2 Continued.

	Groups			
	White	Black	Hispanic	Asian[a]
Item	(N=331)	(N=102)	(N=49)	(N=46)
Number of instrumental activities of daily living dependencies				
0 (Most independent)	30	23	18	22
1–2	24	25	18	13
3–4	23	19	25	28
5–6	16	19	25	20
7–8 (Most dependent)	7	14	14	17
Self-reported health status				
Good	39	52	37	41
Fair	44	32	42	54
Poor	17	16	20	5
Average number of chronic conditions	5.4	4.5	3.8	2.2

[a] "Asian" includes only Chinese and Japanese.

functional intellectual capability that is not reflected by this index. In other words, they knew what they had to know. The SPMSQ may be more sensitive at more severe levels of impairment, but it appears to be less useful, for some racial/ethnic groups or with illiterate groups, at the intact or mild ranges.

Results of the SPMSQ highlight a measurement problem that occurs throughout this chapter to one degree or another and for any cross-cultural research: "We may not be adequately sampling the culturally relevant skills. What we may be asking is the question: 'How well can *they* do *our* tricks?', whereas what we should be asking is, 'How well can *they* do *their* tricks?' " (Dasen, 1977).

Since our focus is on functional status, family structure and interaction, and use of services rather than on more abstract domains such as cognitive structures, we feel that although the items in the CSS questionnaire may be culturally "tricky," they do not confound our results, with the probable exception of the SPMSQ.

Our functional data show more similarities than differences. The Activities of Daily Living (ADL) Index (Katz, 1963) are six personal-care tasks such as bathing and eating. As with most elders in general (Shanas, 1979), the majority of all widows report no dependencies in these six areas. The majority of widows do need, however, some personal assistance in carrying out the eight tasks in the Instrumental Activities of Daily Living (IADL) Index (Lawton and Brody, 1969). These instrumental tasks include such items as shopping, travel, and meal preparation. This overall level of dependency is a marked contrast to widows in general (Lopata, 1973; Shanas, 1979).

What is consistent with other survey research findings is that, in general, the elderly tend to be relatively much more independent in the activities of daily living tasks than in the instrumental activities of daily living tasks (Comptroller General of the United States, 1977).

Regarding possible confounding variables in our own analyses, both indices, ADL and IADL, are performance oriented (e.g., "Do you . . . ,") and the degrees to which independence or dependence in roles such as shopping is culturally determined are not known. For example, one respondent's daughter told the interviewer, "No la dejo a mi mama salir sola, las calles son muy peligrosas." ("I don't let my mother go out alone, the streets are very dangerous.") To what degree this sentiment and similar feelings that tend to foster dependency—even if appropriate—are idiosyncratic to particular groups is an empirical question that presently must go unanswered due to our measurement limitations.

Family Structure and Family Interaction

Table 10.3 illustrates the situation where the majority of white and black widows live alone, whereas Hispanic and Asian widows live with others. All groups of widows who do live alone, however, have children living close by, and the majority of all groups have three generations or more in their families.

Besides differences in living arrangements between groups, another difference appears to be in household size and in the number of living children. Hispanic widows have both the largest household size and number of offspring, while white widows have the smallest household size and number of offspring. For those who have living children, we see that their children maintain frequent contact (a "contact" can be face-to-face, telephone call, or letter).

Table 10.3 Family Structure and Family Interaction of CSS Noninstitutionalized Widows.

	Groups			
	White	Black	Hispanic	Asian[a]
Item	($N=331$)	($N=102$)	($N=49$)	($N=46$)
Percentage distribution				
Others at residence				
Alone	76	68	48	48
With others	24	32	57	52
Number of generations in family				
Kinless	5	10	0	0
One	4	21	3	2
Two	16	15	9	3
Three or more	75	54	99	95
Living siblings				
Yes	79	58	88	98
No	21	42	12	2
Living children				
Yes	79	58	88	98
No	21	42	12	2
Living grandchildren				
Yes	75	54	88	95
No	25	46	12	5
Frequency of contact by children if there are children				
Today/yesterday	56	75	86	62
Within week	28	11	17	33
Within month	7	11	2	2
More than month	9	3	0	2

Table 10.3 Continued.

	Groups			
	White	Black	Hispanic	Asian[a]
Item	($N=331$)	($N=102$)	($N=49$)	($N=46$)
Have children within one hour if living alone				
Yes	80	75	79	78
No	20	25	21	22
Mean number in household if not living alone				
Mean number	1.5	1.8	3.6	2.0
(*SD*)	(.934)	(1.203)	(1.532)	(1.138)
Mean number of living children				
Mean number	2.5	2.8	4.3	3.1
(*SD*)	(1.765)	(2.242)	(2.517)	(1.740)

[a] "Asian" includes Chinese and Japanese only.

In an attempt to achieve a better understanding of the relationship between frequency of contact and racial/ethnic groups, we carried out a series of regression analyses. First, we constructed a model with only the minority groups as the independent variables and frequency of contact as the dependent variables to establish what the frequency of contact is in relation to white widows. We found that this equation explained 3 percent of the variance that both blacks and Hispanics were significant at the $p \leq 0.10$ level. From this we conclude that some minorities (i.e., blacks and Hispanics) tend to keep in more frequent contact with their parent(s) than do whites but that there is no statistically significant difference between Asians and whites.

We then constructed a more complex model to tease out the relationship between ethnicity and frequency of contact. This model included 11 dependent variables that explained 18.6 percent of the variance. Results are shown in table 10.4. The only variables significant at the $p \leq 0.10$ level were the number of instrumental activities of daily living dependencies (positive correlation), the number of children (positive correlation), and living alone (negative correlation). For this equation, the racial/ethnic groupings did not prove to be significant at the $p \leqslant 0.10$ level. For this we conclude that contact with children is a function of having children and living with others (including children) and need as measured by the number of dependencies in instrumental tasks, all irrespective of racial/ethnic groupings.

Support: Formal and Informal

The CSS questionnaire contains a section dealing with 20 areas of possible support. These areas range from such personal-care tasks as bathing and toileting to such instrumental tasks as laundry and shopping. Respondents were asked about each of these areas and research assistants coded the responses in one of five ways:

1. Respondent says does not need support;
2. Respondent says does not need and has informal support;
3. Respondent says does need and support provided by other than informal support system;
4. Respondent says does not have support and needs support; or,
5. Not applicable.

No combination of responses was permitted and, when faced with a combination response, the CSS research assistants were instructed to probe and code the *primary* source of support. Table 10.5 shows results of those who responded that support was needed and how it was distributed between formal and informal support systems.

Although not shown in table 10.5, it should be kept in mind that the only area that the majority of all groups received assistance from either the informal or formal systems combined was shopping. Other areas where a majority of at least one group received assistance were: home repair (white and Hispanic only); housework (Hispanic only); accompanying (Hispanic only); and, travel (Asian only).

In regard to unmet need, again not shown in table 10.5, the highest response was for white widows in the area of home repair (5 percent reported an unmet need). Home repair was followed by 4 percent of white widows reporting an unmet need in the area of housework, and 4 percent of black widows reporting an unmet need in home repair. Hispanic widows reported only two areas of unmet need: housework (2 percent) and laundry (less than 1 percent). Asian widows did not

Table 10.4 Regression Results with Frequency of Contact by Children as the Dependent Variable.

Variable[a]	Estimate	t value
Intercept	3.035	12.06
Number of IADL dependencies	0.071	3.60
Number of children	0.092	4.68
Living alone	−0.392	−4.24
$R^2 = 0.186$		

[a] Other independent variables in the equation but that did not prove to be significant at the $p \leq 0.10$ level were race, age group, siblings, grandchildren, and number of activities of daily living dependencies.

report a single area of unmet need. This latter finding may be attributable to a culturally derived reticence about admitting to unmet needs. On the other hand, given the Asian widows' living arrangements and household sizes, this finding is not totally unreasonable.

Results shown in table 10.5 reinforce the pattern, well-known among gerontologists and students of the elderly, of reliance on the informal support system rather than on the formal support system. Although the numbers are too small in the "personal care" activities to allow generalizations, the relatively larger numbers in the "instrumental care" activities permit us to see this pattern more clearly. White and black widows tend to receive more help from the formal system and Asian widows the least. Conversely, Hispanic widows received the most from the informal system (mean numbers of areas was 4.8) and white widows received the least (mean number of areas was 2.4).

To understand more about the informal support system and investigate the relationships between racial/ethnic groups and support provided, we carried out two regressions. The first equation included only the minority groups that showed the three groupings to be significant at the $p \leq 0.05$ level and that explained 4.7 percent of the variance. This result lends credence to the belief that minorities have a "stronger" informal support system than do whites. On the other hand, keeping in mind that white widows do receive an average of 2.4 supports, we cannot conclude that the white informal support system is "weak."

To explain more fully the relationship between racial/ethnic groupings and the informal support system, we constructed a regression equation that included 11 independent variables and that explained

Table 10.5 Proportion of Assistance Received from Either the Informal or Formal Support Systems.

Assistance area	White Informal/Formal		Black Informal/Form	
Personal care				
Eating				
%	58	42	100	0
(*N*)	(7)	(5)	(4)	(0)
Bathing				
%	50	50	68	32
(*N*)	(18)	(18)	(13)	(6
Transfer[b]				
%	80	20	100	0
(*N*)	(8)	(2)	(3)	(0
Walking				
%	54	46	85	15
(*N*)	(12)	(10)	(6)	(1
Wheelchair use				
%	40	60	100	0
(*N*)	(4)	(6)	(2)	(0
Toileting				
%	85	15	80	20
(*N*)	(6)	(1)	(4)	(1
Dressing				
%	58	42	100	0
(*N*)	(10)	(7)	(10)	(0
Medications				
%	80	20	92	8
(*N*)	(12)	(3)	(13)	(1
Instrumental care				
Laundry				
%	50	50	50	41
(*N*)	(61)	(59)	(29)	(2
Telephoning				
%	82	18	78	2
(*N*)	(14)	(3)	(11)	(
Money management				
%	92	8	92	8
(*N*)	(59)	(5)	(25)	(

Hispanic Informal/Formal		Asian[a] Informal/Formal	
66	34	100	0
(2)	(1)	(1)	(0)
100	0	83	27
(5)	(0)	(5)	(1)
66	34	100	0
(2)	(1)	(2)	(0)
100	0	100	0
(6)	(0)	(1)	(0)
100	0	100	0
(1)	(0)	(1)	(0)
100	0	100	0
(4)	(0)	(1)	(1)
83	17	50	50
(5)	(1)	(1)	(1)
50	50	83	17
(2)	(2)	(5)	(1)
80	20	79	21
(20)	(5)	(19)	(5)
100	0	100	0
(12)	(0)	(13)	(0)
94	6	100	0
(17)	(1)	(20)	(0)

Table 10.5 Continued.

Assistance area	White Informal/Formal		Black Informal/Fo
Travel			
%	77	23	85
(*N*)	(104)	(31)	(42)
Shopping			
%	76	24	73
(*N*)	(138)	(42)	(45)
Housework			
%	40	60	51
(*N*)	(51)	(75)	(24)
Meal preparation			
%	53	47	53
(*N*)	(31)	(27)	(17)
Outside mobility			
%	77	23	85
Stair climbing			
%	60	40	100
(*N*)	(12)	(8)	(5)
Social network[c]			
%	88	12	93
(*N*)	(66)	(9)	(27)
Accompanying[c]			
%	76	24	80
(*N*)	(69)	(21)	(25)
Home repair			
%	34	66	33
(*N*)	(64)	(123)	(12)

[a] "Asian" includes only Chinese and Japanese.

[b] "Transfer" means receiving personal assistance getting out of bed into a chair and vice v

[c] The difference between "Social network" and "Accompanying" is that "Social netwo

65 percent of the variance. These results are shown in table 10.6. In this more-complete equation, we see that the only minority group to be significant in contrast to the white widows is Hispanic widows. The other significant variables are all related to some indication of need and living with others. From these results we conclude that support provided by the informal system is mostly a function of need and having children to supply that support. As in frequency of contact by

Hispanic Informal	Hispanic Formal	Asian[a] Informal	Asian[a] Formal
95	5	100	0
(21)	(1)	(24)	(0)
84	16	83	17
(28)	(5)	(26)	(5)
72	28	76	24
(18)	(7)	(16)	(5)
68	32	83	17
(11)	(5)	(15)	(3)
77	23	100	0
87	13	75	25
(7)	(1)	(3)	(1)
91	9	100	0
(22)	(2)	(14)	(0)
86	14	100	0
(26)	(4)	(16)	(0)
45	55	88	12
(16)	(19)	(8)	(1)

ed to visiting friends and neighbors for social purposes and "Accompanying" is limited to ng public agencies such as the Social Security Administration.

children, Hispanic widows seem to have the "strongest," or at least the most active, support system in contrast to white widows.

Interestingly, these findings are similar to those found in a Massachusetts state-wide sample of predominantly white females with mixed income levels (Branch and Jette, 1983) as well as those found in a sample from a nonmetropolitan area in northeastern New York (Stoller and Earl, 1983). Our findings here are also consistent with Cantor's

Table 10.6 Regression Results with Number of Areas of Support Provided by the Informal Support Systems as the Dependent Variable.

Variable[a]	Estimate	t value
Intercept	0.869	1.69
Hispanic	0.222	1.98
Age group	0.325	8.66
Number of ADL dependencies	1.061	13.13
Number of children	0.211	3.72
Living alone	−1.560	−5.8
$R^2 = 0.659$		

[a] Other independent variables included but which did not prove to be significant at the $p. < 0.10$ level were black, Asian, siblings, grandchildren, and the number of formal services received.

New York inner-city sample of elderly (1979). What is particularly striking between her analysis and our own is that our sample was drawn approximately 10 years after hers, and the patterns still remain the same as on the other side of the country.

The CSS questionnaire contained a separate subsection that listed 37 individual services provided through publicly funded social and medical agencies. Research assistants went through each service and asked if the respondent had received the service within the last month. Over half of all racial/ethnic groupings reported no services received within the last month; and black widows reported the most received, with an average of 1.04 services, while Asian widows reported the least, with an average of 0.17 services.

To explore more thoroughly the relationship between racial/ethnic groupings and utilization of formal services, we carried out two regression analyses. The first equation had the number of formal services as the dependent variable and only the minority racial/ethnic groupings as independent variables. We found that, in contrast to the white widows, black widows were predicted to receive more services, while Asian and Hispanic widows were predicted to receive less than the white widows (all were significant at the $p \leqslant 0.10$ level). Overall, this equation explained 3.9 percent of the variance.

The second equation had 11 independent variables and explained 18.8 percent of the variance. Results are shown in table 10.7, which reveals a more complex set of relationships. First, we see that black widows are predicted to receive more formal services than white widows, while Asian widows are predicted to receive less than their

Table 10.7 Regression Results with Number of Formal Services Received in Last Month as the Dependent Variable.

Variable[a]	Estimate	t value
Intercept	0.261	
Black	0.378	2.56
Asian	−0.242	−2.89
Number of ADL dependencies	0.187	3.16
Living alone	0.176	5.81
Number of informal support areas provided	−0.101	−4.66
$R^2 = 0.18$		

[a] Other independent variables entered but which did not prove to be significant at the $p. < .10$ level were Hispanic, age group, siblings, grandchildren, and number of children.

white counterparts, and no statistically significant difference is expected between Hispanic and white widows.

One possible explanation for Asian widows receiving fewer formal services than white widows is that agencies providing services have instituted some sort of administrative barrier to access by Asian widows. We do not believe this to be true. As we showed in table 10.1 most Asian widows, as well as black widows, are from the San Francisco Bay area. It is through the county departments of social services that the most-frequently used service, In-Home Support Service, is provided, and both county departments have a large number of minorities as staff who determine eligibility and award services. In addition, as we stated above, Asian widows reported no unmet needs. Two of the significant variables in table 10.7 relate to need, indicating that the public welfare system, at least in this stance, responds to need. The other significant variable in table 10.7, the number of areas of support provided by the informal system, also indicates that the welfare system shies away from potential clients who have an active informal support system. In sum, that Asian widows receive fewer formal services than do white widows appears to be more a matter of need than a case of overt or covert discrimination. It remains to be seen what fate would meet Asian widows if their informal support systems should disappear. Whether they would suffer in silence or seek public assistance is an empirical question.

Discussion

The topic of ethnicity and the elderly has its fair share of myths, or more formally, of contending hypotheses. Our results will support some of these hypotheses while testing the validity of others. We summarize and discuss our findings below.

Racial Crossover in Life Expectancy

Our data show the racial crossover in life expectancy to be valid. It appears to hold true for Asian and Hispanic women as well as for black women. Up to now this notion was presumed valid only for whites and blacks. Apparently, it is more generalizable.

Functional Independence

We found that among our very-aged sample the majority of widows were taking care of themselves in the areas of personal care (activities of daily living) but that the majority needed personal assistance in at least three areas of instrumental care. This division among areas of need is consistent with other survey research (Branch and Jette, 1983; Stoller and Earl, 1983; Cantor, 1979; Shanas, 1979; and, Comptroller General of the United States, 1977).

Reliance on the Informal Support System

When the widows needed some personal assistance, we saw that they relied on the informal support system for assistance rather than on the publicly funded formal support system. This also is consistent with the other survey research already cited.

Strength of the Informal Support Systems

Our findings in tables 10.3, 10.4, 10.5, and 10.6 point out a fact that is sometimes lost in debates about elderly white and non-white widows; that is, *all* have active informal support systems and that their children keep in frequent contact. These findings lead us to believe that discussions about the differences between white and non-white elderly and the support they receive are discussions about *marginal* differences. Support seems to be more a function of need and the number of children to supply it than it does to be a function of culturally derived behaviors. Given that our findings are consistent with those based on samples as diverse as nonmetropolitan upstate New York, New York City, and the state of Massachusetts, we conclude that ethnicity is not *the* decisive factor in predicting informal support to the elderly. Holzberg's (1982) statement (made after reviewing the gerontological literature on the minority elderly) that, ". . . the extent to which culture-ethnicity has been treated as an independent variable has been uneventful," overstates the case but not by much.

Utilization of Formal Services

We found that black widows used more publicly funded services than did the whites, Hispanics, or Asians. This is in contrast to Jackson's statement (1980) that ". . . the minority aged are usually excluded from or poorly served by most social programs." We believe, rather, that a reasonable interpretation of this finding is that these widows live in service environments that allow for the exercise of personal preferences and that are positively responsive to their needs to some degree. In service environments less responsive, unmet needs for formal services could increase dramatically.

When a formal service was used by a widow, the most frequently used services during the previous month of the interview were In-Home Supportive Services (19 percent of the sample) and Medicaid-funded medical services (17 percent of the sample). No other services were reported being used by more than 3 percent of the sample.

In-Home Supportive Services (IHSS), funded through Title XX (Social Services Block Grant) of the Social Security Act, provides a variety of personal care and housekeeping tasks that include laundry, light housekeeping, heavy housekeeping, shopping, and bathing. IHSS is presently the largest single social-service program in California and was funded during Fiscal Year 1983–84 at $0.297 billion with 100,770 recipients (Legislative Analyst Office, 1984). This represents an annual cost per recipient of approximately $2,900, and the recipient population aged 65 years and older represents about 17 percent of the total California SSI/SSP population.

When one considers that the single largest publicly funded social program is reaching only approximately 17 percent of the poor elderly at a cost of almost a third of a billion dollars, and that the informal support system is providing similar kind of care to at least half of the poor elderly widows at no public cost, one begins to realize how valuable is the informal support system.

Multiple Jeopardy Versus Age-As-Leveler

What about the multiple-jeopardy hypothesis—the additive effects of being old and in a racial/ethnic minority—mentioned at the beginning of this chapter and fully described elsewhere (Dowd and Bengston, 1978)? Our experience with this concept of double, triple, or multiple jeopardy is a lot like our experience with the concepts of romantic love, pornography, or good and evil. It depends upon a context, under what conditions, and a multitude of intervening variables. Toward the end of specifying variables relevant to the multiple-jeopardy hypothesis, a recent review and critique of the concept concluded that the whole notion of double jeopardy was of little analytic value (Coons, 1983).

We found, in our own case, mixed evidence of this phenomenon. Since all our respondents are poor, we do not believe that socioeconomic status confounds our results. On the other hand, since our sample is so aged, the hypothesis of age-as-leveler may be operating ad extremum (Kent, 1971).

Regarding educational achievement, our white widows progressed to high school or beyond, while the minority widows achieved significantly lower levels. In fact, from the level of schooling achieved, we can conclude that the ethnic minority widows are either functionally illiterate or simply illiterate. Clearly, in this case, ethnicity is associated with the jeopardy of a lack of formal schooling. Interestingly, if educational achievement is related to increased income and knowledge and skills, it did not protect the white widow from a fate of poverty.

Regarding health and functional status, our widows score relatively equally—regardless of ethnic group. Again, the two possible areas of imprecision in measuring independence/dependence involve a cultural reluctance to self-report need or a cultural role that fosters dependence.

Concerning living arrangements, the potential jeopardy of living alone is suffered most by white widows and then by blacks. The majority of Hispanic and Asian widows live with others.

Regarding family structure and interaction, most widows—regardless of ethnic group—are part of families with three or more generations. All have children who live within a one-hour drive, and over 80 percent of all widows have been in contact with at least one child within the week. As children are the primary providers of informal support, white widows appear to be at greatest risk of unmet needs due to their smallest household size and number of offspring. On the other hand, a plurality of black widows report not having any living children. This may reflect the high rate of black infant mortality of 60 years ago and that continues to be almost twice as high as the white infant mortality rate (U.S. Department of Health and Human Services, 1983).

Regarding potential institutional discrimination, we find that black widows are predicted to receive the greatest number of publicly funded formal services, followed by whites, Hispanics, and Asians. If services are indeed responding to need, then black and white widows are the most needy. Given the relatively larger household sizes and greater number of children of the Hispanic and Asian widows, their informal systems appear to be willing and able to meet the needs of the widows.

The one dimension where there does seem to be some evidence supporting the double-jeopardy hypothesis—income levels—is not applicable to our sample since all our widows are poor and connected with the welfare system.

Overall, we are left with the muddled concept of multiple jeopardy and our mixed findings. Basically, our belief is that the notion has very limited analytic applications and we suspect that "the immensity of the problems in old age pale the issues of racial differentiation" (Coon, 1983).

Social Policy Implications

What relevance do our findings have for social policy? First, given that the majority of non-English-speaking widows are illiterate in both their own language and in English, translators should be available where social and health services are provided. Translated written materials will not be effective for these groups.

Second, the Instrumental Activities of Daily Living measures those areas where the elderly widows need the most personal assistance. From what we have seen, those widows who do need assistance receive it from the informal support system. Accordingly, those widows in need and without children should receive priority attention from the publicly funded service agencies.

Third, in regard to the debate about how best to adapt social services so that they are culturally appropriate and accessible, we believe that this debate misses the point. The "point" we have observed is that all of these widows are poor. Elsewhere, minority groups have separately reported that their major concern is financial (Asociacion Nacional Pro Personas Mayores, 1981). What kind of life can one lead when one's monthly income is $460? And this is in a state with the highest cash-assistance levels to low-income elderly! Decision makers, instead of arguing, for example, of how best to deliver ethnic meals in a particular catchment area, would be better addressing the needs of *all* groups by simply increasing the federal Supplementary Security Income levels and/or advocating for the institution of a State Supplementary Payment program in those states that do not have it. Cash is certainly the most culturally neutral policy instrument available.

Finally, we cannot close this section on social policy without expressing a vague sense of something missing in the lives of our widows. The research assistants carrying out the interviews have told us that the widows' participation in a larger social context is very limited. Our data indicate that less than 1 percent regularly visit a senior center. The widow's social world tends to have its perimeter boundaries marked by family care-givers. There is a conspicuous absence of the helping professions from the publicly funded formal support systems. This pattern in also reported elsewhere (Lopata, 1973).

Our own observations have shown that perimeter boundaries of the social world of widows are perhaps most permeable to telecommunications contact and engagement. CSS interviewers reported that otherwise-isolated frail elders are oftentimes linked, engaged—indeed participate—in the larger society by way of television, radio, telephone, and electronic applications.

For example, there is an infrared wireless system, sennhiser, that amplifies sound. Individuals may purchase electronic miniamplifiers with speakers, headphones, and microphones for home use or at public gatherings. There are frequency-modulated systems for listening with a transmitter box that is placed directly in the ear. Available from vendors and the telephone company are amplifier headsets and handheld portable types that run on batteries and couple to any phone. Additionally, the telephone company offers "Life Line," a program of low-cost local service to low-income elders who qualify with the public utilities commission.

Public libraries now offer record-player talking books with directions in braille. Individuals may purchase talking clocks, caption television, TTD (telecommunications for the deaf), and the TTY (telecommunications teletype). Although the latter two systems are of limited use in California, they are growing.

In the realm of television broadcasting, the Public Broadcasting Service's station in San Francisco produced and aired "Over Easy," a series of programs directed at the joys and challenges of aging, a potpourri of information and entertainment with a local emphasis. No doubt every major city in the country has similar efforts underway. Such electronic strategies for engaging the elderly, particularly the frail, aged elderly, may be more effective than a "bricks and mortar" senior center approach.

Directions for Future Research

Doubtless, future research will be carried out regarding ethnicity and the informal support systems of the elderly. However, if we were controlling the last remaining dollars to be invested in social science research about the elderly, we would invest them in a study where female gender was the dependent variable. Aging in the United States, at least, has evolved into a predominantly female experience. The social world of the aged is a world of women, and the more advanced the age and frailty, the more monosexual: from informal support providers (e.g., daughters, granddaughters, wives, and daughters-in-law) to formal care-givers (e.g., nurses, IHSS choreworkers, social workers, and activity directors).

What might be the possible future of our human group where legions of our elders are surviving to a very advanced age? Where these legions are primarily female? Where, at least until now—and if current patterns continue—care is provided by the informal support system, which is itself vastly overrepresented by women?

We urge that directions for future research into human aging be focused squarely upon the changing characteristics of women.

For example, when one considers the astronomical value of informal support—both apparent and latent functions—its potential absence is almost mind-boggling. What are the real current and future costs of informal support paid by women? Regardless if the motivation for care is duty, love, or self-interest, dollar costs are identical and getting higher. For example, for the high-powered woman financial planner with an office to manage and clients all over the country, taking half a day off work to assist with an aged mother's domestic chores is a very costly service indeed. For the female education consultant, an hour spent shopping for mother's groceries is an hour's worth of fees lost. A more likely scenario has the working woman adding on care chores to an existing work schedule. (Here she soon finds herself working sixteen- to eighteen-hour days. She also may find herself consuming health care dollars with ulcers—the latent costs of informal support.)

Another possible future for women, given current patterns, is freedom dependent on social class. The before-mentioned busy financial planner and professional consultant may find it more cost effective to purchase a care-giver rather than lose work time and money. Whom will they then hire? Who and what social stratum has historically done domestic work for the more affluent? One can almost envision a déjà vu picture of a futuristic Third World "mammy" caring for children or elders while her own needs and needy go unattended. As ethnicity and social class are related, freedom of future high-income white women may be bought at the price of freedom for low-income ethnic minority women.

We believe that the future of our society will be profoundly affected by the numbers and needs of the aged. Further, the nature of aging is intimately linked to the nature of the female experience—both structurally and interactionally. Future research would do well to direct an inquiry into the changing status, roles, values, and biology of women. This would include their worlds of work, family structures, and functions, including women's impact and the effects of U.S. politics, social policy, and economics. And finally, and perhaps most important, future research should focus on the reflexive social constructions and constrictions of being both female and aged.

Part III
The Big Picture

11 Support Systems of Widows in Canada

ANNE MARTIN MATTHEWS

Introduction

Patterns of widowhood in Canada have been characterized by both stability and profound change in recent years.[1] In 1981 there were 1,157,670 widowed persons in Canada, representing 6 percent of the population aged 15 and over, a proportion that has remained the same for the entire twentieth century. There has also been relatively little alteration in the long-term sex-specific nature of widowhood in Canada. At the time of the 1981 census only 2 percent of males aged 15 and over were widowed, while 10 percent of women were (Statistics Canada, 1982).

There have, however, been dramatic changes in the median age of the widowed, as well as other features of this status, such as its duration, and age of onset. Table 11.1 provides data from the 1981 census that indicate the age-related nature of the experience of widowhood in Canada; it increases from 2 percent of women in the age group 40–44 to 32 percent of women aged 65–69, and 70 percent of women aged 80–84.

Overall, two factors primarily characterize the incidence of widowhood in the Canadian population: its sex-selective and age-related nature. Eighty-two percent of the widowed are women, and their proportion is increasing. For all ages, widows outnumbered widowers by nearly four to one in Canada in 1971; by 1981 the proportion had

Table 11.1 Widowed Population 15 Years and Over, by Sex and Age Cohorts, Canada 1981.

	Widowers		Widows	
	N	Percentage of age cohort*	*N*	Percentage of age cohort*
Total, 15+ years	199,530	2.2	958,135	9.9
15–19	320	0.03	600	0.05
20–24	430	0.04	1,350	0.1
25–29	640	0.06	3,225	0.3
30–34	1,215	0.1	5,865	0.6
35–39	1,830	0.2	9,200	1.1
40–44	2,905	0.4	14,580	2.2
45–49	5,280	0.8	25,460	4.1
50–54	9,820	1.6	47,155	7.6
55–59	14,885	2.6	79,500	13.0
60–64	19,395	4.2	109,005	21.1
65–69	26,180	6.7	142,985	31.5
70–74	30,395	10.8	155,290	44.1
75–79	31,285	17.3	145,050	57.5
80–84	26,265	27.7	113,600	70.2
85–89	17,815	40.5	68,675	79.0
90+	10,880	55.5	36,610	84.7

Source: 1981 Census of Canada, Catalogue 92-901, September 1982, table 4: Population by selected age groups and sex, showing marital status.
*Percentages are my own calculation.

increased to almost five to one (Statistics Canada, 1982). In recent decades the average age at widowhood has steadily increased, with the proportion of the widowed in each age cohort increasing dramatically from age 50 onward. As a result, widowhood in Canada, as in the United States, is associated not only with women but now also with the elderly. In addition, the years that a widow can expect to live have also increased. Women widowed at age 65 can expect on average, almost nineteen more years of life; those widowed at age 80 can expect an average of nearly nine more years (Statistics Canada, 1984).

In this chapter, we will examine various features of Canadian society that relate to the experience of widowhood for women. We will then examine selected characteristics of the support systems of Canadian widows.

The Country

Canada is a vast land of almost four million square miles, the largest country in the Western Hemisphere and the second largest in the world. About 58 percent of the population of 25 million (Statistics Canada, 1982) hugs the border with the United States in a narrow band across the entire country. Because of this, many Canadians are within easier reach of Americans than they are of Canadians in other regions of the country.

Twenty years ago, in a paper seeking to specify and analyze the similarities and differences between Canada and the United States, S. M. Lipset wrote that "although these two peoples probably resemble each other more than any other two nations on earth, there are consistent patterns of divergences between them" (1965:21). In particular, Lipset postulated that Canada has been a more conservative, traditional, law-abiding, statist, and elitist society than the United States. The ensuing years have witnessed considerable debate on this point, with some sociologists, Lipset among them, "who emphasize the distinctiveness of the *values* of the two countries, and the ways in which these in turn affect behavior, beliefs, and institutional arrangements, and those who place primary importance on various *structural* differences, particularly geographic, economic and political factors" (Lipset, 1985:116). In a current re-examination of both structural and cultural factors that account for variations between the two countries, Lipset concludes that "Canada and the United States continue to differ considerably along most of the dimensions suggested in my previous work" (1985: 156). Let us briefly examine a few of these differences as they relate broadly to the social context within which women experience widowhood.

Perhaps the most readily apparent distinguishing factor lies in Canada's bilingual and multicultural character. "The relationship between different language groups in Canada—English, French, and other minority language groups—has long been one of the central issues in the evolution of Canadian society" (Lindsay, 1980:4). However, while English and French remain the two dominant linguistic and cultural groups, the proportion of Canadians reporting English as their mother tongue is increasing (by 11 percent between 1941 and 1976) and the percentage reporting French mother tongue is declining (by 12 percent in the same period). Nearly two-thirds of Canadians (63 percent) have English as their mother tongue, but there is extensive variation among the 10 Canadian provinces in the distribution of population by mother tongue. For example, among the two most populous Canadian provinces, 82 percent of the population of Quebec is francophone, while 80 percent of Ontario residents state English as their mother tongue (Lindsay, 1980:12).

Canada is also a country of regions "distinguished by geographical setting, economic role, history, culture, and even different ambitions for the same Canada to which they all belong" (Bercuson, 1977:1). The experience of regionalism is distinctive not only in Canadian history, however; it remains today to the extent that "region of residence and factors related to regional identity, regional satisfaction and regional commitment are capable of independently explaining variance in a whole array of attitudes and values" (Matthews and Davis, 1986:351).

Canada and the United States also differ along several fundamental dimensions of population. Despite the perception that the United States is a nation of immigrants, census data show that Canada has a larger proportion of foreign-born: 15 percent compared to 5 percent in the United States. Marriage rates are, however, slightly higher in the United States than in Canada—eight per 1,000 for Canada versus 10 per 1,000 in the United States (Michalos and Fortey, 1980:295), attributable in part to higher remarriage rates following divorce in the United States. Although the Canadian divorce rate has nearly doubled since laws were relaxed in 1968, the current rate of 1,125 per 100,000 married women aged 15 years and over (Statistics Canada, 1985:10) still remains about half the American rate. However, figures derived from recent divorce trends in Canada project that nearly one-quarter of persons marrying between the ages of 15 and 25 (and born between 1946 and 1956) may be expected to obtain a divorce by the time they reach 75.

Canada's population is also generally younger: the median age is 27.8 years compared to 29 years for Americans. Two factors appear to affect this: a higher Canadian birthrate since the early 1950s, and Canada's greater proportion of immigrants, who are generally younger than the total population and who tend to deflate the median age (Michalos and Fortey, 1980:295). Since life expectancy for females is now higher than that for males in both countries, and because the American population is older, it follows that there are proportionally more widows in the United States than in Canada.

Another relevant comparison between Canada and the United States relates to the cost of health care, an issue with direct implications for the experience of widowhood. In 1975, total expenditures on health care in Canada were $520 per person compared to $620 in the United States. In Canada, governments pay approximately 75 percent of total health care expenditures with private outlays accounting for the remainder. In the United States, governments pay 43 percent of the total while the private sector pays the remaining 57 percent (Michalos and Fortey 1980:296). There is no doubt that the Health Insurance Programs in Canada take an enormous psychological burden off sick people and their families.

Issues related to employment and income are also relevant to this cross-national comparison. Labor force participation rates for men are approximately 77 percent in both countries. While the participation rate for women has been typically higher in the United States, Canada's rate had increased to 53 percent by 1983 (Statistics Canada, 1985:48). Median family incomes for both countries showed a drastic change in recent years—increasing by 55 percent from 1965 to 1976 in Canada, but only by 19 percent in the United States during the same period. A comparison of the tax systems between the two countries shows that the total tax burden (expressed as a percentage of Gross National Product) is somewhat higher in Canada than in the United States. However, total personal taxes as a percentage of personal income are nearly equal in the two countries. Additional indicators of living standards show that Americans consume more than do Canadians. In the United States people have more cars, more television sets, and more telephones per 1,000 persons, and their consumption of energy per person is higher than for Canadians (Michalos and Fortey, 1980:297).

Women in the Country

In this brief description of factors influencing women's experiences of life in Canada, issues of educational, legal, and socioeconomic status, and patterns of marriage and mate selection, divorce, and widowhood will be addressed.

Educational Status

Woman's educational status in Canada remains somewhat lower than that of men, although gains have been made in recent years. Among women age 15 and older in 1983, one-fifth had completed less than grade 9; over one half (52%) had completed or attended high school;

and, of the remainder, one-fifth had a postsecondary certificate or diploma or university degree (Statistics Canada, 1985:36). Indeed, one of the major developments in Canadian education since the early 1970s has been the increase in the number of women attending university: the total enrollment of women more than doubled to over 350,000 between 1970–71 and 1982–83. These figures are for all women aged 15 and over. When one looks to the current cohort of middle-aged and older women, those most likely to experience widowhood in the next few decades, it is apparent that their levels of educational attainment fall far short of those identified above. The implications of this will become particularly apparent in later discussions of the financial and employment opportunities available to older women.

Legal Status

The legal status of Canadian women is currently being affected by the introduction of several provisions contained in the Canadian Charter of Rights and Freedoms, with provisions related to equality coming into effect in April 1985. Under these new provisions, "every individual is equal before and under the law and has the right to the equal protection and equal benefit of the law without discrimination and, in particular, without discrimination based on race, national or ethnic origin, colour, religion, sex, age or mental or physical ability" (Government of Canada, 1982:15). The implementation of these provisions on equality rights will mean that "For the first time in Canadian history, the Constitution will make it clear that, for women, equality is not a right to be acquired, but a state that exists. It will ensure that women are entitled to full equality in law—and not just in the laws themselves but in the administration of law as well" (Government of Canada, 1982:16). At present it is assumed that it will be some years before judicial testing of these provisions establishes them as fundamental aspects of women's legal status in Canada.

Within the last decade, legal reforms in various Canadian provinces have also fundamentally changed family law, with wide-ranging implications for both men and women. While the legislation associated with such reform is a provincial responsibility, and hence will vary from one province to the next, an overview of legislative provisions in Canada's most populous province, Ontario, illustrates several implications of this reform for the widowed. The Succession Law Reform Act in Ontario, for example, governs the right of surviving spouses and other family members on the death of a family member. If a person dies without a will, the surviving spouse receives the first $75,000 of the estate plus half of any remainder if there is one child, or one-third of the remainder if there are two or more children. If there are no children, the surviving spouse receives the entire estate. If the deceased left a will, the surviving family members receive what the will says is to go to them. However, if this is inadequate, they can apply to a court for a greater share of the estate. This right is available to the spouse, parents, children, brothers, and sisters of the deceased if the deceased was supporting them or was under a legal obligation to support them (Schlesinger, 1979:190).

Socioeconomic Status

Assessments of socioeconomic status typically include analyses of occupational and income measures. In measuring the socioeconomic status of women, it is important to acknowledge that such an examination is invariably confounded by the fundamental issue of the assessment of the occupation homemaker or housewife. In Canada in 1983 just under half of women with a husband at home and preschool-age child(ren), over a third of those with child(ren) 6–15 years, and over half of those without children under 16 years did not participate in the paid labor force (Statistics Canada, 1985:49). Many of these women may list their occupation as homemaker or housewife and may, therefore, derive their socioeconomic status from their partner or spouse (Eichler, 1976). Because of the inherent difficulties and philosophical complexities of the attribution of socioeconomic status in relation to this group of Canadian women, the following discussion will focus on the majority of Canadian women currently participating in the paid labor force, a group for whom occupational and income data are readily available. In so doing, however, we recognize that the occupational sector not represented in these discussions is one likely to be most at risk in terms of the financial supports available in widowhood.

In the past 15 years women's rate of participation in the paid labor force has shown dramatic change, increasing from 38 percent to 53 percent between 1970 and 1983 (Statistics Canada, 1985:41). Even during the period of economic slowdown in the early 1980s, the female labor force grew by 233,000, over five times the increase recorded for the male labor force. Most women, however, continue to work in female-dominated occupations: in 1983, 77 percent of all female employees worked in just five occupational groups—clerical, service, sales, medicine and health, and teaching. There have, nevertheless, been increases in women's share of jobs in all occupational groups, with gains being most impressive in the managerial and administrative category (Statistics Canada, 1985:44). Much of women's employment in Canada remains part-time, however. In 1983 almost 1.2 million women, representing just over one quarter of the female labor force, worked part-time.

Another socioeconomic indicator that not only reflects women's current status but that has profound implications for their experience of widowhood in Canada, is income. The 1982 average earnings of women who were employed full-time was $16,100, representing just 64 percent of those of full-time male employees. Progress in this regard has, however, been steady, if somewhat slow: a decade earlier, women's average annual earnings had been just under 60 percent of those of men (Statistics Canada, 1985:46).

About nine out of 10 Canadians marry at least once in their lifetime. In 1981 close to two-thirds (62 percent) of women aged 15 and over were married. This rate reflects a long-term trend of increasing proportions of adult Canadians who marry (from 52 percent of the adult population in 1909, through 56 percent in 1931, to 64 percent in 1976) (Statistics Canada, 1979). The remainder of Canadian women in 1981 were either formerly married (ten percent widowed, and 3 percent divorced), or had never married (25 percent). The average age at first marriage in 1982 was 23.7 years for women, almost a full year more than in 1970 (Statistics Canada, 1985:10). The mating gradient, the pattern of husbands typically being several years older than their wives, has shown notable consistency over the past 15 years: at first marriage males continue to be an average of two years older than women.

In recent years, however, the marriage rate for women has been falling: from 70 marriages per 1,000 eligible women in 1970 to 51 in 1982. This decline is related to both the increasing trend to delay marriage, and an increase in the number of couples who live together without marrying. There has also been an increase in the rate of remarriage in Canada. Nearly 13 percent of annual marriages in recent years have involved at least one partner who had been married previously, with nearly three-quarters of these (71 percent) divorced and 29 percent widowed. The average age at second marriage for a widower in 1981 was 59 years and for a widow 53 years (Statistics Canada, 1983:9). Rates of remarriage do however remain consistently higher for men than for women.

Nearly every tenth Canadian family is headed by a single parent, 80 percent of these by women. The primary reasons for this relate to increases in divorce and separation rather than widowhood. Overall trends from 1941 to 1981 also show notable changes in family size in Canada. There has been a marked decline in very large families, increases in childless and one-child families, and a striking convergence on the two-child family (Statistics Canada, 1985:4).

Widowhood in Canada

A fundamental characteristic of widowhood in Canadian society is its stress-related nature. There is consensus in the field of life event scaling that the death of a spouse is among the most, if not *the* most, stressful of role transitions (Holmes and Rahe, 1967; McFarlane et al., 1980). This was recently corroborated in a study of the social, emotional, service, and economic supports of widowed women living in a small city in southern Ontario. Without exception, these widows, all a minimum of five and a maximum of 10 years into widowhood, indicated that the loss of the spouse had affected them more than any other single life event (Martin Matthews, 1982). In another Canadian study of recently retired men and women in Ontario, the death of a spouse consistently emerged as the life-cycle experience that had had the greatest impact on respondents. It ranked first of 34 life events in an assessment of crisis; by contrast, retirement ranked twenty-eighth of 34 life events, and the end of a marriage through separation or divorce ranked seventeenth (Martin Matthews et al., 1982).

In recent decades there have been substantial changes in the causes of death (and, by association, causes of widowhood) in Canada. Since 1931, for example, four major communicable diseases and tuberculosis have all but disappeared as causes of death. Other diseases, such as influenza, have been substantially reduced. On the other hand, diseases that occur later in life have assumed a prominent role as causes of death. Cancer, for instance, has registered a 50 percent increase in 50 years. Age-specific death rates due to cancer have, however, remained fairly stable over the years, even though the actual number of cases does show considerable increase (Kubat and Thornton, 1974:48).

Rituals associated with funerals and mourning remain virtually the same throughout North American society, and there are no substantial differences between the United States and Canada in this regard. Recent

Canadian research has, however, identified several important features of grief and mourning. It has been found that "lack of opportunity for anticipatory grieving (i.e., short final illness) may lengthen the grief process" (Vachon et al., 1982:1002). Another study makes the important point that "not until 2 years after bereavement did a difference in overall disturbance between intervention and control groups become apparent.... The estimate of the duration of adjustment to conjugal bereavement has been steadily extended" (Vachon et al., 1980:1384).

Support Systems of the Widowed Woman in Canada

At the outset of this discussion it is important to note the paucity of information on the issues that the remainder of this chapter will address. While there is now a growing body of Canadian research on women in widowhood, in contrast to the situation only five years ago (Martin Matthews, 1980), this area of research is still very much in its infancy. In a broad sense most of the current and completed research falls into one of three classifications: those studies focused on temporal dimensions of the *process of adjusting to bereavement*; those focused on *correlates of the status of widowhood itself*; and those focused on the postgrieving period of later widowhood when issues of the *reconstruction of one's identity and social world* become salient.

The focus of the first type of research is on the process of adaptation to bereavement, which covers a period of time up to approximately two years after the death of the spouse. Haas-Hawkings et al. (1980), for example, examined the relatively immediate (four to 12 weeks) psychosocial adjustment to widowhood, finding positive correlations between preparation for loss and self-report of adjustment. While also focused primarily on the bereavement process, Vachon's research on widowed women is unique in Canada in its longitudinal design, examining the widow's situation at one, six, 12, and 24 months after the death of the spouse. Reports on this quite comprehensive study (Vachon et al., 1976; Vachon et al., 1977; Walker et al., 1977; and Vachon, 1981) indicate that high stress at one month after bereavement is a strong predictor of distress two years later, and also that bereavement typically alters patterns of interaction with significant others, frequently in association with high levels of stress. The research of Haas-Hawkings et al. and Vachon and associates thus exemplifies a type of investigation that deals with the more immediate or short-term consequences for women of the bereavement experience, with the focus primarily on adjustment as outcome.

A second body of research on widows in Canada considers the characteristics of older widowed women in a variety of settings, with the focus being on the correlates of the status of widowhood itself. Christiansen-Ruffman (1976:457) observed some time ago that frequently in social science "concepts such as age and sex . . . simply characterize the individual but ignore the social meaning given to these characteristics in a particular setting." In this second type of Canadian research, this is true of the concept of marital status. Investigations are made of elderly women who happen also to be widowed. Such research contributes substantially to our knowledge of the characteristics of widows' lives but does not as such focus on the issue of the social meaning of the status widow in and of itself.

Examples of this kind of research include provincial government profiles of the correlates of the status widowed for both women and men. One such study, for example, identifies low income as the major problem for women, and social isolation as the major problem for men (Saskatchewan Senior Citizens' Provincial Council, 1979). Other, federally sponsored, projects include a report on the living arrangements of older women in Canada, most of whom are widowed (Fletcher and Stone, 1980) and a joint federal-provincial project identifying elderly widowed females who live alone as accounting for one in five of all admissions to home-care programs (Health and Welfare Canada, 1982a:16).

In the third classification are those studies of the later widowhood period (usually four or more years after bereavement) where the focus of analysis shifts from adaptation per se to the examination of the reconstructed social world, identity, and the social meaning of the status of widow. Such research is generally cross-sectional and frequently comparative in design. For example, Stryckman's (1981) analysis of the decision to remarry compares the attitudes and social circumstances of elderly remarried and widowed persons, and focuses on the social meaning that potential or actual remarriage has for the widowed and their kin relationships. Similarly, Norris (1980) examines the characteristics of the social personality of elderly widows as contrasted with never-married older women. Her data indicate widows' ongoing involvement in and emotional commitment to the role of wife as long as 10 years after the death of the spouse. Another example is a pilot survey of the support systems of women widowed five to 10 years

(Martin Matthews, 1982). This research will be discussed more fully later.

Despite the relative paucity of Canadian data on widows and the limitations of existing studies, the remainder of this chapter will develop a profile of the support systems of these widowed women, focusing on their economic, social, emotional, and service supports.

Economic Supports

Since, as discussed earlier, the vast majority (69 percent) of widows in Canada are over the age of 65, it is instructive to examine the patterns of economic supports available to widows in this age group. In 1982 slightly more than 50 percent of the income of unattached elderly women came from federal old-age security or public pension plans, a proportion largely unchanged for more than a decade. Investments made up 29 percent of the income of these women, while earnings contributed only 5 percent. In addition, because public pension plans are tied to labor-force participation, and benefits depend on the length of time worked and size of contributions, fewer women receive benefits (only 29 percent in 1980), and the benefits they do receive are only 68 percent of those received by men (Statistics Canada, 1985:67). It is apparent that most elderly women, who have spent their lives as homemakers and largely outside the paid labor force, rely in old age almost completely on government assistance programs, and their own accumulated savings.

Women who are "unattached" in old age (either because they never married or were widowed, separated, or divorced) are financially the worst-off segment of the Canadian population in terms of their financial status. In 1982 an estimated 60 percent of unattached elderly women, most of them widows, were poor, compared to 49 percent of unattached men aged 65 and older (National Council of Welfare, 1984). In addition, increasing age raises the risk of poverty for the unattached elderly woman; while just over half (54 percent) aged 65 to 69 were poor in 1981, the rate increased to 65 percent for unattached women aged 70 years and older, "the highest low-income rate of all age groups in 1981" (National Council of Welfare, 1984:26). Indeed, in 1981, there were more aged unattached women below the poverty line than above it!

While there has been much recent discussion in Canada of ways in which to improve the financial circumstances of unattached older women, gains are not likely to be made in the near future. Discussions of pensions for homemakers have been fraught with controversy. In the private sector in 1979 only 49 percent of males and 30 percent of females were members of employer-sponsored pension plans (Health and Welfare Canada, 1982b:6), and few such plans have survivor benefits. More than two million women work in the private sector, earning less than the average wage and have no private pension protection at all. A factor that does not bode well for the future of women's financial status in widowhood is the finding that in the 25–44 and 45–64 age groups only one-third of females in the private sector were members of pension plans in 1979. These findings are significant because of the fact that "for women to build up adequate pension credits, it is important to have pension protection for their early years spent in the labor force" (Health and Welfare Canada, 1982b:9–10).

Social Supports

Several Canadian studies highlight the central importance of social support in the lives of women after widowhood. This research varies in its focus on support in the early versus later years of widowhood and will be overviewed in this context. In a longitudinal study of 162 widows in Toronto, "the social support variables were the most important in explaining the level of distress 1 month after bereavement." Among these, the most relevant was the woman's perception that she was seeing old friends less than before the death of her husband (Vachon et al., 1982:1000). In a follow-up of 99 of these widows two years later, "low satisfaction with help at one month was the only social support variable to retain importance in the 24-month regression analysis" (Vachon et al., 1982:1000).

In an analysis of a subset of 81 of these widows aged 55 to 69, several dimensions of social support were examined in relation to age. Older widows were more likely to be living alone, less likely to have children, and more likely to have children living outside Toronto. One month after bereavement, the older widows were more likely than the younger ones to rate themselves as having received help from children over age 18, from other widows, and from clergy. Overall, the most frequent sources of social support to these widows were their children, members of their family of origin (parents, siblings), and friends.

Further analyses found that 73 percent of the widows experienced at least one change in their social relationships over the first two years of adaptation to bereavement (Vachon, 1981). There was a significant association between the number of relationship changes a woman experienced and her score on a measure of distress. In this research a "Perceived Lack of Social Support Index" was developed that included such items as the feeling that no one cares; finding it hard to carry on social activities alone; seeing old friends less; receiving less help than wanted, in general, from family and friends, and from professionals (if such help was desired); and being able to count on not more than one person to understand how one is really feeling. This perceived lack of social support accounted for fully 25 percent of the variance in distress levels one month after bereavement. In follow-up interviews it accounted for 12 and 13 percent at six and 12 months, respectively, and only at 24 months did it decrease to 5 percent (Vachon, 1981).

In an analysis of the effect of new relationships and activities on the level of distress, significant association was found between the development of relationships and bereavement outcome. Seventy-six percent of the low-distress women had developed new relationships two years after bereavement, compared to 57 percent of the high-distress women.

Social networks served three major functions in the lives of the recently bereaved: to smooth the transition to a traditional widow role; to offer support and guidance as the widow sought to establish a new identity that may or may not have correspondence with what her social network might have chosen or expected; to reject or ignore the widow, which either led to a lonely, isolated life or may have provided an incentive to develop new relationships (Vachon, 1981).

This research indicates that friendships were the crucial relationships most likely to change during bereavement. Vachon and associates conclude that families have certain role responsibilities they are *expected* to fulfill in interaction with a recent widow. Friendship, on the other hand, based on reciprocity and mutual need fulfillment, will deteriorate or cease to exist if these criteria are not fulfilled. Many widows came to the realization that the significant others they had previously considered close friends had not even been seen in several months. Half of the women noted a decrease in social relationships from six months after bereavement. The widows typically responded to these changes in two ways: the high-distress group tended to withdraw in anger and resentment, thus becoming increasingly isolated;

the low-distress group took these changes as the opportunity to initiate new relationships.

In terms of adult children as sources of support the patterns varied among different types of widows. As Vachon notes, the traditional widow role was usually assumed by older working-class widows or those from a more traditional ethnic background. These were the women who moved to be closer to adult children, who were sources of practical assistance. These were also the women who had a social network composed mostly of both children and other widows and unattached women. A primary focus of the support of adult children involved getting their mothers into new activities. They also worked hard to encourage their mothers to retain old contacts as sources potentially of remarriage or employment.

As a final observation from Vachon's research on patterns of social support in the early years of widowhood, it should be noted that, given a deterioration in her health, a widow may experience high distress even in the presence of social supports. How the social support network responds to health problems in the widow may well be a matter of timing, with less support forthcoming during the first year as adjustment to widowhood and the sick role overlap.[2]

Other Canadian research, focusing on the later period of widowhood —typically some five to 10 years after the event—provides some interesting parallels, but also some contrasts, with these findings. Research by Martin Matthews (1982) on widowed women found there to be stability over time in the contact with adult children but also found substantial evidence for the support of members of the "family of origin," as did Vachon. These findings, it must be pointed out, are quite in contrast to Lopata's findings in Chicago, where she notes that children are by far the most viable members of the widow's support system (1978;1979). Siblings, in-laws, and other relatives were not actively involved in most of the support systems Lopata studied.

In the Canadian research by Martin Matthews (1982), using the same instrument as developed by Lopata, over half of the respondents with living siblings saw at least one as frequently as several times a month. More significantly, siblings and other extended kin also emerged as important figures in the social and emotional support systems. In all, 54 percent of the widows listed at least one sibling (typically a sister) as being involved in at least one exchange in the social support system. Sixty-five percent listed an extended kin member (sibling, sibling-in-law, cousin, aunt, or niece) as involved in their emotional support system. Half the respondents specifically referred to a sister as one of the three people to whom they felt closest, either currently or in the year before their husband's death.

While these findings will be examined more fully in a major project currently under way (Martin Matthews, 1985; Dickinson and Martin Matthews, 1986), there is presently no ready explanation for the disparate findings in the Canadian pilot study and the Chicago survey. It may be that because a higher proportion of the Canadian than the Chicago widows grew up in the local area, they have been able to retain more contacts with siblings and other extended kin over the years. It may also be that because almost half the Chicago widows have at least one child still living at home (in contrast to 15 percent of the Canadian widows), the presence of children makes them more salient resources than are extended kin at this stage in the life cycle. It is interesting to note, however, that in another Canadian study focused on the supports of both widowed and non-widowed elderly men and women, siblings were also identified as close family members (Martin Matthews et al., 1984).[3] Vachon and associates also found evidence of the important supportive role of members of the family of origin, although they do not specify whether or not they were siblings.

Similarly, in a study of widowed women in Winnipeg, Manitoba, Harvey and Harris (1985) have found that median contact with siblings is two to three times per month. Ten percent of the sample of 141 women widowed an average of two years have contact with siblings more than once a week, while a further 15 percent have once-weekly contact. Harvey and Harris postulate that the residential stability of these women (a median 35 years residence in Winnipeg) may account in part for the extent of sibling involvement in their supports in widowhood. These data raise questions about the generalizability to the Canadian context of Lopata's (1978) conclusions about the limitations of the modified extended-kin network in widowhood. There is a clear need for more research in this area.

Two other Canadian studies add an interesting dimension to the consideration of patterns of social support in widowhood. One study focuses on the role of the late husband in the ongoing support system of the widow, and the other study looks at the issue of social support among francophone Canadians. In the first study Norris (1980) took the novel approach of contrasting the patterns of social involvement of widows with that of never-married older women. The mean age of her sample was 71, and the widowed had experienced a mean of 10 years since the death of their spouse (Norris, 1980:137). She found that widows were more socially engaged than singles primarily because of their involvement in kinship roles. On the other hand, the never married were overall more adjusted and happier in old age. She concluded that the differences that did emerge between the two groups reflect involvement in the roles of wife and worker that have been maintained beyond the loss of these roles. The widows' higher average score on global measures of involvement was no doubt due to their engagement in activities created by the role of spouse: parenting and grandparenting. The widow's score was also influenced by responses to questions about marriage as if the husband were still alive. For example, rather than view statements about married life as personally no longer relevant, widowed women frequently expressed strong agreement with the statement, "Being married makes my daily activities more satisfying and easy to deal with." "Through an inability or a desire not to relinquish the role, they remained emotionally committed to being wives. . . . Widows . . . had apparently maintained the central role of their lives, spouse . . . into old age" (Norris, 1980:142).

These findings echo a pattern recently observed in U.S. research on widows (Anderson, 1984), and observations made by Unruh (1983:72): "Social worlds in aging lives may be rooted in the past, as well as the present . . . Involvements and activities in which the aged were no longer actively engaged have continued to be sources of integration through memories that provided linkages into social worlds. These kinds of linkages, and their importance to the lives of older people, are crucial to a full understanding of social integration."

Another Canadian study that examines social supports in relation to long-term adaptation to widowhood is that by Stryckman (1982) on 574 men and women aged 55 and over living in urban and rural environments in francophone Quebec. As one measure of social support, relations with children exhibited quite complex, and somewhat contradictory patterns. For example, while frequency of interaction with children decreased over time in widowhood, these fewer interactions were characterized by the widowed as being more positive; such findings have implications for the many studies that measure social support in terms of frequency of contact only. However, residence with children (itself frequently considered an indicator of social support) did not significantly reduce the emergence of loneliness as a major problem of widowhood. Indeed, 63 percent of widowers ($N = 51$) and 33 percent of widows ($N = 64$) living with children identified loneliness as their major problem (1982:79). Stryckman also found that relations with children constituted the biggest obstacle for those who wished to remarry, particularly so for widows who strongly identified themselves as mothers.

While much of this discussion of social support in the later period of widowhood has focused on the role of the deceased spouse in memory, on older parent-adult child relations, and sibling relations, there are also Canadian data on the role of friendship and neighbor support in widowhood. The potential supportive function of friends and neighbors is apparent when one recognizes that a third (32 percent) of women aged 65 and over were living alone in 1981 (Statistics Canada, 1985:8).[4] In other studies of widowed women, proportions as high as 73 percent living alone (Martin Matthews, 1982) and 78 percent living alone (Martin Matthews et al., 1984) were found. In Stryckman's research, only 23 percent were living alone, but fully a third were living in quasi-family settings, typically with a sister or a female friend. Such an arrangement was described as bringing satisfaction to the widowed in terms of needing someone to take care of them (Stryckman, 1982: 144–45).

Research by Elias (1977) on elderly widows living in age-segregated apartment complexes emphasizes the importance of neighbors as friends and as social supports to the widowed. She found that most women had a neighbor who had become a close friend, and about 90 percent of respondents felt that neighbors in the current age-segregated environment were friendlier than in their previous housing. The majority had made casual friendships with neighbors who lived on the same floor of the building (Elias, 1977:62).

Peer relationships other than those with neighbors were also important in the social support systems of these elderly widows. The vast majority (92 percent) reported associations limited to other older widows; and 92 percent indicated that their closest friend was also a widow, with the friendship originating for the most part (62 percent) after bereavement. The importance of the friendship role is also confirmed in the finding that "close friendship was the second best significant predictor of the criterion variable, social adjustment" (Elias, 1977:77).

Yet another indicator of the importance of friendship roles in the social support systems of the widowed elderly is the finding that 8 percent of a sample of widowed elderly included at least one friend in descriptions of their "family" compared to 4 percent of the nonwidowed

(Martin Matthews et al., 1984). In another study of widowed women, nearly three-quarters identified neighbors as helpful resources to them in bereavement, and over 80 percent identified friends as being similarly helpful (Martin Matthews, 1982).

Before leaving the issue of social supports in widowhood, it is important to acknowledge how the personal resources of the widow influence both the extent of the social supports utilized and the response and attitude toward available social supports. Lopata has recognized that the widow "needs to 'make herself over,' from a dependent person, living vicariously through the husband and children, into an independent person" (1979:32), and that "many of the women are aware of themselves as a resource for supplying supports" (1979:75). To further explore this issue, a recent pilot study of support systems in widowhood incorporated several questions that allowed for an extensive discussion of the widow's personal supports (Martin Matthews, 1982). These primarily focused on the issue of how the respondents felt that the years since being widowed had changed them personally. Data collected in response to these questions provided information that proved vital in understanding the context in which changes in the widows' support systems took place. Three quite varied responses by women who each experienced a contracting of their social support system in widowhood illustrate this point.

> It made me bitter, awfully bitter. I know now that all those friends who came here all those years, all those great parties we had, well, they were never *really* our friends, now were they? Oh, we thought they were, at the time. But where were they when I needed them? The kids say I should forget it, but I won't. You can't depend on anybody in this life, just your family. That's the lesson I learned the hard way.

> I feel removed from life now. You feel like you're always a third wheel at cards. It's not quite the same when you play with another woman. You also hesitate to ask couples in, even for dinner. It's a lonelier, quieter life. I'm okay . . . I understand that, I accept it now. But it's a different life.

> I'm more independent. I just couldn't keep relying on people. I had to stop being dependent on my children and my friends. I had to *force* myself to start standing on my own two feet. That wasn't easy, I tell you. I did it, though. And I'm proud of myself that I did it, too.

These three comments illustrate distinctly different contexts in which the change in social support in widowhood takes place, is interpreted, and has meaning for these widows. These varied responses—embitterment, resignation, and satisfaction—yield quite different *interpretations* of changes in the support systems of widows, be they social, emotional, service, or economic. Each of these responses also has quite different implications for strategies of intervention by those working with the widowed.

These preliminary findings from a pilot study suggest the need for research on later widowhood to examine more fully the social *meaning* of widowhood for women. Lopata's research on Chicago-area widows clearly recognizes this point in the finding that over half the widowed women felt that they personally had been changed by the experience of widowhood (1973). In any study of changes in patterns of social support in widowhood, the possibility of change in the widow herself as an influencing factor must be considered.

Emotional Supports

Few Canadian studies examine emotional supports of the widowed, and those that do deal primarily with these supports in the longer-term adaptation to widowhood. One example is research by Strain and Chappell (1982) in Winnipeg, Manitoba, focused on the maintenance of confidante relationships among the aged, with the widowed comprising one sub-sample of the larger study. One-fourth had been widowed less than five years, a third from six to 15 years, a quarter 16 to 25 years, and 17 percent more than 26 years. Strain and Chappell (1982) found no statistically significant differences among the single/separated/divorced, the married, and the widowed in terms of number of confidants in the emotional support system. Significant differences were apparent, however, in the number of confidants reported by the widowed males and females. "The females are more likely than the males to report at least one confidant: 18 percent of the [male] widowed reported no confidant, but over one-half (54 percent) of the widowed females reported having two or more confidants." This finding corroborates other Canadian research, such as that of Haas-Hawkings (1978) and others who note that "widowed women . . . are more likely to have established intimate relationships outside their marriages" than are other women or men (Strain and Chappell, 1982:489).

Marital status does differentiate the types of confidant utilized in the emotional support system. While there were no significant marital-status differences in naming peer family (siblings, cousins, aunts, and uncles) as confidants, the widowed were the most likely to name other relatives (grandchildren, nieces/nephews, and second cousins) as confidants compared to the single/separated/divorced and the married, while the single/separated/divorced were more likely than the other two groups to name friends (Strain and Chappell, 1982:493).

The finding that women were significantly more likely than men (35 percent versus 23 percent) to name peer family as confidants is particularly noteworthy. Previously discussed Canadian studies have clearly identified siblings, especially sisters, as major contributors to the support systems of the widowed. While Strain and Chappell (1982) do not specify the relatives named as confidants, one might conjecture, on the basis of other Canadian studies (Harvey and Harris, 1985; Martin Matthews, 1982; Stryckman, 1982; Vachon, 1979, 1981), that sisters played some significant part in the emotional support systems of these women. The finding that the widowed were most likely to name such other relatives as nieces, nephews, and grandchildren as confidants is also striking. It supports other Canadian research which found that the widowed are more likely than the non-widowed elderly (20 percent versus 14 percent) to identify nieces and nephews in discussions of family relationships (Martin Matthews et al., 1984).

Service Supports

Just as Lopata (1979) described for Chicago-area widows, there is evidence that Canadian widows do not rely extensively on a service support system, reciprocal or otherwise. Only two Canadian studies have in fact addressed this aspect of the support systems of widowed women, however, and conclusions must necessarily remain tentative. One such study examined patterns of receipt and giving of various kinds of service support: transportation, household repairs, help with housekeeping, help with shopping, yard work, child care, sick care, help in decision-making, and provision of legal aid (Martin Matthews, 1982). While overall there was relatively little involvement in most of these supports, some types of service were engaged in by many of the widows. For example, assistance with minor repairs was received by 65 percent, yard work by 46 percent, transportation by 43 percent, and legal aid by 42 percent. The areas where assistance was most frequently given to others were transportation (54 percent), help to others in times of illness (46 percent) and child care (35 percent). While these figures indicate the service supports most frequently given to and received by the widows, they hardly represent extensive service involvement in the lives of others. Only in one case (assistance received for minor repairs) do a majority of the widows avail themselves of the service. Nevertheless, these figures do represent a somewhat more pervasive pattern of service support than that found by Lopata. Until a more comprehensive examination of the service support systems of Canadian widows is available, however, there is no ready explanation for these differences, particularly in the *giving* of such service supports as the provision of child care (in which 35 percent of the Canadian widows but only 20 percent of the Chicago widows were engaged). We can only conjecture that, because of the large proportion of Chicago-area widows with at least one child still living at home, their need for involvement with service supports outside the immediate household was somewhat reduced. Although the Canadian widows were more involved in service supports, they were not *extensively* involved in them, and they did not indicate any desire for supports which others might have provided. Less than 4 percent wished for some type of service support that had not materialized (Martin Matthews, 1982).

A study of the decision-making patterns of Canadian widows provides some further insight into this pattern of service supports. In examining patterns of decision making along a range of issues (car sale/purchase, medical visit, house sale/purchase, job acquisition, car and house repair, husband's estate, relocation, and remarriage), Harvey and Harris found that the widows who had made decisions had infrequently sought help in arriving at a course of action. The cases where support in decision making was sought most typically involved car sale or purchase (52 percent) and the spouse's estate (55 percent). Decisions about medical visits and remarriage rarely involved consultation with others (11 percent and 8 percent, respectively) (Harvey and Harris, 1985).

These data suggest that a strong ethic of independence, the pattern of seeking "help" only in extraordinary circumstances, characterizes widowed women in both Canada and the United States. An intriguing issue for future Canadian research is the indication that the services which the U.S. widows were *most* likely to give (sick care) and receive (transportation and help in illness) were not uniformly the ones characteristic of the Canadian widows.

Circumstances Complicating Support Systems

A variety of circumstances specific to Canadian society and culture bear directly upon the availability and potential value of support systems in the lives of widows. These include issues of labor-force participation and unemployment rates among older women, patterns of migration, and location in a rural versus an urban environment.

Issues of labor-force participation and rates of unemployment have a direct bearing on the availability of economic supports in widowhood. In recent years Canada has witnessed a significant rate of growth in the female labor force, particularly among middle-aged women. While this appears to auger well for the economic supports of the widowed, Dulude recently concluded that "almost 2/3 of widows in their fifties who are in the labor force hold low-paying unskilled jobs" (1978:10). Data from the 1981 Census of Canada show that while the labor-force participation rate for females over the age of 15 as a whole is 51.8, the participation rate for the widowed and divorced female is 31.3 (Statistics Canada, 1984). In addition, while mature women workers have a substantially lower rate of unemployment than their younger counterparts (in 1981 it was 7 percent for widowed and divorced women), the bad news is that "older women suffer longer periods of unemployment than do younger women" (1979:11). Dulude observes that while this phenomenon has received very little attention in Canada, it has been extensively studied in the United States where "it was found to be at least partially due to age discrimination." Indeed, it is generally acknowledged that "to be old and female is the best combination to ensure being poor in Canada . . . and to be old and a widow is an even better one" (1979:40). The main cause of the widows' poverty is the extreme financial vulnerability of most elderly married women, at least one-third of whom have no personal income at all. Dulude (1979) further notes that "More than half of all married women aged 55 to 64 have no income at all. When their husbands die, it appears that most of them will inherit nothing other than poverty." These factors have significant implications for the perpetuation of patterns of economic support available to the widowed woman in Canada, and reflect her reliance on savings and other forms of family-generated assistance in order to ensure her livelihood.

Another phenomenon with direct relevance to the social supports of the widowed is the high rate of migration characteristic of Canadian society. Nearly half (48 percent) of the Canadian population changed residence between 1976 and 1981; 20 percent moved from a different municipality, and 15 percent from a different province (Statistics Canada, 1983). Although national data indicating the availability of children in geographical proximity to their elderly or widowed kin are not available, there is reason to believe that these high rates of mobility can and do have an impact on the availability of kin as resources in the social support systems of the widowed.

Another factor complicating the issue of mobility is the recognition that rates of out-migration are high among the young residents of rural areas, and that in these areas the elderly and the elderly widowed in particular are over-represented. For example, while widows comprise 12 percent of women living in urban areas, they comprise fully 18 percent of women residing in rural areas of the country.[5] Among widowed rural women, fully 93 percent reside in non-farm areas, typically small towns and villages. The sheer demography of rural Canada suggests this pattern will continue and likely even intensify in the future. For example, a recent Health and Welfare Canada report notes that "only 9.4 percent of the total population of large urban centres was age 65 and over in 1981. . . . Small towns, on the other hand, had an unusually large proportion of elderly persons in their populations. In towns with 1,000 to 2,499 people, 13.5 percent of the population was aged 65 and over or more . . ." (1983:26). Indeed, census data show that small towns had a larger than average proportion of persons aged 80 and over relative to their total population, 3.1 percent compared to the national average of 1.9 percent (Health and Welfare, 1983). Table 11.1 has illustrated the proportions of widowed women among this age group; it is therefore apparent that many rural areas of Canada have, and will continue to have, high concentrations of elderly widows in their populations. These environments, frequently characterized by few or no formalized support services to the aged, and reduced availability of younger family members as potential supports, create particular circumstances that may affect the widow's access to supportive services and individuals.

Also relevant to this discussion of circumstances that may complicate the availability of and access to supports are several demographic characteristics of Canada's current aged population. As Marshall has recently noted, "the cohort now in old age has very few children compared to earlier cohorts and also compared to most later cohorts. The cohort now in their forties has more children than the preceding and following cohorts" (Marshall, 1981:17–18). As we have seen,

Canada's aged women represent a substantial proportion of the widowed. Their extremely low birthrate will therefore make this cohort of widows fundamentally different from preceding and succeeding cohorts of widows in terms of their access to intergenerational family contacts as potential supports.

In sum, a range of socioeconomic and cohort-related factors serve to complicate the experience of widowhood in Canadian society. Not the least of these for the group of aged widows who have been the focus of this analysis is the fact that the very nature of widowhood has changed in terms of its location and duration in the life course of women: "Widowhood is now a typical family life course stage for women, located at the end of the life course. In an earlier era—as recently as for the cohorts born in the last quarter of the nineteenth century—many more women could expect to die in childbirth, or to either predecease their husbands or to enter widowhood at a much younger age" (Marshall, 1981:21).

Conclusions

This paper has examined various features of Canadian society that relate to the experience of widowhood for women, as well as selected characteristics of the support systems of Canadian widows. In comparing the findings of Canadian studies with those from Lopata's research in the United States, striking parallels as well as intriguing contrasts are evident. Parallels in the economic support system of widows are readily apparent: Canadian widows, as did those studied by Lopata, suffer significant declines in income in widowhood, and many live on incomes below the poverty line. Parallels also exist in the patterns of service support utilized by widows in both countries. Lopata has noted the "failure of widows to use many of the supports deemed beneficial in the modern urban environment" (1979:355), a statement largely corroborated by Canadian research.

In terms of social and emotional supports, however, there are both comparisons and contrasts in the findings. Canadian researchers have indeed found evidence that "a husband in memory can also provide a form of support" (Lopata, 1979:352). The importance of female relatives, particularly daughters, in the social and emotional support systems of widows is striking in both the Canadian and Chicago research. In addition, the role of the personal resources of the widow in shaping her reliance upon, and response to, her support system is evident in the Canadian and Chicago-area studies. However, as noted earlier in the chapter, the role of the extended family in the support system of the widow is apparently quite different in Canada. While Lopata found almost a complete absence of meaningful support from family members other than children, several Canadian studies identified other members of the extended family as involved in the social and emotional support systems of the widowed. While none of the Canadian studies are individually of the scope and comprehensiveness of Lopata's research, collectively they do point to a notable consistency in the identification of the supportive role played by extended family members in all stages of widowhood. This is most evident in reference to the role of peer family, especially siblings, a finding made more significant by its contrast to Lopata's statement that "one of the most unexpected findings of this study . . . is the absence of siblings from the emotional support systems of widows" (1979:242).

This review of the Canadian literature on the support systems of widows also serves to highlight the fact that, while widowhood research in Canada has grown significantly in the last five years, there are substantial gaps in our knowledge. Specific subgroups of widows identified by Lopata as having somewhat distinctive patterns of social support ("off time" widows and minority widows) have simply not been systematically studied in Canada. In addition, the many features of Canadian society that both contribute to our uniqueness as a nation and add potential complexity to the experience of widowhood for women (bilingualism, multiculturalism, regional diversity, and concentrations of the widowed aged in rural areas) have not been systematically investigated in relation to this most disruptive of life-cycle transitions.

12 Activities, Religiosity, and Morale of Canadian Widowed Persons

CAROL D. H. HARVEY, GORDON E. BARNES,
LEONARD J. GREENWOOD,
ROSE KABAHENDA-NYAKABWA

Widowhood is a major life event, and in this chapter we will consider it in relationship to activities, religiosity, and morale. Although the effect of widowhood on morale has previously been investigated with the same data (Harvey, Barnes, and Greenwood, 1986), we will extend the analyses here to include the possible moderating or buffering effects of activities and religiosity on morale of the widowed. We will trace the effect of demographic and structural conditions upon morale directly as well as their effect indirectly through activities and religiosity. Using a large national sample, originally drawn for a study of the health of Canadians, we have investigated the relationships among demographic, structural variables, activity variables, religiosity, and morale. A discussion of results showing both male and female widowed people in the Canadian context are drawn at the end of the chapter.

Review of the Literature

In order to study widowhood and the relationships with which we are interested, it is necessary to review evidence presented in past research. What we shall be reporting here are results from a variety of North American sources, although some are also drawn from Great Britain and European samples. A group of independent predictors of morale (including positive and negative feelings) will thus be considered, namely, demographic and structural conditions (marital status, income, education, age, gender, health status, family size, and labor force participation), activities (both solitary and social), chores, and religiosity.

The effects of demographic and structural conditions upon morale of widowed persons have been investigated quite thoroughly since the mid-1960s. The impact of these personal characteristics has a profound effect upon the coping strategies and morale that evolve for people after the death of a spouse.

Widowhood and Morale

Relationships between widowhood and global happiness and morale indicators have been found to exist. Furthermore, a relationship exists between stressful life events and psychiatric symptoms, particularly depression (Brown and Harris, 1978; Cadoret et al., 1972; Paykel, 1979; Tennant et al., 1981; Warheit, 1979). "Attempts to clarify the types of events that are most relevant in depression have shown that loss or exit events (e.g., widowhood, marital separation) occur more frequently among depressed than non-depressed persons" (Harvey, Barnes, and Greenwood, 1986:1). Stated differently, "people with spouses are more likely to enjoy psychological well-being than those without" (Pearlin and Johnson, 1977:704).

Although depression is a common problem of the elderly, recent research seems to suggest that loss of a spouse (widowhood), education, income, health, living arrangements, and lack of social support from family, confidant, friends, neighbors, or community—as well as failure to engage in social activities—could heighten negative feelings and depression among the elderly; they may also be important predictors of depression. Since many elderly are widowed, these effects may be interrelated.

When we look at subjective well-being (instead of the psychiatric literature), we also find that a similar relationship exists between morale and marital status. Diener (1984) reviewed this literature recently and found that married persons have higher morale than do the non-married. Bankoff (1983) used Bradburn's Affect Balance Scale to measure positive and negative feelings and found widowhood had a significant impact on both components of the scale. Harvey and Bahr (1980) used the same scale and found that widows were similar to married women in positive aspects but reported more negative affect.

Life satisfactions have been examined as well when considering morale. Here researchers found that community and friendships were similar for the married and the widowed but that family life was less satisfactory and life generally less exciting for widowed persons (Harvey and Bahr, 1980; Hyman, 1983). Widowed persons have reported much less satisfaction with family income than do married ones (Harvey and Bahr, 1980; Hyman, 1983). In fact, Harvey and Bahr concluded that family income satisfaction was more highly correlated with personal happiness than were other satisfaction items, including satisfaction with children, house and furniture, or community. It is known also that a drop in income occurs with death of spouse. This drop has been observed to persist over the rest of the life span (Harvey and Harris, 1985; Martin Matthews, 1986).

Income

Income is directly and negatively related to age. Older widowed people have been found to be poorer in Canada, compared to their married cohorts (Martin Matthews, 1980), and this is true in the United States as well (Atchley, 1975).

Income differences in morale show consistent patterns in the research. People with more money are happier (Bradburn, 1969; Edwards and Klemmack, 1973; Harvey and Bahr, 1974, 1980; Myers, Lindenthal, and Pepper, 1974). Furthermore, widowed people with more money also report more happiness and greater satisfaction with their incomes.

With age held constant, income itself appears to be a stronger predictor of morale than marital status (Harvey and Bahr, 1974). In other words, the somewhat lower morale of widowed individuals is due to their low incomes rather than to marital status. Economic circumstances are powerful factors influencing negative attitudes of widows (Atchley, 1975; Lopata, 1971), and reduced income has a negative impact on self-image, especially for people at the lower end of the socioeconomic scale.

Education

Better educated widows cope better (Harvey and Bahr, 1974, 1980; Lopata, 1979). Widows with more education appear to have more money, and they are also more likely to belong to formal organizations. Both more income and more ties to their community may serve as resources that are used along with education to deal with the effects of widowhood.

Age

Happiness or positive mood is also affected by age (younger people are more positive than older ones), by education (better educated people are more positive), and by health, with good health meaning a more positive outlook (Harvey, 1986; Harvey and Bahr, 1974, 1980; Hyman, 1983; Lopata, 1979). Balkwell (1985) found a weak age difference among widowed Mexican-Americans and Anglos and married persons; for blacks, no relationship existed.

Older and better educated widows are said to show better adjustment (Carey, 1979–80). The relationship appears to be curvilinear, with young and extremely old widows having more trouble coping, while the "young-old" do this task more easily (Balkwell, 1981).

When considering anomie, Hyman (1983) found little difference between married and widowed people in either feelings of "the lot of the average person" or feelings about "living for today and letting tomorrow take care of itself." This did not change much by age, income level, or by length of time widowed.

Gender

Inconsistent relationships between gender and morale in widowhood have been found. Being a widow or a widower appears to have a differential impact on adjustment or coping in some studies, but it appears to be of little effect in others. Berardo (1967) found that males had more trouble adapting to widowhood than did females. Leaf et al. (1984) found more psychiatric disorders among formerly married men than among comparable women. In assessing health risks, Stroebe and Stroebe (1983) found widowed men to be less healthy than widowed women. Contrasting results were found by Carey (1979–80) and by Gallagher et al. (1983), who found widows to have more adjustment difficulties than did widowers. Arens (1982–83) found no gender differences in morale of widowed individuals; health, social participation, and socialization with friends were more important predictors of morale in Arens's work.

Living Arrangements

Widowed persons in Canada often live alone. Their children are grown, and they retain for a time the housing they had when they were married—then they move into a smaller place. A majority of elderly in Wister and Burch's sample agreed that, "In this age of pensions and welfare, it isn't necessary anymore for older persons to be taken care of by their adult children" (1985:9). They found that elderly persons did not want to share accommodations with nonrelatives and generally considered living alone the only possible option. Wister and Burch concluded that ". . . while some elderly individuals are dissatisfied with separate living, many do not perceive viable alternatives" (1985:10). These perceptions were colored by past histories of personal tastes and preferences, cultural norms, and social roles.

Younger widowed women (average age 50–55) in one western Canadian city were likely to live with their children or to have children close enough to visit several times a week (Harvey and Harris, 1985). They also had frequent, weekly contact with siblings. It appeared that these Canadian urban widows were preparing for old age, with its norms of independence and privacy. They will likely be influenced, as were those in the Wister and Burch sample in central Canada, by health status and domestic competence in their continuing ability to fulfill these norms as they grow older and continue in the widowed status. Past fertility will also continue to be an indicator of availability of kin who might provide support for an independent living arrangement (Wister and Burch, 1985). Opinions of friends are also important. If friends think it is not appropriate for the widow to live with children or siblings, then proscriptions on alternative behaviors will deter her (Wister and Burch, 1985).

Health

Good physical vigor appears to have a positive effect on widows' morale (Harvey and Bahr, 1980). Using step-wise multiple regression to predict morale, Harvey and Bahr found that when widows perceived their own health to be "excellent" or "good," they tended to rate higher on morale scales. In conjunction with age, income, and employment status, health was an important predictor of morale.

In combination, possession of adequate income and good health is positively related to the life satisfaction and morale of the elderly

(Edwards and Klemmack, 1973; Palmore and Luikart, 1972; Spreitzer and Snyder, 1974). Quinn (1983) predicted an inverse relationship of health and income with activity level and hence on nonfamilial associations; greater restrictions on activity develop among those with poor health.

Labor Force Participation

Between 1970 and 1983 in Canada, the rate of women participating in the labor force increased from 18 percent to 53 percent (Martin Matthews, 1986). However, in a report for the Advisory Council on the Status of Women, Dulude (1978) reported that "almost 2/3 of the widows in their fifties who are in the labour force held low paying unskilled jobs." Widowed and divorced women are reported to suffer extended periods of unemployment. This and the fact that they are widowed leaves them economically more disadvantaged than their married counterparts (Martin Matthews, 1986).

Activities and Morale

In addition to the above-mentioned demographic and structural variables, activity patterns appear to have an effect on the morale of widowed persons. The extent of social participation and contact with others is highly and positively related to morale (Arling, 1976; Atchley, 1975; Lopata, 1970; Walker, MacBride, and Vachon, 1977). With a female sample, widows who attended meetings and who had greater diversity of organizational affiliations had greater happiness (Harvey and Bahr, 1980). Conversely, widows with no organizational activity reported less personal happiness. As the extent of activity increased, so too did the level of reported happiness (1980:98).

Leisure-time activities of widows in two American samples revealed no differences with other women of comparable ages. Widows wrote letters about the same amount as did other women in Harvey and Bahr's 1980 sample, and Lopata found that most of the widows in her study did not use the mails as a means of active involvement in the lives of relatives or friends living far away (Lopata 1973:135).

Hours spent in solitary leisure activities—such as reading, watching television, sewing, baking, or fishing—had little effect on levels of happiness for either the married or the widowed samples (Harvey and Bahr, 1980).

Friendship patterns appear to be altered among widowed women. Harvey and Bahr (1980) found, in interviewing a sample of women widowed by an industrial fire, that they saw less of their married friends six months after the fire. The frequency of communication with friends was similar, however, to two comparison groups of married women. In that community, widows had fewer kin available than did the comparison groups and had had consistently lower levels of involvement with relatives prior to and during the fire (Harvey and Bahr, 1980).

Glick, Weiss, and Parkes (1974), using a sample of young widowed men and women in the United States, found that, "By the end of the first year of bereavement, most widows had returned to fairly active social participation" (1974:222). In a different study of young widows six months after bereavement, widows were "more apt to belong to recreational organizations such as bridge clubs or bowling leagues" than were married comparison samples (Harvey and Bahr, 1980:55).

Lopata found education to be a key in the Chicago-area widows' community participation, including neighboring, working, or belonging to voluntary organizations (Lopata, 1973). This was also true for the Harvey and Bahr sample of younger widows (1980).

Religion and Morale

Other activities in which widowed persons may participate are related to their churches. Although church participation appears not to change at widowhood, widows do report an increase in the importance of religion in their lives (Harvey and Bahr, 1980). Using successive panels of the population in the United States, Hyman (1983:69) reported that widows "are no more likely to reject formal religion or to seek the solace and social benefits such participation provides," a finding that holds constant across gender and age lines. Religiosity appeared to have an effect on morale of widowed persons in the Harvey and Bahr (1980) sample as well. Using the same Canadian sample reported in this chapter, religiosity had a consistent and positive relationship to morale for both men and women across marital statuses (Harvey, Barnes, and Greenwood, 1986).

We can thus conclude that religiosity is a main-effect variable that has a positive influence on morale. We thus interpret the role of religion as a resource that can provide meaning or spirituality for the widowed individual. People who have a strong faith before widowhood are also likely to have it afterward and are more likely to report positive feelings and general well-being than do those for whom religion is unimportant.

Circumstances of Death, Time, and Morale

Circumstances surrounding the death of the spouse also affect morale, with sudden deaths generally demanding more dramatic shifts in mood than expected ones (Vachon et al., 1982). Effects of widowhood upon morale seem to change over time, with negative feelings easing as length of widowhood expands. Vachon and colleagues (1982) used a Toronto sample and found that 162 widows in four time periods showed highest distress levels one month after their husbands' deaths—by two years the norm had moved to low distress. The small part of the sample who were distressed two years after bereavement were more likely to have experienced multiple stressors before the death of the husband and did not find religion helpful.

Resources

Widowhood can bring about a new resource, the self, as an evolving strength upon which one can rely (Martin Matthews, 1982). When asked to list some advantages of widowed status, women told Harris and Harvey, "I rely on myself more. There is nobody else to help with decisions, and so I have learned to do things for myself" (1986). Lopata (1979) also listed the self as a resource.

Other resources include personal ones of finance, education, health, and psychological independence (George, 1980). Family systems can contribute to resources, including the organization of the family, the role relationships within it, and its management and problem-solving styles (McCubbin et al., 1983). Social resources of friends, membership in social organizations, and religious beliefs and affiliations are also available and used by some widowed individuals to cope with their new lives after the death of their spouses (Clark et al., 1986).

One very important resource is a confidant. Many researchers report that the presence of a confidant, a person with whom the widowed person can share close, intimate details of life, is highly correlated with high morale and positive mood states (Bowling and Cartwright, 1982; Faletti and Berman, 1983; Harvey and Bahr, 1980; Lopata, 1973; Martin Matthews, 1986). Individuals with confidants (Breslau and Haug, 1983) are best able to survive social losses. Siblings, particularly sisters, play an important role as confidants to widowed women and are very important sources of support for them (Martin Matthews, 1986).

There seems to be a difference in the use of the resources of income and money by men and women. Women place a higher value on social support because of the different emphasis put upon it in their socialization. Men place a higher value on income because of the success ethic (Elwell and Maltbie-Crannell, 1981). Glick and colleagues (1974) found that men adjusted their social lives more quickly after widowhood than did women, who adjusted their emotional lives more quickly than did men.

Relationship of Variables to Morale

This review of literature has led us to think that there are some important predictors of morale in widowhood. These can be listed in a brief outline.

Relationships are expected in particular patterns. More formally, we expect to support the following hypotheses:

1. The relationship between widowhood and morale is direct, with widowed people having more negative feelings than others. Positive feelings are not expected to be affected by widowhood.

2. The relationship between other demographic variables and morale is direct, with lower morale among the poor, the less-educated, those with poorer health, the unemployed, and those with a large number of family members. (Exceptions are age and gender, where these relationships are not expected to hold.)

3. The relationship between solitary activities and chores and morale is weak, but a strong positive relationship will exist between religiosity and social activities and morale.

Methodology

Data and Data Analysis

The present research used data from the Canadian Health Survey, which were collected over a period of ten months, July 1978 to March 1979, using random-selection techniques. The sample consisted of 31,668 persons across Canada. Various methods were used to collect the data, including questionnaires, interviews, and physical-health measures taken by trained practitioners. Only the self-reported items were used in this research.

From the large sample, samples of women and men over 40 years of age were drawn, including 5,155 women, 1,135 of them widows, and 4,776 men, 237 of whom were widowers. Our previous experience had suggested that widowhood had different implications on the social and economic resources of widows and widowers; thus, males and females were analyzed separately (Harvey et al., 1986). Since widowed and married persons are distinguished only by the event of death of a spouse, and since divorced, separated, and single persons have several contrasting characteristics, only the widowed and married groups were included in this study.

For analysis of the Canadian Health Survey data, we employed the following strategies:

For the dependent variables that measure morale, separate analyses have been conducted for positive and for negative feelings. Although Bradburn (1969) did present positive and negative feelings separately, he also combined these into an Affect Balance Scale. We have chosen to use these dependent variables separately since the factors that affect them are different, as shown in our own previous analyses of these same data (Harvey et al., 1986). This is in contrast to the findings of Harding (1982), who used the Affect Balance Scale as well as the two subscales.

Data for men and for women were analyzed separately. No gender comparisons were made. Categorical variables such as widowhood, labor-force participation, and education were dummy coded for correlation and regression purposes.

Data were analyzed first by exploring the univariate differences in means between widowed and married on resources, activities, religiosity, and morale. Simple correlations were computed to check for multicolinearity among the predictors and to observe the simple associations between predictor variables and morale.

Regression equations were computed as the primary mechanism of hypothesis testing. Regressions were computed for men and women separately and within gender groups on widowed and married separately. Each regression examined the predictive association of individual resources and activities on morale.

Measures

The Positive Affect Scale (PAS) and Negative Affect Scale (NAS) of the Bradburn Affect Balance Scale (1969) were used as indices of positive and negative morale. PAS and NAS scores are each the sum of five item scores. Scale scores hypothetically range from five to 15. Low PAS scores indicate more positive affect, and low NAS scores indicate more negative affect. The five PAS items asked the degree to which one had been feeling pleased, excited or interested, on top of the world, things were going their way, and proud over the last few weeks. The NAS asked the degree to which one was restless, lonely, worried, depressed, and upset over the last few weeks. Harvey et al. (1986) reported coefficients of internal reliability in excess of .70 for each scale.

Aside from conceptual arguments for considering the PAS and the NAS as separate indices of morale, factor analyses found the PAS and NAS item scores for the Canada Health Survey data to load on two separate factors (Harvey et al., 1986). Correlational analyses of the data for purposes of the present study reported a PAS–NAS correlation of –.09 for men, and –.20 for women.

Activity Scale Construction

Three measures of activity were scaled: solitary physical activity, social physical activity, and home-based chores. These scales measured individual activities using separate items for the number of occurrences in the last two weeks as well as the usual number of minutes spent at that activity each time. The product of these two measures (number of occasions and time per occasion) provided a cumulative number of minutes spent at an activity over a two-week period. The hypothetical range for each item was zero to 480 minutes. Each of the three scales reflects an average time per activity. Hypothetical scale ranges and items ranges were therefore identical.[1]

The Solitary Activity Scale reflects the average time spent at walking, jogging, doing calisthenics, bicycling, or swimming. All of these are activities that are individually focused and do not require the presence of others, although for some the activity may be done with others. The real range of scores for this scale was zero to 360.

The Social Activity Scale is the average time spent bowling, dancing, skating, skiing or curling, or playing racket sports, baseball, golf, or other team sports. All these, excepting skating and skiing, require social exchange. Skating and skiing were included because they were judged to usually take place in a social context. Scores on this scale ranged from zero to 180 minutes.

The Home-based Chores Scale reflects the average time spent on any of ten activities: mowing grass, shoveling snow, cleaning floors, raking leaves, gardening, making beds, carpentry, handicraftsman work, ironing, and other chores. Obtained scores for this scale ranged between zero and 240 minutes.

For all three scales, higher scores reflect more activity. High interitem correlations were not anticipated, and reliability coefficients will not be reported. One limitation applying to all of the scales was the high degree of positive skew. A large percentage of the sample reported zero levels of physical activities (40 percent for solitary activity, 62 percent for social activity, and 16 percent for chores).

Religiosity was measured by a one-item scale indicating the degree to which religion was important. The scale was inversely scored, with the lowest score (1) given for a response of "very important" and a high score of (4) for a response of "of no importance." Response frequencies for this item, for men and for women, are presented in table 12.2.

Results

Demographic Characteristics and Health Status

The demographic characteristics of the widowed and married respondents included in this study are summarized in table 12.1. The data show that widowed people are much more commonly women than men. Within the male sample the widowed respondents were significantly older, had lower income, less education, smaller family size, less labor-force participation, and more health problems than did married males. The same differences applied in comparing female widowed respondents with married ones. It is interesting to note that lower incomes for widowed persons applied in both the male and female comparisons, with the widows reporting the lowest family income. Because there are so many important demographic differences between widowed and married people in this study, these differences represent important confounding factors that needed to be addressed in the data analyses examining the relationship between widowhood and morale.

Table 12.1 Married Versus Widowed Comparisons of Demographic Factors for Men and Women in Canada (in percentages).

	Men		Women	
	Widowed (N=237)	Married (N=4,539)	Widowed (N=1,135)	Married (N=4,020)
Age				
40–44	3	17	2	19
45–49	4	17	4	19
50–54	4	17	7	17
55–59	10	15	8	16
60–64	11	12	12	12
65–69	11	9	15	8
70+	57	13	52	9
Mean	64.3 years	53.3 years	68.0 years	56.0 years
Univariate F	F=280 (1,4774) $p \leq .001$.		F=1468 (1,5153) $p \leq .001$.	
Income				
$ 0–6,500	43	9	55	11
$ 7,000–13,500	20	22	20	22
$14,000–20,500	15	19	12	23
$21,000–27,500	9	25	6	19
$28,000–34,500	3	11	3	11
$ 35,000+	8	14	3	12
Mean	$12,620	$19,941	$9,658	$19,598
Univariate F	F=122 (1,4429) $p \leq .001$		F=913 (1,4823) $p \leq .001$	
Education				
Some secondary	89	81	87	83
Postsecondary	11	18	13	17
Univariate F	F=6.56 (1,4724) $p \leq .01$.		F=13 (1,5114) $p \leq .001$.	
Family size				
Unattached	53	<1	58	<1
2–3 members	28	57	28	62
4–6 members	16	38	13	34
7 or more	3	5	1	4
Univariate F	F=392.9 (1,4774) $p < .001$		F=1623 (1,5153) $p < .001$	

Table 12.1 Continued.

	Men		Women	
	Widowed ($N=237$)	Married ($N=4,539$)	Widowed ($N=1,135$)	Married ($N=4,020$)
Labor force participation				
Work or school	21	65	12	24
Housework	1	<1	56	69
Retired	78	35	32	7
Univariate *F*	$F=169$ (1,4774) $p<.001$		$F=169$ (1,4774) $p<.001$	
Health status				
No problems	21	31	13	23
1 problem	22	28	18	27
2 problems	22	18	20	20
3 problems	14	11	17	13
4 or more	21	11	32	17
Mean	2.1	1.5	2.8	1.9
Univariate *F*	$F=29.5$ (1,4774) $p<.001$		$F=217$ (1,5153) $p<.001$	

Widowhood and Activities and Religiosity

Comparisons of widowed and married respondents on various activities and religiosity are presented in table 12.2. In the male sample there were no significant differences observed between widowed and married respondents on any of the activities variables or on religiosity. In the female sample differences did occur. Widows were much less active in all areas, including solitary activities, social activities, and chores. They also scored lower on the religiosity scale than did married women, indicating that they were more religious.

Widowhood and Morale, One-way Analyses

A one-way analysis of variance comparing widowed and married subjects in the male and female samples is provided in table 12.3. In the male sample, significant differences occurred on the Positive Affect Scale. Widowed respondents had higher scores on this scale, reflecting less positive affect than the married respondents. No significant difference was found on the Negative Affect Scale. In the female sample significant differences occurred on both the Positive and Negative Affect

Table 12.2 Canadian Widowed Versus Married: Between-Group Comparisons of Means on Activity Variables and Religiosity.

	Men		Women	
	Widowed	Married	Widowed	Married
Solitary activities				
$\bar{X}$	22.26	22.55	15.72	17.89
(*N*)	(182)	(3,345)	(879)	(3,164)
Univariate *F*	$F = .012$ (1,3525) ns		$F = 3.89$ (1,4041) $p \leq .05$	
Social activities				
$\bar{X}$	4.17	2.58	1.29	2.94
(*N*)	(182)	(3,347)	(879)	(3,164)
Univariate *F*	$F = 3.74$ (1,3527) ns		$F = 28.07$ (1,4041) $p < .001$	
All chores				
$\bar{X}$	21.03	20.94	23.5	36.55
(*N*)	(169)	(3,247)	(843)	(3,011)
Univariate *F*	$F = .002$ (1,3414) ns		$F = 106$ (1,3852) $p < .001$	
Religiosity*				
$\bar{X}$	1.95	1.96	1.52	1.68
(*N*)	(194)	(3,717)	(979)	(3,547)
Univariate *F*	$F = .03$ (1,3909) ns		$F = 34.3$ (1,4524) $p < .001$	

*Lower score reflects higher religiosity.

subscales, with the widowed respondents being less positive and more negative in their affect scores.

Correlational Analyses

Prior to conducting regression analyses predicting morale, correlational tables were prepared and examined. The results are provided in tables 12.4 and 12.5. Results showed that while there were indeed several high correlations among some of the variables that we intended to use as predictors of morale, the correlations were not generally high enough to warrant serious concern about problems of multicolinearity. In the male sample high correlations were observed between age and family size (−.52) and between labor-force activity and income (−.51) and age (.59). In the female sample the highest correlations observed were between family size and income (.57) and age and family size (−.55).

Table 12.3 Canadian Widowed Versus Married: Between-Group Comparisons of Means on Bradburn Scales.

	Men		Women	
	Widowed	Married	Widowed	Married
Positive Affect Scale*				
$\bar{X}$	9.71	9.28	9.36	9.12
(N)	(159)	(3,245)	(829)	(3,127)
	$F=7.29$ (1,3401) $p=.007$		$F=10.62$ (1,3954) $p=.001$	
Negative Affect Scale*				
$\bar{X}$	12.09	12.33	11.76	12.01
(N)	(164)	(3,241)	(831)	(3,119)
	$F=7.2.1$ (1,3403) ns		$F=8.44$ (1,3948) $p=.004$	

*Lower scores indicate more affect.

In the male sample there were seven significant correlations with widowhood. Males who were widowed tended to have lower incomes, smaller family size, more health problems, less education, less positive morale, and to be older and thus less likely to be in the labor force than were married men. Among women, even more of the correlations with widowhood were significant. Widows, like their male counterparts, tended to have lower incomes, smaller family size, more health problems, less education, less positive morale, and be older and less active in the labor force than married women. In addition, widows reported that they participated less in both solitary and social activities, were more religious, and were more negative and less positive in their morale.

Widowhood and Morale, Regression Analyses

In order to examine the effect of widowhood on morale while controlling for demographic and health problems, simple multiple regression analyses were conducted. The roles of activities and religiosity in predicting morale were also examined in these analyses, conducted within each sex. Results are presented in table 12.4.[2] In the male sample there were eight significant predictors of positive morale and seven significant predictors of negative morale, with somewhat different patterns emerging. Positive morale in male respondents was associated with (1) being married as opposed to being widowed, (2) having more income,

(3) having better health, (4) living in smaller family units, (5) spending more time in solitary activities, (6) spending more time in social activities, (7) spending more time participating in chores, and (8) being more religious. Negative morale in male respondents was associated with (1) being widowed, (2) having low education, (3) being younger, (4) having more health problems, (5) being less likely to be in the labor force, (6) participating less in social activities, and (7) being less religious. For both the positive and negative morale scales the variables explained a fairly low percentage of the variance (6 percent for positive morale and 7 percent for negative morale).

In the female sample there were eight significant predictors of positive morale and eight significant predictors of negative morale. Females with more positive morale tended to (1) be married, (2) have better income, (3) be better educated, (4) have fewer health problems, (5) have smaller families, (6) participate more in solitary activities, (7) participate more in social activities, and (8) be more religious. Females with more negative morale tended to (1) be widowed, (2) have less income, (3) have less education, (4) be younger, (5) have more health problems, (6) have larger family size, (7) participate less in solitary activities, and (8) be less religious. In the female sample the predictors explained 5 percent of the variance in positive morale and 10 percent of the variance in negative morale.

In order to explore whether or not the predictors of morale might differ within the widowed as opposed to the married sample, another series of regression analyses were conducted separately within the widowed and married sample. These analyses were done to determine what factors might be exerting a stronger influence in the widowed sample, possibly buffering the widowed person against the effects of widowhood. Results of these analyses are presented in table 12.5.

There was a somewhat smaller sample of widowers than for the other groups, and fewer significant predictors of morale were observed for these men. In the sample of widowers, two significant predictors of positive morale were found. More positive morale was observed among widowers who spent more time participating in social activities and chores. The higher beta weight for these factors in the widowed as opposed to the nonwidowed group suggests that they may have a buffering effect in the widowed group. Only one significant predictor of negative morale was observed among widowers. Younger widowed men were less positive in their morale than older ones.

Among widows three significant predictors of positive morale

Table 12.4 Beta Weights of Demographic and Activity Factors as Predictors of Positive and Negative Affect Scores, Canada Health Survey Data.

	Men		Women	
	PAS*	NAS**	PAS	NAS
Widowed	.04[a]	−.04[a]	.05[a]	−.07[c]
Income	−.07[b]	.04	−.08[c]	.10[c]
Education	−.01	.07[c]	−.04[a]	.08[c]
Age	.04	.16[c]	−.02	.15[c]
Health	.10[c]	−.22[c]	.10[c]	−.26[c]
Family size	.09[c]	−.04	.10[c]	−.10[c]
Labor force participation	.01	−.05[a]	—	—
Solitary activities	−.05[b]	.00	−.12[c]	.03[a]
Social activities	−.06[c]	.04[a]	−.07[c]	.02
All chores	−.11[c]	.01	−.03	.02
Religiosity	.12[c]	−.05[b]	.09[c]	−.08[c]
R	.25[c]	.26[c]	.23[c]	.32[c]
R^2	.06	.07	.05	.10
	(N=3,009)	(N=3,013)	(N=3,430)	(N=3,419)

*PAS is Positive Affect Score.

**NAS is Negative Affect Score.

[a] $p<.05$.

[b] $p<.01$.

[c] $p<.001$.

N=Minimum pairwise with nonmissing value.

emerged. These predictors were (1) health problems, (2) time spent in solitary activities, and (3) time spent in social activities. More positive morale was reported by those who were healthier and more active. The somewhat stronger relationships between these factors and morale in the widowed group suggests a possible buffering effect. As to negative morale, the most negative mood states were reported by widows who had less education, were younger, had more health problems, had larger families, and who were less religious. Most of these predictors had approximately the same effect in the married group, except for family size, which seemed to be a somewhat stronger predictor in the widowed group. In other words, being a widow with a large family may be more detrimental than being a widow with a small family.

Discussion

Using the Canada Health Survey data, analyzing people over 40 years of age, and comparing widowed to married people, we have presented some interesting results. We will now discuss the meaning of these findings and draw implications for practitioners and researchers.

First, we used the Bradburn (1969) Positive and Negative Affect Scales as measures of morale, our dependent variable. We found that widows and widowers in Canada in 1978–1979 were very similar to those in the United States in 1969 in regard to these morale measures. Both in data presented here and in Bradburn's (1969) samples, the rank order of results were identical. For Positive Feelings, ranks (from high to low) were married women, married men, widowed men, and widowed women; for Negative, ranks (from high to low) were widowed women, married women, widowed men, and married men. Thus, married people are clearly higher in positive feelings and lower in negative ones than their widowed counterparts in both countries, even when the data is separated by 10 years in time.

Widowed people had less positive morale than did married ones in Canada. This is consistent with the findings of Bankoff (1983), Diener (1984), and Pearlin and Johnson (1977). It is in contrast to the findings of Harvey and Bahr (1980), although their female sample was much younger than the women in this Canadian study.

Income did not show the strong, independent effect on morale among the widowed that we had anticipated. Instead, other factors were more important to predict both positive and negative feelings. Since our analyses included chores and solitary activities, both of which have not been consistently included in previous research on widowhood, we can suggest that being independent and enjoying health and ability to do things alone may alter previous income-morale relationships found in other research. Clearly, this notion warrants further study. Additionally, since Canada provides medical care for all citizens at little or no cost and has other social insurance programs, variability in income is less extreme than in the United States. Thus, fewer very poor people and less overall variability in income could account for the lesser importance of income as a predictor with Canadian data compared to that of the United States.

Age results are consistent with current epidemiological findings in regard to depression. These findings show that younger samples show

Table 12.5 Beta Weights of Demographic, Activity, and Religiosity Factors as Predictors of Positive and Negative Affect Scores Considering Widowed and Married Separately, Canada Health Survey Data.

	Men			
	Positive Affect		Negative Affect	
	Widowed	Married	Widowed	Married
Income	.15	−.08[c]	−.00	.03
Education	−.07	−.01	.11	.07[c]
Age	−.20	.05[a]	.28[b]	.14[c]
Health	.17	.09[c]	−.16	−.22[c]
Family size	−.13	.10[c]	.05	−.04
Labor	.09	.01	−.18	−.04
Solitary activities	−.10	−.05[b]	.05	.00
Social activities	−.22[a]	−.05[b]	.05	.04[a]
All chores	−.17[a]	−.11[c]	−.04	.02
Religiosity	.03	.12[c]	−.02	−.05[b]
R	.43[b]	.24[c]	.31[c]	.26[c]
R^2	.18	.06	.10	.07
	(N=141)	(N=2,868)	(N=237)	(N=2,868)

[a] $p<.05$, [b] $p<.01$, [c] $p<.001$, N=Minimum pairwise with nonmissing value.

higher amounts of depression than do older ones (Barnes, Currie, and Segall, forthcoming).

Sex differences were observed here, but since we conducted our analyses separately for men and women, we are not able to specify probability levels associated with the differences that were presented. By comparing results of men and women, however, some clearly different patterns of morale emerge.

Living alone is a clear preference for Canadians of older ages, as shown by Wister and Burch (1985). Our data showed that living alone does not have a detrimental effect on mood; thus, other factors of good health and social involvement are better predictors, in general, of morale than is size of family.

Health clearly emerges as a sensitive predictor of morale. This is consistent with earlier findings of Edwards and Klemmack (1973), Harvey and Bahr (1980), Palmore and Luikart (1972), Quinn (1983), and Spreitzer and Snyder (1974). Researchers and practitioners both should thus be sensitive to good health as a correlate of positive morale.

Women

Positive Affect		Negative Affect	
Widowed	Married	Widowed	Married
−.00	−.08[c]	−.10	.10[c]
−.05	−.04[a]	.07[a]	.09[c]
−.02	−.02	.13[c]	.14[c]
.15[c]	.08[c]	−.24[c]	−.26[c]
.08	.08[a]	−.16[b]	−.06[b]
—	—	—	—
−.16[c]	−.11[c]	.08[a]	.02
−.09[b]	−.06[b]	.05	.02
−.07	−.02	−.03	.03
.11	.09[c]	−.08[c]	−.08[c]
.31[c]	.21[c]	.34[c]	.32[c]
.09	.04	.11	.10
(N=733)	(N=2,688)	(N=731)	(N=2,688)

Activity patterns show interesting things in this Canadian sample, especially for men. Men who are able to look after themselves, do their own chores, and who are healthy have better outlooks, both among the married and the widowed. This finding also applies to women, although for women other items are also correlated with morale. We think practitioners and family members should be encouraging independence of widowed people, particularly widowers. It is probably no help to widowers to do chores for them; instead it may have a more positive long-term outcome to teach them to do chores for themselves.

Religiosity results presented here were consistent with other studies. Again, family members, practitioners, and researchers should be sensitive to the religious feelings of people with whom they live or work. Encouraging consistent religious participation after widowhood with what was the case before it seems warranted, as shown in Harvey and Bahr's (1980) longitudinal study.

We conclude that many factors associated with widowhood in the United States appear to apply in Canada as well. However, we add that solitary participation patterns ought to be investigated further. It is also important to keep country differences in mind, as shown by Martin Matthews (1986).

Limitations of the present data set also prevent exploring two items that we think might affect our results. The low explained variation on morale these data showed could also be due to the two variables not collected in the original study of Canadians and their health. First, the amount of time since the spouse's death and the circumstances surrounding the death were unknown. Second, availability of a confidant was also not assessed. It is our opinion that these factors may contribute greatly to the morale of the widowed, and we suggest they be added to further studies of widowed people in Canada.

13 Brief Conclusions

HELENA ZNANIECKA LOPATA

The first idea that strikes the reader of volume 2 of *Widows* is this great heterogeneity alluded to in chapter 1. Here we have two societies, Canada and America, that are allegedly the most "socially developed" and with an extreme complexity of scale. According to some observers, this should make their members alike in their individuality and complexity of involvement. Yet we see tremendous variation in life frameworks, social roles and relations, support systems, life-styles, and self-concepts. In simplest terms, we might say that the widows under study in these societies can be located in various positions along a continuum between traditional and modern, except that none but the very highly educated can be fully located at the modern extreme. Which criteria can we use to place, for example, the widows in a Florida retirement community vis-à-vis those in urban Nebraska or the participants in the widowed self-help groups? Complicating the picture is the fact that we do not have comparable data; each scholar used different methods of selecting and studying people. It would be folly to try a single line of placement of the widows described in this volume.

In volume 1 we stressed the differences in the societies and communities in which the various categories of widows are living. The cultural and structural divergences were so overwhelming that less attention was paid by the authors (and in the volume as a whole) to variations within each society, although comments were made about the importance of age, social class, urban–rural, and presence and availability of children and other relatives. In volume 2 we have two similar societies, and the contrasts drawing the attention of many of our contributors are often between widows and other categories of members of these societies. The research team at the University of Manitoba has the largest and most complex sample, which enabled them to make contrasts between men and women and the married versus the widowed. This study finds widowed women lowest in positive feelings and highest in negative feelings. For the latter feelings, widows were followed by married women, widowed men, and married men. Widows were also less involved in all kinds of activities. The comparison between wives and widows in the Florida retirement community, among urban blacks, among urban Nebraskans, and among the Canadians finds widows worse off than wives. The measures of social involvement and morale indicate this to be true, even when controlling for age, health, and socioeconomic status, as Anderson did. In Nebraska, the absence of a husband made other relations, including those with siblings, more important. A significant conclusion of that study is the continuity in support networks from marriage to widowhood. The same is true of the Columbus homeowning widows studied by O'Bryant who have been able to remain in the same environment, with its advantages and sources of vulnerability.

Pelham and Clark's comparison between white, black, Hispanic, and Asian poor widows in California documents the importance of knowing the relationship between informal and formal support resources as well as the difficulty in determining need. They feel that ethnicity per se is not the important independent factor. However, the social organizational and cultural differences among these groups are significant. The Asian and Hispanic widows are not only illiterate, which makes independent living very restrictive, but they also are embedded in a culture that does not favor women living alone. The blacks are less likely than the whites to live alone. Their social resources are much less likely to include living children, siblings, and grandchildren than do those of the other three groups.

While the four groups of California widows have widely varied resources for informal support systems, they all live in a state that makes available highly developed formal resources. Again, however, because of the complexity of the informal network it appears impossible to predict the level of utilization of these state-run economic and service supports. This is due to the influence of intervening variables of self-defined need, knowledge of what is available, and willingness to use the formal resources. For example, we found in Cairo, Egypt, that even highly uneducated widows were tied into the formal services because relatives and neighbors, who were otherwise responsible for their welfare, provided connections to many of the formal supports (not reported elsewhere).

Several of our authors suggested some policy implications of their data, particularly the importance of targeting widows who are without the "normal" informal network of family in the form of children or their substitutes (O'Bryant, Pelham and Clark). The presence in American and Canadian societies of people illiterate in English and who are poor and require help brings Pelham and Clark to recommend the hiring of translators by public agencies. I came across a Polish immigrant in Chicago who was being evicted from her home for not obeying a rule described in English in letters that were sent to her. Whenever she called the number given by the agency to get an explanation, no one could understand her, and it was assumed that she purposely broke the law.

Pelham and Clark make an important point, echoed by other researchers studying the elderly poor, that what is needed is an increase in the federal Supplementary Security Income—increase the amount of money available to all these people rather than arguing, for example, how best to deliver ethnic meals in a particular catchment area. I would add to this the need to provide nationalized health care, as available in Australia and Canada, to the whole population. Medicaid and Medicare have obvious limitations and certainly do not cover the majority of the people in our societies.

Finally, most of the authors stress the importance of providing connecting links between widowed women and formal as well as more personal support networks. Most of the widows presently living in America and Canada were socialized in times when women were supposed to limit themselves to the private, home sphere, and not to venture outside of it except to meet its needs. They were not expected to demand attention from the public sphere and its bureaucracies. They were raised in stable communities and automatically engaged in networks of family, neighbors, church groups, and long-lasting friendships. As O'Bryant and others point out, many elderly widows, even if they can remain in their homes, do not have living children or do not have them easily available because of social and geographical mobility.

For others, a whole series of events disorganizes life. The husband dies, the neighborhood changes, the widow moves to a smaller housing unit, she sells the car, married friends no longer include her in their activities, the new church does not seem friendly, and she fears to go out at night. So, she gradually disengages, becomes inwardly oriented, and depends mainly on television for company. Even libraries and television programming are not particularly helpful, according to Pelham and Clark. Of course, for some women, the death of the husband does not create major disorganization of their life frameworks, as Fry and Gavrin explain, because of the sex-segregated nature of these frameworks. Some are even relieved of the problems of the marriage and/or feel free to engage in activities restricted by the presence of a husband or that particular husband.

There are, of course, many widows to whom these descriptions do not apply because they have the feelings of independence and competence reported by Silverman, which enables them to create a new life framework for themselves. Very few of the widowed persons who answered Silverman's questionnaire feel that only the past is meaningful and all "happiness was being married." The Chicago respondents included members of a cosmopolitan world, those with a complex social life space utilizing many formal and informal support resources; these widows are quite pleased with this phase of life.

In comparing the widows whose life frameworks are analyzed by our authors, I was struck by how these frameworks reflect the different categories of widows in the Chicago area. Momence widows resemble the working-class women I studied, with sex-segregated life-styles and easy reintegration following official grief. Of course, the town is much smaller, but most widows, especially the older ones, live in a small geographical area. The same is true of the homeowners in Columbus and the women living in that part of Omaha studied by Anderson. The retirement community is a different situation—people moved there to be with others like themselves, older, Jewish, and from the Detroit area. Activities abound, although the widows seem even here less integrated into the community. We in Chicago had some respondents living in age-segregated subcommunities, but the climate is very different and winter months decrease mobility. The same is true, of course, of Omaha or Columbus. Beck's population is also located in Florida, which tends to be overrepresented by the elderly, but they were not living in the protected environment of an organized retirement community. The blacks studied by McDonald and by Pelham and Clark resemble the poorer Chicago area blacks, although California and northern cities are not very much alike. The Canadians appear more stable in residence than many of our Chicagoans. There is definitely a difference between many of the women I studied and the Canadians reported upon by Anne Martin Matthews, as well as those in Columbus and Omaha, in the frequency with which siblings and other members of the extended family appear in the support systems of the widows.

Religion and church organizations appear as part of the support system unevenly, possibly because of differences in research emphasis. There does appear to be a significant variation in their salience between whites and blacks, as reported by several studies.

All in all, these two volumes contain a wealth of information about widows in many communities the world over. It would be nice if someday all of us could undertake truly comparative research. In the meantime, although the methods and theoretical frameworks vary considerably, we have moved ahead on this previously understudied area of sociological and psychological thought.

About Our Contributors

Trudy B. Anderson is a postdoctoral fellow with the Midwest Council for Social Research on Aging at Iowa State University. She received her Ph.D. from the University of Nebraska-Lincoln and previously was an Assistant Professor of Sociology at East Texas State University at Texarkana. Her research interests include the kinship and friendship networks of widows and the relationship between older husbands and wives. Her work has appeared in the *Journal of Marriage and the Family* and in *Research on Aging*. Currently she is on the Editorial Board of *Family Relations*.

Gordon E. Barnes, Ph.D., is Head and Associate Professor, Department of Family Studies, Faculty of Human Ecology, University of Manitoba, Winnipeg. He had been a national Health Scholar for five years, attached to the Department of Psychiatry at the University of Manitoba. Raised in Winnipeg, he received two bachelor's degrees, one in Science from the University of Manitoba and one in Arts from the University of Winnipeg. His master's and doctorate degrees are in psychology from York University. His research interests are in depression and alcohol and drug use in families.

Rubye Wilkerson Beck received her Ph.D. in sociology from the University of Florida in 1986. She is currently a part-time faculty member in the department of sociology and anthropology at East Tennessee State University in Johnson City. Her interests include marriage and family issues, widowhood, the influence of religion on social variables, family stress, and teenage parenthood.

William F. Clark, M.P.P., is currently Systems Director for the California Department of Aging's Multipurpose Senior Services program. He obtained his degree from the Graduate School of Public Policy at the University of California, Berkeley. He is coeditor with Dr. Pelham of *Managing Home Care for the Elderly* and, along with Marleen L. Clark, D.S.W., coauthor of *Old and Poor*.

Christine L. Fry is professor of anthropology at Loyola University in Chicago and co-director of a crosscultural research project on aging with Jennie Keith of Swarthmore

College. Sponsored by the National Institute on Aging, this project is a major program with global scope on the well-being of older people. She has published articles in the *Journal of Gerontology* and the *International Journal of Aging and Human Development* and has edited two books, *New Methods for Old Age Research* and *Aging in Culture and Society.*

Lauree Garvin is a doctoral student at Loyola University of Chicago. Her interests are in crosscultural research on aging, with an emphasis on Canadian studies.

Margaret Gentry is Assistant Professor of Psychology at Hamilton College in Clinton, New York. She received her Ph.D. in social psychology from Washington University in St. Louis. Her research interests include gender roles, self-perception, and coping.

Leonard J. Greenwood, B.A., is a doctoral candidate in the Department of Psychology, University of Manitoba, Winnipeg and is majoring in clinical psychology. He was raised in rural Alberta and received his bachelor's degree at the University of Alberta, Edmonton. His research interests are in the family and chemical dependency.

Carol D. H. Harvey, Ph.D., is currently Associate Professor of Family Studies, Faculty of Human Ecology, University of Manitoba, Winnipeg. She was raised on a farm in Idaho, earned a bachelor's degree in home economics extension at the University of Idaho and later a master's in family studies and a doctorate in sociology from Washington State University. She came to Canada in 1982 from a position in sociology at Boise State University. Her research interests are in widowhood and intergenerational relationships.

Rose Kabahenda-Nyakabwa, B.A. (Dip. Ed.), is a master's candidate in the Department of Family Studies, Faculty of Human Ecology, University of Manitoba, Winnipeg, Manitoba, Canada. She was raised in Kabarole, Uganda, and received her bachelor's degree and diploma in education from the University of Makerere, Kampala, Uganda. Her research interests are in widowhood and immigrant family adaptation.

Helena Znaniecka Lopata is professor of sociology and director, Center for the Comparative Study of Social Roles, Loyola University of Chicago. Her other works on widowhood include *Widowhood in an American City* (1973), *Women as Widows: Support Systems* (1979), and *Widows and Dependent Wives: From Social Problem to Federal Policy* (1986). She has recently studied the occupations of women (*City Women: Work, Jobs, Occupations, Careers*) and is planning a replication of a 1956 study of 300 homes in 12 suburbs of Chicago, called *This Old House: Social Integration in Post-World War II Suburban Homes*.

Jessyna M. McDonald is currently the chairperson of the Recreation Studies Section, Department of Physical Education, Health and Recreation Studies, at Purdue University. Her university experience also includes teaching undergraduate and graduate courses in therapeutic recreation, aging, and management at the University of Maryland, the University of Missouri, and Howard University. Practical experience includes various positions in clinical and community-based services for multiple handicapped adults and the aged. Dr. McDonald has also presented several professional workshops and presentations with organizations such as the National Recreation and Park Association; the American Alliance for Health, Physical Education, Recreation, and Dance; the Gerontological Society of America; the Western Gerontological Association; and other state and regional organizations. In addition, she has served as project director and principal investigator for grants funded by the Office of Special Education and Rehabilitation Services.

Anne Martin Matthews, Ph.D., is director of the Gerontology Research Center and associate professor, Department of Family Studies at the University of Guelph, Ontario, Canada. She has studied rural widows and will also compare rural to urban ones using a very similar interview to one used in Chicago.

Anne Victoria Neale, Ph.D., is currently on the faculty of the Department of Family Medicine at Wayne State University, where she works in the areas of social epidemiology, health promotion, and occupational health. She obtained a doctorate in social psychology at Wayne State University, where she studied social/psychological well-being among the widowed living in a retirement community. She also received a master's in public health from the University of Texas Health Science Center at Houston, School of Public Health. She is particularly interested in marital status differences in morbidity and mortality and has published an article on marital status, length of delay in seeking treatment, and survival from breast cancer.

Shirley L. O'Bryant, Ph.D., is a developmental-social psychologist, with a Ph.D. from The University of Texas at Austin. From 1974 to 1977 she served as associate director of a research project studying the effects of television on families. In the autumn of 1977 she joined the faculty of the Department of Family Relations and Human Development, The Ohio State University. There she specializes in the area of gerontology through teaching, research, and service to the community. Her special interest centers on the issues that societies face in understanding and assisting their elderly. Among her accomplishments has been a research analysis of "attachment to home," the psychological phenomenon that explains the high levels of housing satisfaction expressed by the elderly in America and why they usually do not wish to move from their homes. Her most recent research project, funded by AARP Andrus Foundation, is a study of older widows—their circumstances, well-being, and decision making in regard to relocation. Dr. O'Bryant has published in a number of professional journals and has presented the results of her research at conferences in the United States and abroad.

Anabel O. Pelham, Ph.D., is an associate professor and director of gerontology programs at San Francisco State University. From 1980 to 1983 she was also the northern coordinator of the California Senior Survey. She is a medical sociologist specializing in gerontology and health policy. She is the author of various papers in the field of aging, health, and adult education and is a graduate of the University of California, San Francisco. Her most recent books are *Managing Home Care for the Elderly*, about community-based long-term care, and *Old and Poor: A Study of Low Income Elders and the Continuum of Care*.

Linda Rosenman, Ph.D., is an Australian who is currently associate dean of Arts and Sciences Extension and associate professor of social work at the University of Missouri–St. Louis. She has done considerable cross-national research and publication on older women in Australia and the United States. The research on which this chapter is based was partly funded by the National Institute of Aging and was carried out while she was on the social work faculty at Latrobe University in Melbourne and subsequently as a visiting fellow at the Social Welfare Research Centre in Sydney. This chapter was coauthored with her husband. Linda and Arthur also contributed to volume I on widowhood in Australia.

Arthur D. Shulman, Ph.D., is an associate professor of psychology at Washington University in St. Louis. His research was carried out jointly while he was the Inaugural Ashworth Fellow at the University of Melbourne. This research was part of a larger research project funded by the National Institute of Aging on Widowed Women in St. Louis and in Melbourne.

Phyllis R. Silverman, Ph.D., is a professor in the social work and health program of the Massachusetts General Hospital Institute of Health Professions. She also holds an appointment in the Department of Psychiatry at Harvard Medical School, where she developed the concept of the widow-to-widow program and directed the research project that demonstrated its effectiveness. Her publications include *Helping Each Other in Widowhood, If You Will Lift the Load I Will Lift It Too, Mutual Help Groups: A Guide for Mental Health Professionals, Mutual Help Groups: Organization and Development, Helping Women Cope with Grief,* and *Widow-to-Widow*.

Notes

1 Widows: North American Perspectives

1 The role modification study, which included 301 widows aged 50–64 and 65+, was funded by the Administration on Aging, Department of Health, Education and Welfare, United States Government (Grant No. AA46703001A1). The sample was selected and interviews conducted by the National Opinion Research Center, University of Chicago. Thanks also go to Roosevelt University. The support systems sample was stratified and drawn up by the Social Security Administration's (SSA) statisticians from lists with different ratios to insure sufficient cases in the less-populous strata. The five samples include: (1) current beneficiaries because of dependent children, (2) current old age beneficiaries, (3) former beneficiaries whose children grew up, (4) former beneficiaries who remarried, and (5) widows who received only the "lump sum" payment to help defray funeral costs. The study was funded with a contract from the Social Security Administration (Contract No. SSA71-3411), with the cooperation of Loyola University of Chicago. Special thanks go to Dr. Henry Brehm of the SSA, to the staff of the Survey Research Laboratory of the University of Illinois, Circle Campus, and to the staff of the Center for the Comparative Study of Social Roles at Loyola University, especially Frank Steinhart, Sister Gertrud Kim, Suzanne Meyering, and Sue Dawson.

References

Berger, Peter, and Hansfried Kellner. 1970. Marriage and the construction of reality: An exercise in the microsociology of knowledge. In Hans Dreitzel (ed.), *Patterns in Communicative Behavior*. Pp. 50–73. London: Collier-Macmillan.

Blau, Z. 1961. "Structural constraints of friendship in age." *American Sociological Review* 26:429–39.

Blumberg, R. 1985. Personal communication.

Bohannan, P. J. 1963. *Social Anthropology*. New York: Holt, Rinehart and Winston.

Chicago Mayor's Office for Senior Citizens. 1973. "Chicago Needs Assessment Survey." Unpublished.

Cumming, E., and W. Henry. 1961. *Growing Old*. New York: Basic Books.

Decker, D. L. 1980. *Social Gerontology*. Boston: Little, Brown.

Farrell, W. 1975. *The Liberated Man: Beyond Masculinity: Freeing Men and Their Relationships with Women*. New York: Bantam Books.

Fisher, L. R. 1986. *Linked Lives: Adult Daughters and Their Mothers*. New York: Harper and Row.

Fowlkes, M. 1980. *Behind Every Successful Man: Wives of Medicine and Academe*. New York: Columbia University Press.

Goode, W. 1963. *World Revolution and Family Patterns*. New York: Free Press.

Hareven, T. K. 1976. "Modernization and family history: Perspectives on social change." *Signs* 2:190–206.

Hess, B. B., and E. W. Markson. 1980. *Aging and Old Age*. New York: Macmillan.

Hochschild, A. R. 1973. *The Unexpected Community*. Englewood Cliffs, N.J.: Prentice-Hall.

Hyman, H. H. 1983. *Of Time and Widowhood*. Durham, N.C.: Duke University Press.

Kanter, R. M. 1977. *Men and Women of the Corporation*. New York: Basic Books.

Komarovsky, M. 1967. *Blue-Collar Marriage*. New York: Random House.

Lindemann, E. 1944. "Symptomatology and management of acute grief." In R. Fulton, E. Markusen, G. Own, and J. L. Scheiber (Eds.), *Death and Dying: Challenge and Change*. Pp. 221–28. 1978. Reading, Mass.: Addison-Wesley.

Lipset, S. M. 1979. *The First New Nation: The United States in Historical and Comparative Perspective*. 2d ed. New York: W. W. Norton.

Litwak, E. 1965. "Extended kin relations in an industrial democratic society." In E. Shanas and G. Streib (Eds.), *Social Structure and the Family: Generational Relations*. Pp. 290–323. Englewood Cliffs, N.J.: Prentice-Hall.

Lopata, H. Z. 1969. "Loneliness: Forms and components." *Social Problems* 17(2, Fall):248–72.

———. 1971. "Living arrangements of urban widows and their married children." *Sociological Focus* 9(1, Autumn):41–61.

———. 1972. "Social relations of widows in urbanizing societies." *Sociological Quarterly* 13(Spring):259–71.

———. 1973a. "The effect of schooling on social contacts of urban women." *American Journal of Sociology* 79(3, November):604–19.

———. 1973b. *Widowhood in an American City*. Cambridge, Mass.: Schenkman.

———. 1978a. "The absence of community resources in support systems of urban widows." *The Family Coordinator* (October):383–88.

———. 1978b. "Contributions of extended families to the support systems of metropolitan area widows: Limitations of the modified kin network." *Journal of Marriage and the Family* 40(May):355–64.

———. 1979. *Women as Widows: Support Systems*. New York: Elsevier-North Holland.

———. 1981. "Widowhood and husband sanctification." *Journal of Marriage and the Family* 43(2, May):439–50.

———. 1984. "The self-concept, identities and traumatic events: The death of a husband." Paper presented at the International Conference on Self and Identity. Cardiff, Wales (July 9–13).

———. 1986a. "Time in anticipated future and events in memory." *American Behavioral Scientist* 29(6, July/August):695–709.

———, and H. Brehm. 1986. *Widows and Dependent Wives: From Social Problem to Federal Policy*. New York: Praeger.

Ostrander, S. A. 1984. *Women of the Upper Class*. Philadelphia: Temple University Press.

Papanek, H. 1973. "Men, women and work: Reflections on the two-person career." *American Journal of Sociology* 78:852–72.

———. 1979. "Family status production: The 'work' and 'non-work' of women." *Signs* 4(Summer):775–81.

Rosow, I. 1967. *The Social Integration of the Aged*. New York: Free Press.

Rubin, L. B. 1979. *Women of a Certain Age*. New York: Harper and Row.

Seidenberg, R. 1973. *Corporate Wives—Corporate Casualties*. New York: American Management Association.

Shanas, E. 1979. "The family as a social support system in old age." *The Gerontologist* 19(2):169–74.

Stack, C. B. 1976. "Divorce and child custody decisions in middle-class families." *Social Problems* 23(4):505–14.

Sussman, M., and L. Burchinal. 1966. "Kin family network: Unheralded structure in current conceptualization of family functioning." In B. Farber (Ed.). *Kinship and Family Organization*. Pp. 123–33. New York: John Wiley and Sons.

Townsend, P. 1968. "Isolation, desolation and loneliness." In E. Shanas, P. Townsend, D. Wedderburn, J. Friis, P. Milhoj, and J. Stehouwer (Eds.), *Old People in Three Industrial Societies*. Pp. 258–87. New York: Atherton.

Working Woman. 1986. "How working women have changed America." (November.)

Znaniecki, F. 1952. *Modern Nationalities*. Urbana: University of Illinois Press.

2 American After Lives

1 Funding for the research reported in this chapter was granted by the National Institute on Aging, grant PO1-AG03110. The authors gratefully acknowledge the careful reading and commentary on an earlier draft of this chapter by Jennie Keith, Robert Fry, and Cheryl Woosnam.

2 This is a Program Project supported by the National Institute on Aging. The project systematically investigates the same problem with comparable research designs in seven communities around the world. Christine L. Fry (Loyola) and Jennie Keith (Swarthmore) are codirectors of the project. The communities selected are Hong Kong (Charlotte Ikels, Case Western Reserve); Swarthmore, Pa. (Jennie Keith, Swarthmore); Momence, Ill. (Christine L. Fry, Loyola); Blessington and Clifden, Ireland (Anthony P. Glascock, Drexel University); Kung Bushmen, Botswana (Patricia Draper, Pennsylvania State University); and Herero of Botswana (Henry Harpending, Pennsylvania State University).

3 Ethnosemantics is a distinctive research strategy to examine the cognitive organization of the phenomena under investigation. Language and semantic domains are seen as organizing principles people use in making decisions and negotiating social transactions. Research strategies involve eliciting frames to understand native or emic classifications. For a consideration of this approach salient to aging see Fry, 1986.

4 Since respondents made their own groupings, we found considerable variation. The range in Momence was between zero (age is not important) to nine divisions of life. The median number of divisions seen was five, with the vast majority of variance ranging between three–seven groups. In the statistics presented, we have analyzed those who see three groups, four groups, five groups, and six groups separately. The older groups for people who see three divisions are somewhat different from those who see six life stages. These differences have been analyzed using multidimensional scaling and cluster analysis.

5 They are not visible, but when needed the information usually is not too difficult to obtain. For instance, when the senior author's mother became ill and was scheduled to come to Momence, she had, within a few days of this becoming known in the community, the names of three women who provide home support for people who need extra assistance.

References

Bott, E. 1957. *Family and Social Network*. London: Tavistock Institute of Social Relations.

Fry, C. L. 1986. "The emics of age: Age differentiation and cognitive anthropological strategies." In C. L. Fry and J. Keith (Eds.), *New Methods for Old Age Research*. Pp. 105–30. South Hadley, Mass.: Bergin and Garvey.

Levine, S. E. 1986. "Widowhood in Los Robles: Parent-child relations and economic survival in old age in urban Mexico." *Journal of Cross-Cultural Gerontology* 1:223–38.

Lopata, H. Z. 1972. "Role changes in widowhood: A world perspective." In D. O. Cowgill and L. D. Holmes (Eds.), *Aging and Modernization*. Pp. 275–304. New York: Appleton-Century Crofts.

———. 1973. *Widowhood in an American City*. Cambridge, Mass.: Schenkman.

———. 1979. *Women as Widows: Support Systems*. New York: Elsevier-North Holland.

Moore, S. F. 1978. "Old age in a life-term arena: Some Chagga of Kilimanjaro in 1974." In B. G. Myerhoff and A. Simic (Eds.), *Life's Career: Aging*. Beverly Hills, Calif.: Sage Publications.

Ortner, S. B. 1974. "Is female to male as nature is to culture?" In M. Z. Rosaldo and L. Lamphere (Eds.), *Women, Culture and Society*. Stanford, Calif: Stanford University Press.

Silverman, P. R. 1986. *Widow to Widow*. New York: Springer.

Spradley, J. P. 1979. *The Ethnographic Interview*. New York: Holt, Rinehart and Winston.

Treiman, D. J. 1977. *Occupational Prestige in Comparative Perspective*. New York: Academic Press.

Turner, V. W. 1969. *The Ritual Process*. Chicago: Aldine.

Van Gennep, A. 1960. *The Rites of Passage*. London: Routledge and Kegan Paul.

Warner, W. L., M. Meeker, and K. Eells. 1949. *Social Class in America*. Chicago: Science Research Associates.

3 Attachment to Home and Support Systems

1 This figure for percentage of population differs from the national figure of 11 percent due to several factors, the major one being the 77,000 university and college students

who reside in the county and substantially increase the number of younger persons counted in the census figures.

2 Because the time of interview varied from seven to 21 months after the death of the husband, several preliminary analyses were conducted. Number of days widowed was not significantly correlated with any of the types of supports or with the frequency of receipt of support. However, some longitudinal data have been collected that may help determine if support diminishes in the long run, as has been proposed by other researchers, including Lopata (1979). These data will be reported on at a later time.

3 In Franklin County, whites account for 89 percent of all owner-occupied housing units; this is in line with national figures, which indicate that black elderly are less likely to own their own homes (Struyk and Soldo, 1980). Also, using data abstracted from the census, Chevan and Korson (1972) determined that older black households included more relatives and nonrelatives than white households, hence fewer older blacks live alone. Finally, with respect to the "attachment to home" phenomenon, one might raise questions about the meaning of home for various ethnic and cultural groups. Without a sufficient number of cases in each group, such questions cannot be adequately examined.

4 Interestingly, there was no relationship between age and health. Perhaps self-rated health is relative to one's age; consequently, when considering the health status of one's peers, one's own poor health may be rated "good" by comparison. Or, perhaps, only the older widows who were in the best of health remained alone in their homes. Age data from a small sample of movers suggests that this is indeed the case—the older the widow is the more likely she is to move, or be moved involuntarily, after her husband's death.

5 Nine percent of the group still worked either part-time or full-time; however, the relationship for income and work history did not change when these workers were excluded from the correlational analysis.

6 Unfortunately, comparative figures from national or census data related to older women's labor-force participation could not be located. Szinovacz (1983) observes that, for particular cohorts, the percentages of women who were never employed are confused because official data sources often collapsed housewives and retirees into the category of "nonworkers." These figures vary from those reported by Lopata (1979), wherein there were more widows (40 percent) who had never worked during marriage. Among the variables differentiating the Chicago-area widows from the Columbus widows are age at widowhood, the presence of children in some of the households, and some educational, income, and ethnic differences. In addition, as Lopata suggests, perhaps we are witnessing some changes in the level of commitment to jobs over the past decade.

7 Seven percent of the sample had stepchildren. When a stepchild was of long duration and was mentioned as a "child" by the widow in terms of her support network, the stepchild was counted as a child. This occurred in only a few cases.

8 Thirty-one widows, 14 percent of the respondents, were in their eighties. The mother of the 69-year-old "child" was 88; her husband had passed away at age 92.

9 The majority of these supports are "service" supports. This group of items was chosen because they appeared to be the most crucial in terms of whether the older widow could remain in her home or would have to move. In addition to these 11 types of support, other parts of the interview schedule called for a series of responses

with respect to neighbor networks, social/religious activities, and availability of a confidant. The data related to neighbor support has been analyzed and reported on elsewhere (O'Bryant, in press). Findings with respect to confidant relationships and social/religious activities will be reported on at a later date.

10 Friends and neighbors were coded separately on the basis of the widows' actual responses. In an earlier part of the interview, the widow had already responded with regard to her neighbors, how many were friends, and what they did for each other. Consequently, it was assumed she responded "friend" for those whom she had already counted within her network of friends and "neighbor" for those she had not mentioned earlier.

11 Self-reported health and income were used as covariates in all analyses conducted and reported here.

References

Anderson, T. B. 1984. "Widowhood as a life transition: Its impact on kinship ties." *Journal of Marriage and the Family* 46:105–14.

Arling, G. 1976. "The elderly widow and her family, neighbors and friends." *Journal of Marriage and the Family* 38:757–68.

Blau, Z. S. 1973. *Old Age in a Changing Society*. New York: Franklin Watts.

Block, M., J. Davidson, and J. D. Grambs. 1981. *Women Over Forty*. New York: Springer.

Bowman, T. F., G. A. Giuliani, and M. R. Mingé. 1981. *Finding Your Best Place to Live in America*. New York: Red Lion.

Bradburn, N. 1969. *The Structure of Psychological Well-Being*. Chicago: Aldine.

Brophy, J. E. 1977. *Child Development and Socialization*. Chicago: Science Research Associates.

Cantor, M. A. 1975. "Life space and the social support system of the inner city elderly of New York." *The Gerontologist* 15:23–27.

Chevan, A., and J. H. Korson. 1972. "The widowed who live alone: An examination of social and demographic factors." *Social Forces* 51:45–53.

Cicirelli, B. G. 1981. "Feelings toward siblings in adulthood and old age." Paper presented at American Psychological Association, Los Angeles.

Columbus Area Chamber of Commerce. 1984. *Columbus . . . Ohio's Capital Gains*. Columbus, Ohio.

Columbus Regional Information Service. 1984. *Growth Areas: Franklin County, 1970–1980*. Columbus, Ohio.

Doborf, R. 1979. "The family relationships and living arrangements of older women." In R. Kastenbaum (Ed.), *Older Women in the City*. Pp. 142–52. New York: Arno Press.

Garrett, B., with E. R. Lentz. 1980. *Columbus: America's Crossroads*. Tulsa, Okla.: Continental Heritage Press.

Goldenberg, L. 1981. *Housing for the Elderly: New Trends in Europe*. New York: Garland.

Hartmann, C. W. 1977. "Social values and housing orientations." In K. Nattress and B. Morrison (Eds.), *Human Needs in Housing: An Ecological Approach*. Pp. 63–81. Washington, D.C.: University Press of America.

Hays, J. A. 1984. "Aging and family resources: Availability and proximity of kin." *The Gerontologist* 24:149–53.

Hing, E., and B. K. Cypress. 1981. *Use of Health Services by Women 65 Years of Age and*

Over. DHHS Publication No. PHS 81-1720. Washington, D.C.: U.S. Government Printing Office.

Kahana, E. F., and H. A. Kiyak. 1980. "The older woman: Impact of widowhood and living arrangements on service needs." *Journal of Gerontological Social Work* 3:17–29.

Kohen, J. A. 1983. "Old but not alone: Informal social supports among the elderly by marital status and sex." *The Gerontologist* 23:57–63.

Lawton, M. P., M. H. Kleban, and E. diCarlo. 1984. Psychological well-being in the aged. *Research on Aging* 6:67–97.

Lopata, H. Z. 1973. *Widowhood in an American City*. Cambridge, Mass.: Schenkman.

———. 1979. *Women as Widows: Support Systems*. New York: Elsevier-North Holland.

———. 1980. "Loneliness in widowhood." In J. Hartog, J. R. Audy, and Y. A. Cohen (Eds.), *The Anatomy of Loneliness*. Pp. 237–58. New York: International Universities Press.

———. 1982. "Lifestyles of American widows and widowers in urban America." *Educational Horizons* 60:184–90.

Lopata, H. Z., and F. Steinhart. 1971. "Work histories of American urban women." *The Gerontologist* 11:27–36.

Mutran, E., and D. C. Reitzes. 1984. "Intergenerational support activities and well-being among the elderly: A convergence of exchange and symbolic interaction perspectives." *American Sociological Review* 49:117–30.

National Institute of Health. 1979. *The Older Woman: Continuities and Discontinuities*. NIH Publication No. 79-1897. Washington, D.C.: U.S. Government Printing Office.

O'Bryant, S. L. 1982. "The value of home to older persons and its relationship to housing satisfaction." *Research on Aging* 4:349–63.

———. 1983a. "The subjective value of 'home' to older homeowners." *Journal of Housing for the Elderly* 1:29–43.

———. 1983b. *The relationship of "attachment to home" and other factors to the residential choices of recent widows*. Final report to AARP Andrus Foundation, Washington, D.C.

———. "Neighbors' support of older widows who live alone in their own homes." *The Gerontologist*, in press.

O'Bryant, S. L., and D. Nocera. "The psychological significance of 'home' to older women." *Psychology of Women Quarterly*, in press.

O'Bryant, S. L., and S. M. Wolf. 1983. "Explanations of housing satisfaction of older homeowners and renters." *Research on Aging* 5:217–33.

Ohio Bureau of Employment Services. 1984. *Ohio Labor Market Information*. January, 1984. Columbus, Ohio.

Ohio Department of Aging. 1984. *Facts on Older Ohioans*. Columbus, Ohio.

Pastalan, L. A. 1983. "Demographic characteristics." *Journal of Housing for the Elderly* 1:85–87.

Patterson, A. H. 1978. "Crime and fear of crime among the elderly." In *Crime Prevention Through Environmental Design*. Washington, D.C.: National Institute of Justice.

Peirce, N. R., and J. Hagstrom. 1984. *The Book of America: Inside 50 States Today*. New York: Warner.

Pihlblad, C. T., and D. L. Adams. 1972. "Widowhood, social participation, and life satisfaction." *Aging and Human Development* 3:323–30.

Powers, E. A., P. M. Keith, and W. Goudy. 1975. "Family relationships and friendships." In R. C. Atchley (Ed.), *Rural Environments and Aging*. Pp. 67–90. Washington, D.C.: Gerontological Society.

Rix, S. E. 1984. *Older Women: The Economics of Aging*. Washington, D.C.: Women's Research and Education Institute.

Scholen, K. 1980. "Stereotypes, demographics, and independence: The needs of elderly subpopulations." In K. Scholen and Y. P. Chen (Eds.), *Unlocking Home Equity for the Elderly*. Pp. 41–46. Cambridge, Mass.: Ballinger.

Scholen, K., and Y. P. Chen. 1980. *Unlocking Home Equity for the Elderly*. Cambridge, Mass.: Ballinger.

Scott, J. P. 1983. "Siblings and other kin." In T. H. Brubaker (Ed.), *Family Relations in Later Life*. Pp. 47–62. Beverly Hills, Calif.: Sage Publications.

Smith, B., and J. Hiltner. 1977. "Multifactor uniform areas of elderly housing." *Professional Geographer* 29:366–73.

Struyk, R. J., and B. J. Soldo. 1980. *Improving the Elderly's Housing*. Cambridge, Mass.: Ballinger.

Szinovacz, M. E. 1983. "Beyond the hearth: Older women and retirement." In E. W. Markson (Ed.), *Older Women: Issues and Perspectives*. Pp. 93–120. Lexington, Mass.: D. C. Heath.

U.S. Bureau of the Census. 1981. *Current Population Reports*. Series P-23, nos. 58 and 100. Washington, D.C.: U.S. Government Printing Office.

Wood, V., and J. F. Robertson. 1978. "Friendship and kinship interaction: Differential effect on the morale of the elderly." *Journal of Marriage and the Family* 40:367–75.

4 Widows in a Florida Retirement Community

References

Adams, D. L. 1971. "Correlates of satisfaction among the elderly." *The Gerontologist* Part II:64–68.

Babchuk, N., G. R. Peters, D. R. Hoyt, and M. A. Kaiser. 1979. "The voluntary associations of the aged." *Journal of Gerontology* 34:579–87.

Barrett, C. J. 1977. "Women in widowhood." *Signs* (Summer):857–68.

Barsby, S. L., and D. R. Cox. 1975. *Interstate Migration of the Elderly*. Lexington, Mass.: Lexington Books.

Beck, A. A., and B. Leviton. 1976. "Social support mediating factors in widowhood and life satisfaction among the elderly." Paper presented at the Twenty-Ninth Annual Meeting of the Gerontological Society of America, New York.

Bennett, R., and J. Eckman. 1973. "Attitudes toward aging: A critical examination of recent literature and implications for future research." In C. Eisdorfer and M. P. Lawton (Eds.), *The Psychology of Adult Development and Aging*. Washington, D.C.: APA Associates.

Berardo, F. M. 1967. "Social adaptation to widowhood among a rural-urban aged population." Washington State University, Washington Agricultural Experiment Station, Bulletin 689.

———. 1968. "Widowhood status in the United States: Perspective on a neglected aspect of the family life-cycle." *The Family Coordinator* 17:11–25.

———. 1970. "Survivorship and social isolation: The case of the aged widower." *The*

Family Coordinator 19:11–25.
Biddle, B. J., and E. J. Thomas (Eds.). 1966. *Role Theory: Concepts and Research*. New York: John Wiley and Sons.
Biggar, J. C. 1980. "Reassessing elderly sunbelt migration." *Research on Aging* 2:177–90.
Biggar, J. C., C.F. Longino, Jr., and C. B. Flynn. 1980. "Elderly interstate migration: Impact on sending and receiving states, 1965–1970." *Research on Aging* 2:217–32.
Blau, Z. 1961. "Structural constraints on friendships in old age." *American Sociological Review* 26:429–39.
Bock, E. W., and I. L. Webber. 1972. "Suicide among the elderly: Isolating widowhood and mitigating alternatives." *Journal of Marriage and the Family* 34:24–31.
Booth, A. 1972. "Sex and social participation." *American Sociological Review* 37:183–92.
Boursetom, N., and P. Pastalan. 1981. "The effects of relocation on the elderly: A reply to Borup, J. H., Gallego, D. T., and Heffernan, P. G." *The Gerontologist* 21:4–7.
Bultena, G. F., and V. Wood. 1969. "The American retirement community: Bane or blessing?" *Journal of Gerontology* 24:209–17.
Carp, F. M. 1975. "Impact of improved housing on morale and life satisfaction." *The Gerontologist* 15:511–15.
———. 1978. "Effects of the living environment on activity and use of time." *International Journal of Aging and Human Development* 9:75–91.
Christopherson, V. A. 1972. "Retirement communities: The cities of two tales." *Social Science* 47:82–86.
Cleveland, W. P., and D. T. Gianturco. 1976. "Remarriage probability after widowhood: A retrospective method." *Journal of Gerontology* 31:99–103.
Deimling, G. T., L. S. Noelker, and A. C. Beckman. 1979. "The impact of race on the resources and well-being of aged public housing residents." Paper presented at the Thirty-Second Annual Meeting of the Gerontological Society of America, Washington, D.C.
Edwards, J. M., and D. L. Klemmack. 1973. "Correlates of life satisfaction: A re-examination." *Journal of Gerontology* 28:497–502.
Ferraro, K. F., E. Mutran, and C. M. Barresi. 1984. Widowhood, health and friendship support in later life." *Journal of Health and Social Behavior* 25:245–59.
Gibbs, J. M. 1978. "Role changes associated with widowhood among middle and upper class women." *Mid-American Review of Sociology* 3:17–33.
Glick, I. G., R. S. Weiss, and C. M. Parkes. 1974. *The First Year of Bereavement*. New York: John Wiley and Sons.
Golant, S. M. 1975. "Residential concentrations of the future elderly." *The Gerontologist* 15, Part II:16–23.
Gubrium, J. P. 1970. "Environmental effects on morale in old age and the resources of health and solvency." *The Gerontologist* 10:294–97.
Harvey, C. D., and H. M. Bahr. 1974. "Widowhood, morale, and affiliation." *Journal of Marriage and the Family*, February:97–106.
Havighurst, R. J., B. L. Neugarten, and S. S. Tobin. 1968. "Disengagement and patterns of aging." In B. Neugarten (Ed.), *Middle Age and Aging*. Chicago: University of Chicago Press.
Heintz, K. M. 1976. *Retirement Communities, For Adults Only*. New Brunswick, N.J.: Center for Urban Policy Research, Rutgers University.
Heyman, D. K., and D. T. Gianturco. 1973. "Long-term adaptation by the elderly to

bereavement." *Journal of Gerontology* 28:359–62.
Hochschild, A. R. 1973. *The Unexpected Community*. Englewood Cliffs, N.J.: Prentice-Hall.
Kahana, E. F., J. Liang, and B. J. Felton. 1980. "Alternative models of person-environment fit: Prediction of morale in three homes for the aged." *Journal of Gerontology* 35:584–95.
Kivett, V. R. 1978. "Loneliness and the rural widow." *The Family Coordinator* 27:389–94.
Kline, C. 1975. "The socialization process of women: Implications for a theory of successful aging." *The Gerontologist* 15:486–92.
Knapp, M. R. J. 1976. "Predicting the dimensions of life satisfaction." *Journal of Gerontology* 31:595–604.
Kohen, J. A. 1983. "Old but not alone: Informal social supports among the elderly by marital status and sex." *The Gerontologist* 23:57–63.
Koskenvuo, M., J. Kaprio, A. Kosaniemi, and S. Sarno. 1980. "Differences in mortality from ischemic heart disease by marital status and social class." *Journal of Chronic Diseases* 33:95–106.
Kraus, A. S., and A. M. Lilienfeld. 1959. "Some epidemiologic aspects of the high mortality rate in the young widowed group." *Journal of Chronic Diseases* 10:207–17.
Larson, R. 1978. "Thirty years of research on the subjective well-being of older Americans." *Journal of Gerontology* 33:109–25.
Lemon, B. W., V. L. Bengston, and J. A. Peterson. 1972. "An exploration of the activity theory of aging: Activity types and life satisfaction among in-movers to a retirement community." *Journal of Gerontology* 27:511–23.
Longino, C. F., Jr. 1980. "Retirement communities." In F. J. Berghorn and D. E. Schafer (Eds.), *The Dynamics of Aging: Original Essays on the Experience and Process of Growing Old*. Boulder, Colo.: Westview Press.
Longino, C. F., Jr., and A. Lipman. 1981. "Married and spouseless men and women in planned retirement communities: Support network differentials." *Journal of Marriage and the Family* 43:169–77.
Lopata, H. Z. 1970. "The social involvement of American widows." *American Behavioral Scientist* 14:41–57.
———. 1973. "Self-identity in marriage and widowhood." *Sociological Quarterly* 14:407–18.
———. 1979. *Women as Widows*. New York: Elsevier-North Holland.
Lowenthal, M. F., and C. Haven. 1968. "Interaction and adaptation: Intimacy as a critical variable." *American Sociological Review* 33:20–30.
Lowenthal, M. F., and B. Robinson. 1976. "Social networks and isolation." In R. H. Binstock and E. Shanas (Eds.), *Handbook of Aging and the Social Sciences*. N.Y.: Van Nostrand Reinhold.
Mangum, W. P. 1973. "Retirement villages." In R. Boyd, R. Oakes, and C. G. Oakes (Eds.), *Foundations of Practical Gerontology*. Columbia: University of South Carolina Press.
Martin, W. C. 1973. "Activity and Disengagement: Life satisfaction of in-movers into a retirement community." *The Gerontologist* 13:224–27.
Messer, M. 1967. "The possibility of an age concentrated environment becoming a normative system." *The Gerontologist* 7:247–51.
Morgan, L. A. 1976. "A re-examination of widowhood and morale." *Journal of Gerontology* 31:687–95.
Morgan, M. 1980. "Marital status, health, illness and service use." *Social Science and Medicine* 14:633–43.
Mutran, E., and D. C. Reitzes. 1981. "Retirement, identity and well-being: Realignment of

role relationships." *Journal of Gerontology* 36:733–40.

Neugarten, B. L., R. J. Havighurst, and S. S. Tobin. 1961. "The measurement of life satisfaction." *Journal of Gerontology* 16:134–43.

Palmore, E. 1968. "The effects of aging on activities and attitudes." *The Gerontologist* 8:259–63.

Parkes, C. M., B. Benjamin, and R. G. Fitzgerald. 1969. "Broken heart: A statistical study of increased mortality among widowers." *British Medical Journal* 1:740–43.

Patrick, C. H. 1980. "Health and migration of the elderly." *Research on Aging* 2:233–41.

Petrowsky, M. 1976. "Marital status, sex, and the social networks of the elderly." *Journal of Marriage and the Family* November:749–56.

Pihlblad, C. T., and D. L. Adams. 1972. "Widowhood, social participation, and life satisfaction." *Aging and Human Development* 3:323–330.

Poulin, J. E. 1984. "Age segregation and the interpersonal involvement and morale of the aged." *The Gerontologist* 24:266–69.

Rees, W. D., and S. G. Lutkins. 1967. "Mortality of bereavement." *British Medical Journal* 51:547–55.

Rosow, I. 1967. *Social Integration of the Aged*. New York: Free Press.

———. 1973. "The social context of the aging self." *The Gerontologist* 13:82–87.

Schultz, R., and G. Brenner. 1977. "Relocation of the aged: A review and theoretical analysis." *Journal of Gerontology* 32:323–33.

Serow, W. J. 1978. "Return migration of the elderly in the U.S.A.: 1955–1960 and 1965–1970." *Journal of Gerontology* 33:288–95.

Shely, J. F. 1974. "Mutuality and retirement community success: An interactionist perspective in gerontological research." *Aging and Human Development* 5:71–80.

Sherman, S. R. 1975. "Mutual assistance and support in retirement housing." *Journal of Gerontology* 30:479–83.

Slivinske, L. R., and J. I. Kosberg. 1984. "Assessing the effect of a personal health management system within retirement communities: A preliminary investigation." *The Gerontologist* 24:280–85.

Sommers, T., and L. Shields. 1979. "Social Security: Adequacy and equity for older women." *Gray Paper No. 2, Issues for Action*. Oakland, Calif.: Older Women's League Educational Fund.

Talbott, E., L. H. Kuller, V. Perper, and P. A. Murphy. 1981. "Sudden unexpected death in women." *American Journal of Epidemiology* 114:671–82.

Teaff, J. D., M. P. Lawton, L. Nahemow, and D. Carlson. 1978. "Impact of age integration on the well-being of elderly tenants in public housing." *Journal of Gerontology* 33:126–33.

Tobin, S. S., and B. L. Neugarten. 1961. "Life satisfaction and social interaction in the aging." *Journal of Gerontology* 16:344–46.

Treas, J., and A. VanHilst. 1976. "Marriage and remarriage rates among older Americans." *The Gerontologist* 16:132–35.

U.S. Bureau of the Census. 1978. Current Population Reports, Special Studies Series P-23; no. 85. *Social and Economic Characteristics of the Older Population*. Washington, D.C.: U.S. Government Printing Office, 003-001-90847-6.

Ward, R. A. 1978. "Limitations of the family as a supportive institution in the lives of the aged." *The Family Coordinator* 27:365–73.

Wood, V., M. L. Wylie, and B. Sheafor. 1969. "An analysis of a short self-report measure of life satisfaction: Correlation with rater judgments." *Journal of Gerontology* 24:465–69.

5 The Influence of Religion on the Subjective Well-Being of the Widowed

References

Batson, C. D., and W. L. Ventis. 1982. *The Religious Experience: A Social-Psychological Perspective*. New York: Oxford University Press.

Becker, E. 1973. *The Denial of Death*. New York: Free Press.

Berardo, F. M. 1968. "Widowhood status in the United States: Perspective on a neglected aspect of the family life-cycle." *The Family Coordinator* 17:191–203.

Bryer, K. B. 1979. "The Amish way of death." *American Psychologist* 46:255–61.

Dumont, R. G., and D. C. Foss. 1972. *The American View of Death: Acceptance or Denial?* Cambridge, Mass.: Schenkman.

Feifel, H. 1977. *New Meanings of Death*. New York: McGraw-Hill.

Frankl, V. E. 1963. *Man's Search for Meaning: An Introduction to Logotherapy*. New York: Washington Square Press.

Glick, I. O., R. S. Weiss, and C. M. Parkes. 1974. *The First Year of Bereavement*. New York: John Wiley and Sons.

Glock, C. Y., B. Ringer, and E. R. Babbie. 1967. *To Comfort and to Challenge*. Berkeley: University of California Press.

Gorer, G. 1977. *Death, Grief and Mourning*. New York: Arno Press.

Gray, R. M., and D. O. Moberg. 1977. *The Church and the Older Person*. Grand Rapids, Mich.: Eerdmans.

Hadaway, C. K., and W. C. Roof. 1978. "Religious commitment and the quality of life in American society." *Review of Religious Research* 19:295–307.

Harvey, C. D., and H. M. Bahr. 1980. "Correlates of morale among newly bereaved." *Journal of Social Psychology* 110:219–33.

Hill, S. S., E. T. Thompson, A. F. Scott, C. Hudson, and E. S. Gaustad. 1972. *Religion and the Solid South*. Nashville, Tenn.: Abingdon Press.

Holmes, T. H., and R. H. Rahe. 1967. "The social readjustment rating scale." *Journal of Psychosomatic Research* 11:213–18.

Hunsberger, B. 1985. "Religion, age, life satisfaction and perceived sources of religiousness: A study of older persons." *Journal of Gerontology* 40:615–20.

Jackson, E. N. 1979. "Bereavement and grief." In H. Wass (Ed.), *Dying: Facing the Facts*. New York: McGraw-Hill.

Kalish, R. A. 1981. *Death, Grief and Caring Relationships*. Monterey, Calif.: Brooks/Cole.

Lopata, H. Z. 1980. "The widowed family member." In N. Datan and N. Lohmann (Eds.), *Transitions in Aging*. Pp. 93–118. New York: Academic Press.

O'Dea, T. 1966. *The Sociology of Religion*. Englewood Cliffs, N.J.: Prentice-Hall.

Petrowsky, M. 1976. "Marital status, sex and the social networks of the elderly." *Journal of Marriage and the Family* 38:749–56.

Scheff, T. 1980. "Unresolved grief." *Center Magazine* 13:15–25.

Simpson, M. A. 1979. *The Facts of Death*. Englewood Cliffs, N.J.: Prentice-Hall.

Stack, S. 1983. "The effect of religious commitment on suicide: A cross-national analysis." *Journal of Health and Social Behavior* 24:362–74.

Wuthnow, R., K. Christiano, and J. Kuzlowski. 1980. "Religion and bereavement: A conceptual framework." *Journal for the Scientific Study of Religion* 19:408–22.

6 Widows in Urban Nebraska

References

Adams, B. N. 1968. "The middle-class adult and his widowed or still-married mother." *Social Problems* 16:50–59.

Anderson, T. B. 1984. "Widowhood as a life transition: Its impact on kinship ties." *Journal of Marriage and the Family* 46:105–14.

Babchuk, N. 1965. "Primary friends and kin: A study of the associations of middle class couples." *Social Forces* 43:483–93.

Babchuk, N., and J. A. Ballweg. 1972. "Black family structure and primary relations." *Phylon* (Winter):334–47.

Babchuk, N., and A. P. Bates. 1963. "The primary relations of middle-class couples: A study in male dominance." *American Sociological Review* 28:377–84.

Bell, R. R. 1981. *Worlds of Friendship*. Beverly Hills, Calif.: Sage Publications.

Booth, A., and E. Hess. 1974. "Cross-sex friendships." *Journal of Marriage and the Family* 26:38–47.

Cantor, M. H. 1979. "Neighbors and friends: An overlooked resource in the informal support system." *Research on Aging* 1:434–63.

Johnson, C. L. 1983. "Dyadic family relations and social support." *The Gerontologist* 23:377–83.

Longino, C. F., Jr., and A. Lipman. 1982. "The married, the formerly married and the never married: Support system differentials of older women in planned retirement communities." *International Journal of Aging and Human Development* 15:285–97.

———. 1985. "The support systems of women." In W. J. Sauer and R. T. Coward (Eds.), *Social Support Networks and Care of the Elderly: Theory, Research, and Practice*. Pp. 219–33. New York: Springer.

Lopata, H. Z. 1970. "The social involvement of American widows." *American Behavioral Scientist* 14:41–57.

———. 1975. "Couple-companionate relationships in marriage and widowhood." In N. Glazer-Mabin (Ed.). *Old Family/New Family: Interpersonal Relationships*. Pp. 119–149. New York: D. Van Nostrand.

———. 1978. "Contributions of extended families to the support systems of metropolitan area widows: Limitations of the modified kin network." *Journal of Marriage and the Family* 40:355–64.

———. 1979. *Women as Widows: Support Systems*. New York: Elsevier-North Holland.

Omaha, City Planning Department. 1978. "Intercensual Estimating System (ICES) population and housing estimates." Omaha: The Department.

Peters, G. K., and Kaiser, M. A. 1975. "The role of friends and neighbors in providing social support." In W. J. Sauer, and T. R. Coward (Eds.), *Social Support Networks and the Care of the Elderly: Theory, Research, and Practice*. Pp. 123–58. New York: Springer.

Powers, E. A., and G. L. Bultena. 1976. "Sex differences in intimate friendships of old age." *Journal of Marriage and the Family* 38:739–47.

Shanas, E. 1979a. "Social myth as hypothesis: The case of the family relations of old people." *The Gerontologist* 19:3–9.

———. 1979b. "The family as a social support system in old age." *The Gerontologist* 19:169–74.

SPSS, Inc. 1982. *User's Guide*. Chicago: SPSS, Inc.

Troll, L., S. J. Miller, and R. C. Atchley. 1979. *Families in Later Life*. Belmont, Calif.: Wadsworth.

U.S. Bureau of the Census. 1970. *Census of Housing: Block Statistics, Omaha, Nebraska-Iowa Urbanized Area*. Washington, D.C.: U.S. Government Printing Office.

———. 1981. *1980 Census of Population. Vol. 1: Characteristics of the Population. Chapter A: Number of Inhabitants. Part 29: Nebraska*. Washington, D.C.: U.S. Government Printing Office.

———. 1984. *Demographic and Social Aspects of Aging in the United States*. In Current Population Reports, Series P-23, No. 138. Washington, D.C.: U.S. Government Printing Office.

U.S. National Center for Health Statistics 1985. *Vital Statistics of the United States, Vol. II, Mortality, Part A*. DHHS Publication No. (PHS) 85-1101. Washington, D.C.: U.S. Government Printing Office.

7 Support Systems for American Black Wives and Widows

References

Billingsley, A. 1968. *Black Families in White America*. Englewood Cliffs, N.J.: Prentice-Hall.

Davis, A. Y. 1981. *Women, Race and Class*. New York: Random House.

Gutman, G. G. 1976. *The Black Family In Slavery and Freedom, 1750–1925*. New York: Pantheon Books.

Hooks, B. 1981. *Ain't I A Woman: Black Women and Feminism*. Boston: South End Press.

Ladner, J. A. 1981. "Racism and tradition: Black womanhood in historical perspective." In F. C. Steady (Ed.), *The Black Woman Cross-Culturally*. Cambridge, Mass.: Schenkman.

Lopata, H. Z. 1973. *Widowhood In An American City*. Cambridge, Mass.: Schenkman.

———. 1979. *Women as Widows: Support Systems*. New York: Elsevier-North Holland.

McAdoo, H. P. 1980. "Black mothers and the extended family support network." In L. Rodgers-Ross (Ed.), *The Black Woman*. Beverly Hills, Calif.: Sage Publications.

Martin, E. P. and J. M. Martin. 1978. *The Black Extended Family*. Chicago: University of Chicago Press.

Myers, L. W. 1980. *Black Women: Do They Cope Better?* Englewood Cliffs, N.J.: Prentice-Hall.

Powers, M. 1984. "Falling through the 'safety net': Women, economic crisis, and Reaganomics." *Feminist Studies* 10, no. 1:31–58.

Rodgers-Ross, L. (Ed.). 1980. *The Black Woman*. Beverly Hills, Calif.: Sage Publications.

Scanzoni, J. H. 1971. *The black family in modern society*. Boston: Allyn and Bacon.

Shimkin, D. B., E. M. Shimkin, and D. A. Frate (Eds.). 1978. *The Extended Family in Black Societies*. Paris: Mounton.

Stack, C. S. 1981. "Sex roles and survival strategies in the urban black community." In F. C. Steady (Ed.), *The Black Woman Cross-Culturally*. Cambridge, Mass.: Schenkman.

Staples, R. 1973. *The Black Woman in America*. Chicago: Nelson-Hall.

———. 1982. *Black Masculinity: The Black Male's Role in American Society*. San Francisco: Black Scholars Press.

Steady, F. C. (Ed.). 1981. *The Black Woman Cross-Culturally*. Cambridge, Mass.: Schenkman.

U.S. Bureau of the Census. 1982. *Current Population Reports*, Series P-20. Washington, D.C.: U.S. Government Printing Office.

U.S. Department of Commerce. 1984. *Statistical Abstracts of the United States*. Washington, D.C.: U.S. Government Printing Office.

Williams, L. 1979. "Census data in research, teaching, and studying the conditions of black women." Paper presented at the Black People and the 1980 Census Proceedings from a Conference on the Population Undercount. November 30–December 1. University of Chicago.

8 Comparison of the Needs and Support Systems of Remarried and Nonremarried Widows

References

Berardo, D. H. 1982. "Divorce and remarriage at middle age and beyond." *Annals of the American Academy of Political and Social Science*. 464:132–39.

Bernard, J. 1956. *Remarriage*. New York: Holt, Rinehart and Winston.

Bunch, J. 1972. "Recent bereavement in relation to suicide." *Journal of Psychosomatic Research* 16:36–39.

Clayton, P. J. 1974. "Mortality and morbidity in the first year of widowhood." *Archives of General Psychiatry* 30:747–50.

Cleveland, W. P., and D. T. Gianturco. 1976. "Remarriage probability after widowhood: A retrospective method." *Journal of Gerontology* 31:99–103.

Glick, I. O., R. Weiss, and C. M. Parkes. 1974. *The First Year of Bereavement*. New York: John Wiley and Sons.

Kitson, G. C., H. Z. Lopata, W. M. Holmes, and S. M. Meyering. 1980. "Divorcees and widows: Similarities and differences." *American Journal of Orthopsychiatry* 50:291–301.

Lopata, H. Z. 1973. *Widowhood in an American City*. Morristown, N.J.: General Learning Press.

———. 1979. *Women as Widows: Support Systems*. New York: Elsevier-North Holland.

McKain, W. C. 1969. *Retirement Marriage* (Monograph No. 3.) Storrs, Conn.: Storrs Agricultural Experiment Station.

———. 1972. "A new look at older marriages." *The Family Coordinator* 21:61–69.

Maddison, D., and A. Viola. 1968. "Health of widows in the year following bereavement." *Journal of Psychosomatic Research* 12:297–306.

Parkes, C. M. 1972. *Bereavement: Studies of Grief in Adult Life*. London: Tavistock.

Schlesinger, B., and A. Macrae. 1971. "The widow and widower and remarriage: Selected findings." *Omega* 2:10–18.

Schwartz, L. L., and F. W. Kaslow. 1985. "Widows and divorcees: The same or different?" *American Journal of Family Therapy* 13(4):72–76.

Spanier, G. B., and P. C. Glick. 1980. "Paths to remarriage." *Journal of Divorce* 3:283–98.

Stroebe, M. S., and W. Stroebe. 1983. "Who suffers more? Sex differences in health risks for the widowed." *Psychological Bulletin* 93:279–301.

Vinick, B. H. 1978. "Remarriage in old age." *The Family Coordinator* 27:359–63.

9 Widowhood as the Next Stage in the Life Course

References

Arens, D. A. 1982. "Widowhood and well being: An examination of sex differences within a causal model." *International Journal of Aging and Human Development* 17:27–40.

Berger, P. and H. Kellner. 1974. "Marriage and the construction of reality." In R. L. Coser (Ed.), *The Family: Its Structures and Functions*. New York: St. Martin's Press.

Berger, P. and T. Luckmann. 1967. *The Social Construction of Reality*. Garden City, N.Y.: Doubleday.

Ericson, E. 1968. *Identity: Youth and Crisis*. New York: W. W. Norton.

Gilligan, C. 1982. *In a Different Voice: Psychological Theory and Women's Development*. Cambridge, Mass.: Harvard University Press.

Hummon, D. M. 1986. "City mouse, country mouse: The persistence of community identity." *Qualitative Sociology* 9(1).

Kegan, R. 1982. *The Evolving Self*. Cambridge, Mass.: Harvard University Press.

Lopata, H. Z. 1975. "Grief work and identity reconstruction." *Journal of Geriatric Psychiatry* 8:41–55.

———. 1986. "Time in anticipated future and events in memory." *American Behavioral Scientist* 29:695–709.

Lund, D. A., M. Caserta, and M. Dimond. 1986. "Gender differences through two years of bereavement among the elderly." *The Gerontologist* 26:314–20.

Mahler, M. S., F. Pine, and A. Berman, 1975. *The Psychological Birth of the Human Infant*. New York: Basic Books.

Mead, G. H. 1934. *Mind, Self and Society*. Chicago: University of Chicago Press.

Miller, J. B. 1976. *Toward a New Psychology of Women*. Boston: Beacon Press.

———. 1986. *What Do We Mean By Relationships?* Wellesley, Mass.: Wellesley College, Stone Center Working Papers.

Osterweis, 1984.

Silverman, P. R. 1978. *Mutual Help: A Guide for Mental Health Workers*. Washington, D.C., U.S. Government Printing Office, NIMH, DHEW Publ. No. (ADM) 78-646.

Silverman, P. R. 1980. *Mutual Help Groups: Organization and Development*. Beverly Hills, Calif.: Sage Publications.

———. 1981. *Helping Women Cope With Grief*. Beverly Hills, Calif.: Sage Publications.

———. 1986. *Widow-to-Widow*. New York: Springer.

———. 1987a. "In search of new selves." In L. A. Bond and B. M. Wagner (Eds.), *Families in Transition: Primary Prevention Programs that Work*. Beverly Hills, Calif.: Sage Publications.

———. 1987b. "Research as process: Exploring the meaning of widowhood." In S. Reinharz, and G. Rowles (Eds.), *Qualitative Gerontology*. New York: Springer.

10 Widowhood Among Low-Income Racial and Ethnic Groups in California

References

Asociacion Nacional Pro Personas Mayores. 1981. *White House Mini-Conference on Hispanic Aging, Final Report*. Los Angeles: mimeograph.

Branch, L. G., and A. M. Jette. 1983. "Elders' use of informal long-term care assistance." *The Gerontologist* 23:51–56.

Bureau of the Census. 1980. *A Statistical Portrait of Women in the United States: 1978*. Current Population Reports, Special Studies, Series P-23, No. 100.

———. 1981. *Aging, Sex, Race, and Spanish Origin of the Population by Regions, Divisions, and States: 1980*. Supplementary Reports, PC80-S1-1.

———. 1983a. *Population Profile of the United States: 1982*. Current Population Reports, Special Studies, Series P-23, No. 130.

———. 1983b. *County and City Data Book, 1983*. Washington, D.C.: U.S. Government Printing Office.

———. 1983c. *General Population Characteristics, United States Summary, 1980 Census of Population*. Volume 1, Chapter B, Part 1, PC80-1-B1, Table 41.

California. 1984a. *The Multipurpose Senior Services Project Final Report*. Sacramento: Health and Welfare Agency.

———. 1984b. *In-Home Supportive Services Characteristics Survey*. Sacramento: Department of Social Services, Program Information Series 1984-07.

Cantor, M. H. 1979. "The informal support system of New York's inner city elderly: Is ethnicity a factor?" In D. E. Gelfand and A. J. Kutzik (Eds.), *Ethnicity and Aging*. New York: Springer.

Comptroller General of the United States. 1977. *The Well-Being of Older People in Cleveland, Ohio*. Washington, D.C.: U.S. General Accounting Office (HCD-77-70).

Coons, R. H. 1983. "A theoretical analysis of double jeopardy." Paper presented at the Forty-seventh Annual Meeting of the Midwest Sociological Society, Kansas City, Mo.

Dasen, P. R. (Ed.). 1977. *Piagetian Psychology: Cross-Cultural Contributions*. New York: Halsted; cited in J. B. Thompson and D. Held (Eds.), *Habermas: Critical Debates*. Cambridge, Mass.: MIT Press, 1982.

Dowd, J. J., and V. L. Bengston. 1978. "Aging in minority populations: An examination of the double jeopardy hypothesis." *Journal of Gerontology* 33:427–36.

Estes, C. L. 1979. *The Aging Enterprise*. San Francisco: Jossey-Bass.

Holzberg, C. S. 1982. "Ethnicity and aging: Anthropological perspectives on more than just the minority elderly." *The Gerontologist* 22:249–57.

Jackson, J. J. 1980. *Minorities and Aging*. Belmont, Calif.: Wadsworth.

Katz, S., et al. 1963. "The index of ADL: a standardized measure of biological and psychological function." *Journal of the American Medical Association* 185:914–19.

Kent, D. P. 1971. "The Negro aged." *The Gerontologist* 11:48–51.

Lawton, M. P., and E. M. Brody. 1969. "Assessment of older people: Self-maintaining and instrumental activities of daily living." *The Gerontologist* 9:179–86.

Legislative Analyst Office. 1984. *Analysis of the Budget Bill for Fiscal Year July 1, 1984 to June 30, 1985*. Sacramento: California Legislature.

Lopata, H. Z. 1973. *Widowhood in an American City*. Cambridge, Mass.: Schenkman.

Manton, K. G., S. S. Poss, and S. Wing. 1979. "The black/white mortality crossover: Investigation from the perspective of the components of aging." *The Gerontologist* 19:291–300.

Miller, L. S., M. L. Miller, and W. F. Clark. 1986. "The Comparative Evaluation of California's Multipurpose Senior Services Project." *Home Health Care Services Quarterly* 8 (Spring).

Morris, R. Interview with senior author. San Francisco: June 16, 1985.

National Geographic Society. 1981. *Atlas of the World* (5th ed.) Washington, D.C.: National Geographic Society.

Newton, F., and R. A. Ruiz. 1981. "Chicano culture and mental health among the elderly." In M. Miranda and R. A. Ruiz (Eds.), *Chicano Aging and Mental Health*. Rockville, Md.: U.S. Department of Health and Human Services, Alcohol, Drug Abuse, and Mental Health Administration, National Institute of Mental Health, DHHS Pub. No. (ADM) 81-952.

Pelham, A. O., and W. F. Clark. Forthcoming. "Close encounters of the word kind: Interviewing challenges of the California Senior Survey." In A. O. Pelham and W. F. Clark (Eds.), *At Home to Stay*. New York: Springer.

Pfeiffer, E. A. 1975. "Short portable mental status questionnaire for the assessment of organic brain deficit in elderly patients." *Journal of the American Geriatrics Society* 23:433–41.

Rich, B. M., and M. Baum. 1984. *The Aging: A Guide to Public Policy*. Pittsburgh: University of Pittsburgh Press.

Romo, R. 1983. *East Los Angeles: History of a Barrio*. Austin: University of Texas Press.

Schulz, J. H. 1985. *The Economics of Aging* (3rd ed.) New York: Van Nostrand Reinhold.

Shanas, E. 1979. *National Survey of the Elderly*. Report to the Administration on Aging, Washington, D.C.

Stoller, E. P., and L. L. Earl. 1983. "Help with activities of everyday life: Sources of support for the noninstitutionalized elderly." *The Gerontologist* 23:64–70.

U.S. Department of Health and Human Services. 1983. *Health, United States, 1983*. National Center for Health Statistics, DHHS Pub. No. (PHS) 84-1232. Washington, D.C.: U.S. Government Printing Office.

11 Support Systems of Widows in Canada

1 The research reported in this chapter was funded by University of Guelph Grant 83-909, and Social Sciences and Humanities Research Council of Canada, Grants 492-79-0017, and 492-82-4006 to the Gerontology Research Centre.

The author also wishes to acknowledge the support of the Gerontology Research Centre and its staff, and the assistance of Joseph A. Tindale and Francois Pare of the University of Guelph.

2 The Goldberg General Health Questionnaire was used by Vachon and associates as a measure of overall physical and mental health.

3 In this research on community-dwelling elderly living in four communities along the rural-urban continuum, both widowed ($N=115$) and non-widowed respondents ($N=338$) reported high levels of contact with siblings. In all, 82 percent of the widowed and 88 percent of the nonwidowed reported regular contact with siblings.

4 This large proportion of older women living alone is a relatively new phenomenon in Canada. Between 1961 and 1981, the proportion of women aged 65 and over living

alone doubled from 16 percent to 32 percent (Health and Welfare Canada, 1983:68).

5 One inherent difficulty in the comparison of U.S. and Canadian data on rurality is that each country uses a different census definition. In Canada the criterion is areas with a population of 1,000 or less, while in the United States it is areas with a population of 2,500 or less. Most Canadian researchers in fact use "working" definitions of rurality that are far broader than the "residualist" census definition.

References

Anderson, T. B. 1984. "Widowhood as a life transition: Its impact on kinship ties." *Journal of Marriage and the Family* 46:105–14.

Bercuson, D. J. 1977. *Canada and the Burden of Unity*. Toronto: Macmillan of Canada.

Christiansen-Ruffman, L. 1976. "Newcomer careers: An exploratory study of migrants in Halifax." Unpublished Ph.D. dissertation, Department of Sociology, Columbia University.

Dickinson, L., and A. M. Matthews. 1986. "Elderly widows and widowers: Patterns of social support." Paper presented at the Annual Meeting of the Canadian Association on Gerontology, Quebec City, November 2–6.

Dulude, L. 1979. *Women and Aging: A Report on the Rest of our Lives*. Ottawa: Advisory Council on the Status of Women.

Eichler, M. 1976. "The prestige of the occupation housewife." In P. Marchak (Ed.), *The Working Sexes*. Pp. 151–75. Vancouver: Institute of Industrial Relations, University of British Columbia.

Elias, B. 1977. "Residential environment and social adjustment among older widows." Unpublished M.Sc. thesis, Department of Family Studies, University of Guelph.

Fletcher, S., and L. O. Stone. 1980. "The living arrangements of older women." *Essence: Issues in the Study of Ageing, Dying and Death* 4:115–33.

Government of Canada. 1982. *The Charter of Rights and Freedoms: A Guide for Canadians*. Ottawa: Minister of Supply and Services.

Haas-Hawkings, G. 1978. "Intimacy as a moderating influence on the stress of loneliness in widowhood." *Essence: Issues in the Study of Ageing, Dying and Death* 2:249–58.

———, M. Ziegler, and D. W. Reid. 1980. "An exploratory study of adjustment to widowhood." Paper presented at the Thirty-third Annual Scientific Meeting of the Gerontological Society of America, San Diego.

Harvey, C. D. H., and M. Harris. 1985. "Decision-making during widowhood: The beginning years." Paper presented at the Beatrice Paolucci Symposium, Michigan State University, East Lansing, July 19.

Health and Welfare Canada. 1982a. *The Manitoba/Canada Home Care Study: An Overview of the Findings*. Ottawa: Policy, Planning and Information Branch, Department of National Health and Welfare.

———. 1982b. *Pension Plan Coverage by Level of Earnings and Age 1978 and 1979*. Ottawa: Planning, Evaluation and Liaison Division, Income Security Programs Branch.

———. 1983. *Fact Book on Aging in Canada*. Ottawa: Minister of Supply and Services.

Holmes, T. H., and R. H. Rahe. 1967. "The social readjustment rating scale." *Journal of Psychosomatic Research* 11:213–18.

Kubat, D., and D. Thornton. 1974. *A Statistical Profile of Canadian Society*. Toronto: McGraw-Hill Ryerson.

Lindsay, C. 1980. "Population." In H. J. Adler and D. A. Brusegard (Eds.), *Perspectives*

Canada III. Pp. 3–17. Ottawa: Minister of Supply and Services Canada.

Lipset, S. M. 1965. "Revolution and counterrevolution: The United States and Canada." In T. R. Ford (Ed.), *The Revolutionary Theme in Contemporary America*. Pp. 21–64. Lexington: University of Kentucky Press.

———. 1985. "Canada and the United States: The cultural dimension." In C. F. Doran and J. H. Sigler (Eds.), *Canada and the United States*. Pp. 109–60. Englewood Cliffs, N.J., and Scarborough, Ont.: Prentice-Hall.

Lopata, H. Z. 1973. *Widowhood in an American City*. Cambridge, Mass.: Schenkman.

———. 1978. "Contributions of extended families to the support systems of metropolitan area widows: Limitations of the modified kin network." *Journal of Marriage and the Family* 40:355–64.

———. 1979. *Women as Widows: Support Systems*. New York: Elsevier-North Holland.

McFarlane, A. H., G. R. Norman, D. L. Streiner, R. Roy, and D. J. Scott. 1980. "A longitudinal study of influence on the psychosocial environment on health status: A preliminary report." *Journal of Health and Social Behaviour* 21:124–33.

Marshall, V. W. 1981. "Social characteristics of the future aged." Hamilton, Ont.: Program for Quantitative Studies in Economics and Population, McMaster University.

Martin Matthews, A. 1980. "Women and widowhood." In V. W. Marshall (Ed.), *Aging in Canada: Social Perspectives*. Pp. 145–53. Toronto: Fitzhenry and Whiteside.

———, K. H. Brown, C. K. Davis, and M. A. Denton. 1982. "A crisis assessment technique for the evaluation of life events: Transition to retirement as an example." *Canadian Journal on Aging* 1:28–39.

———. 1982. "Canadian research on women as widows: A comparative analysis of the state of the art." *Resources for Feminist Research* 11:227–30.

———. 1985. "Rural-Urban comparisons of the social supports of the widowed elderly." Social Sciences and Humanities Research Council of Canada (Strategic Grants: Population Aging) 492-84-0028.

———, A. Michalos, A. M. Fuller, C. A. Guldner, J. E. Norris, J. A. Tindale, K. V. Ujimoto, L. W. Wood, and J. S. Wolfe. 1984. "Stability and change in assessments of quality of life of the elderly." University of Guelph Research Board Grant 5089.

Matthews, R., and J. C. Davis. 1986. "Is regionalism dead? Confronting recent interpretations of regionalism in Canada." In *Regionalism and National Identity: Multidisciplinary Essays on Canada, Australia and New Zealand*. Pp. 339–52. Christchurch, N.Z.: Association for Canadian Studies in Australia and New Zealand.

Michalos, A. and S. Fortey. 1980. "Vignettes of Canada and the United States." In H. J. Adler and D. A. Brusegard (Eds.), *Perspectives Canada III*. Pp. 295–97. Ottawa: Minister of Supply and Services Canada.

National Council of Welfare. 1984. *Sixty-Five and Older: A Report by the National Council of Welfare on the Incomes of the Aged*. Ottawa: Minister of Supply and Services.

Norris, J. E. 1980. "The social adjustment of single and widowed older women." *Essence: Issues in the Study of Ageing, Dying and Death* 4:135–44.

Saskatchewan Senior Citizens Provincial Council. 1979. *A Report on Widowed Senior Citizens in Regina and Saskatoon*, August.

Schlesinger, B. 1979. *Families: Canada*. Toronto: McGraw-Hill Ryerson.

Statistics Canada. 1979. *Canada's Families*, Catalogue 98-801E. Ottawa: Minister of Supply and Services.

———. 1982. *Population: Age, Sex and Marital Status, 1981*. Catalogue 92-901.

———. 1983. *Vital Statistics: Marriages and Divorces 1981*. Volume II, Catalogue 92-906. Ottawa: Minister of Supply and Services.

———. 1984. *Life Tables, Canada and Provinces 1980–1982*. Catalogue 84-532. Ottawa: Minister of Supply and Services.

———. 1985. *Women in Canada: A Statistical Report*. Ottawa: Minister of Supply and Services Canada.

Stone, L. O., and S. Fletcher. 1981. *Aspects of Population Aging in Canada: A Chartbook*. Ottawa: Statistics Canada.

Strain, L. A., and N. L. Chappell. 1982. "Confidants: Do they make a difference in quality of life?" *Research on Aging* 4:479–502.

Stryckman, J. 1981. "The decision to remarry: The choice and its outcome." Paper presented at the Joint Meeting of the Canadian Association on Gerontology and the Gerontological Society of America, Toronto.

———. 1982. *Mariages et Mises en Ménage au cours de la Vieillesse*. Université Laval: Laboratoire de gerontologie sociale.

Unruh, D. R. 1983. *Invisible Lives: Social Worlds of the Aged*. Beverly Hills, Calif.: Sage Publications.

Vachon, M. L. S. 1979. "Identity change over the first two years of bereavement: Social relationships and social support in widowhood." Unpublished Ph.D. dissertation, York University, Toronto.

Vachon, M. L. S. 1981. "The importance of social relationships and social support in widowhood." Paper presented to the Joint Meeting of the Canadian Association on Gerontology and the Gerontological Society of America, Toronto, November.

Vachon, M. L. S., A. Formo, K. Freedman, A. Lyall, J. Rogers, and S. Freeman. 1976. "Stress reactions to bereavement." *Essence: Issues in the Study of Ageing, Dying and Death* 1:23–33.

Vachon, M. L. S., W. A. Lyall, J. Rogers, K. Freedman-Letofsky, and S. J. J. Freeman. 1980. "A controlled study of self-help intervention for widows." *American Journal of Psychiatry* 137:1380–84.

Vachon, M. L. S., J. Rogers, W. A. Lyall, W. J. Lancee, A. R. Sheldon, and S. J. J. Freeman. 1982. "Predictors and correlates of adaptation to conjugal bereavement." *American Journal of Psychiatry* 139:998–1002.

Walker, K. N., A. MacBride, and M. L. S. Vachon. 1977. "Social support networks and the crisis of bereavement." *Social Science and Medicine* 11:35–41.

12 Activities, Religiosity, and Morale of Canadian Widowed Persons

1 Scales were treated this way in order to compare scales of unequal item size. We could not assume that scales of a longer list of items reflected more potential for activity of that type. The imbalance would be a scaling artifact.

2 Full regressions were computed using minimum pairwise comparisons (i.e., cases with nonmissing data on all variables). These are the numbers reported in tables 12.4 and 12.5.

References

Arens, D. A. 1982–83. "Widowhood and well-being: An examination of sex differences within a causal model." *International Journal of Aging and Human Development* 15:27–40.

Arling, G. T. 1976. "The elderly widow and her family, neighbors, and friends." *Journal of Marriage and the Family* 38:757–68.

Atchley, R. C. 1975. "Dimensions in widowhood in later life." *The Gerontologist* 15 (April):176–78.

Balkwell, C. 1981. "Transition to widowhood: A review of the literature." *Family Relations* 30:117–27.

———. 1985. "An attitudinal correlate of the timing of a major life event: The case of morale in widowhood." *Family Relations* 34:577–81.

Bankoff, E. A. 1983. "Social support and adaptation to widowhood." *Journal of Marriage and the Family* 45:827–39.

Barnes, G. E., R. R. Currie, and A. Segall. Forthcoming. "Symptoms of depression in a Canadian urban sample." *Canadian Journal of Psychiatry.*

Berardo, F. M. 1967. "Social adaptation to widowhood among a rural-urban aged population." *Washington Agricultural Experiment Station Bulletin* 689(December):31.

Bowling, A., and A. Cartwright. 1982. *Life After Death: A Study of the Elderly Widowed*. London: Tavistock.

Bradburn, N. M. 1969. *The Structure of Psychological Well-Being*. Chicago: Aldine.

Breslau, L., and M. R. Haug. 1983. "Some elements in an integrative model of depression in the aged." In L. Breslau and M. R. Haugh (Eds.), *Depression and Aging. Causes, Care and Consequences*. Pp. 269–79. New York: Springer.

Brown, G. W., and T. Harris. 1978. *Social Origins of Depression*. London: Tavistock.

Cadoret, R. S., G. Winokur, J. Dorzab, and M. Baker. 1972. "Depressive disease: Life events and onset of illness." *Archives of General Psychiatry* 26:133–36.

Carey, R. G. 1979–80. "Weathering widowhood: Problems and adjustment of the widowed during the first year." *Omega* 10:163–64.

Clark, P. G., R. W. Siviski, and R. Weiner. 1986. "Coping strategies of widowers in the first year." *Family Relations* 35:425–30.

Diener, E. 1984. "Subjective well-being." *Psychological Bulletin* 95:542–75.

Dulude, L. 1978. "Women and aging: A report on the rest of our lives." *Canadian Advisory Council on the Status of Women*. Ottawa.

Edwards, J. N., and D. L. Klemmack. 1973. "Correlates of life satisfaction: A re-examination." *Journal of Gerontology* 28:497–502.

Elwell, F., A. Maltbie-Crannell, and D. Maltbie-Crannell. 1981. "The impact of role loss upon coping resources and life satisfaction of the elderly." *Journal of Gerontology* 36:223–32.

Faletti, M. V., and E. Berman. 1983. "Supportive networks and coping in bereaved elderly. Paper presented at the Gerontological Society of America, San Francisco.

Gallagher, D. E., J. N. Breckenridge, L. W. Thompson, and J. A. Peterson. 1983. "Effects of bereavement on indicators of mental health in elderly widows and widowers." *Journal of Gerontology* 38:565–71.

Gallo, F. 1982. "The effects of social support networks on the health of the elderly." *Social Work in Health Care* 8:65–74.

George, L. 1980. *Role Transitions in Later Life*. Monterey, Calif.: Brooks/Cole.

Glick, I. O., R. S. Weiss, and C. W. Parkes. 1974. *The First Year of Bereavement*. New York: John Wiley and Sons.

Harding, S. D. 1982. "Psychological well-being in Great Britain: An evaluation of the Bradburn Affect Balance Scale." *Personality of Individual Differences* 3:167–75.

Harris, M., and C. D. H. Harvey. 1986. "Help-seeking with decision-making among widows." Unpublished paper, Department of Family Studies, University of Manitoba.

Harvey, C. D. H. 1986. "Correlates of morale and loneliness within a middle-aged widowed sample." Unpublished paper, Department of Family Studies, University of Manitoba.

Harvey, C. D. H., and H. M. Bahr. 1974. "Widowhood, morale, and affiliation." *Journal of Marriage and the Family* 36:97–106.

———. 1980. *The Sunshine Widows: Adapting to Sudden Bereavement*. Lexington, Mass.: Lexington Books.

Harvey, C. D. H., G. E. Barnes, and L. Greenwood. 1986. "Correlates of morale among Canadian widowed persons." *Social Psychiatry*, forthcoming.

Harvey, C. D. H., and M. Harris. 1985. "Decision-making during widowhood: The beginning year." Paper presented at the Beatrice Paolucci Symposium, Michigan State University, East Lansing.

Honn, S., J. Breckenridge, L. W. Thompson, D. Gallagher, and J. Peterson. 1973. "Loneliness in bereavement: The role of social supports." Paper presented to the Gerontological Society of America, San Francisco.

Hyman, H. H. 1983. *Of Time and Widowhood: Nationwide Studies of Enduring Effects*. Durham, N.C.: Duke Press Policy Studies.

Leaf, P. J., M. M. Weissman, J. K. Myers, G. L. Tischler, and C. E. Holzer. 1984. "Social factors related to psychiatric disorder: The Yale Epidemiological Catchment Area Study." *Social Psychiatry* 19:53–61.

Lipman, A., and C. F. Longino, Jr. 1983. "Mother is alone now: Sons and daughters of married and widowed mothers." Paper presented at the Gerontological Society of America, San Francisco.

Lopata, H. Z. 1970. "The social involvement of American widows." *American Behavioral Scientist* 14:41–57.

———. 1971. *Occupation: Housewife*. New York: Oxford University Press.

———. 1973. *Widowhood in an American City*. Cambridge, Mass.: Schenkman.

———. 1979. *Women as Widows: Support Systems*. New York: Elsevier-North Holland.

McCubbin, H. I., and J. M. Patterson. 198_. "Family Transitions: Adaptation to Stress." In H. I. McCubbin and C. R. Figley (Eds.), *Stress and the Family, Vol. 1: Coping with Normative Transitions*. Pp. 5–25. New York: Brunner/Mazel.

Martin Matthews, A. 1980. Women and Widowhood. In V. Marshall and D. Mills (Eds.), *Aging in Canada: Social Perspectives*. Pp. 145–53. Ontario: Fitzhenry and Whiteside.

———. 1982. "Review essay: Canadian research on women as widows: A comparative analysis of the state of the art." *Resources for Feminist Research* 11:227–30.

———. 1986. "Women and aging." Keynote address to the Canadian Association for Research in Home Economics, Winnipeg, June 4.

Myers, J. K., J. J. Lindenthal, and M. P. Pepper. 1974. "Social class, life events, and psychiatric symptoms: A longitudinal study." In B. S. Dohrenwend and B. P. Dohrenwend (Eds.), *Stressful Life Events: Their Nature and Effects*. Pp. 191–205. New York: John

Wiley and Sons.

Palmore, E., and C. Luikart. 1972. "Health and Social Factors Related to Life Satisfaction." *Journal of Health and Social Behavior* 13:68–80.

Paloutzian, R. F., and C. W. Ellison. 1982. "Loneliness, spiritual well-being and quality of life." In L. Peplau and D. Perlman (Eds.), *Loneliness: A Sourcebook of Current Theory, Research and Therapy*. Pp. 224–37. New York: John Wiley and Sons.

Paykel, E. A. 1979. "Recent life events in the development of depressive disorders." In R. Depue (Ed.), *The Psychobiology of the Depressive Disorder: Implications for the Effects of Stress*. Pp. 245–61. New York: Academic Press.

Pearlin, L. I., and J. S. Johnson. 1977. "Marital status, life-strains and depression." *American Sociological Review* 42:704–15.

Quinn, W. H. 1983. "Personal and family adjustment in later life." *Journal of Marriage and the Family* 45:57–73.

Spreitzer, E., and E. S. Snyder. 1974. "Correlates of life satisfaction among the aged." *Journal of Gerontology* 29:545–48.

Stroebe, M. S., and W. Stroebe. 1983. "Who suffers more? Sex differences in health risks of the widowed." *Psychological Bulletin* 93:279–301.

Tennant, C., P. Beblington, and J. Hurry. 1981. "The role of life events in depressive illness: Is there a substantial causal relation?" *Psychology and Medicine* 11:379–89.

Vachon, M. L. S., J. Rogers, W. A. Lyall, W. J. Lancee, A. R. Sheldon, and S. J. J. Freeman. 1982. "Predictors and correlates of adaptation to conjugal bereavement." *American Journal of Psychiatry* 139:998–1002.

Walker, K. N., A. MacBride, and M. L. S. Vachon. 1977. "Social support networks and the crisis of bereavement." *Social Science and Medicine* 11:35–41.

Warheit, G. J. 1979. "Life events, coping, stress and depressive symptomatology. *American Journal of Psychiatry* 136:502–7.

Wister, A. W., and T. K. Burch. 1985. "Decision-making traits of the elderly: The case of living arrangement choice." Paper presented at the Twenty-sixth Annual Meeting of the Western Association of Sociology and Anthropology, Winnipeg, February.

Index

Library of Congress Cataloging-in-Publication Data
Widows.
Includes bibliographies and indexes.
Contents: v. 1. The Middle East, Asia, and the
Pacific v. 2. North America.
1. Widows. 2. Widows—Near East. 3. Widows—Asia.
4. Widows—North America. I. Lopata, Helena Znaniecka,
1925–
HQ1058.W53 1987 306.8′8 87-5410
ISBN 0-8223-0680-8 (v. 1)
ISBN 0-8223-0768-5 (pbk.: v. 1)
ISBN 0-8223-0724-3 (v. 2)
ISBN 0-8223-0770-7 (pbk.: v. 2)